CONTENTS

FOREWORD TO
THE THIRD EDITION

This book first appeared in England in 1959, in the United States in 1960. At that time Brecht was still barely known in the English-speaking world. Today he has become a recognized classic, one of the great masters of twentieth-century literature. And there has been a steady stream of books and articles on the man and his work.

Moreover, in the quarter century since Brecht died many of his previously unpublished works have appeared, and a good deal of information about his life and circumstances, letters and diaries have become public. Clearly a book which had been one of the first to attempt only three years after he had died a survey of the man and the artist, the theoretician of drama and the political personality, and for which there seemed a steady continuing demand from students of Brecht and the general public, was in need of revision.

Yet, on rereading what I had written in 1957 and 1958, with an eye on what might have become out of date or been superseded by the new material, I was surprised to what extent the material I had then laboriously assembled has stood up to the test of time. The enormous mass of newly available biographical material and unpublished writings that have recently come to light have, indeed, filled out much that had been reported on the basis of personal reminiscences from friends – and enemies – of Brecht, or from hints contained in newspaper reports of the time. But the basic facts, the basic structure of Brecht's life and personality, the basic outline of his artistic and political profile remain unaffected.

Of course, there has been an immense amount of discussion and often bitter controversy about Brecht, and this book has often been in the centre of such disputes. But here too, in surveying what has been said for and against my point of view, I can merely repeat what I wrote in the foreword to the first paperback edition of the book, in 1960:

'That a study of a highly unorthodox Communist poet, which is appreciative of his genius but critical of his political convictions, would find little understanding in orthodox Communist quarters was only to be expected. There is little point in arguing with criticism on the intellectual level of, say, the London *Daily Worker*. One might as well engage in a debate with a parrot. But there has been another, and outwardly more plausible, line of attack from similar, or at least closely related, quarters which certainly demands strong and categorical refutation.

'I have been accused of wanting to "denigrate" Brecht, the man, and of presenting a "repulsive" picture of a great, and defenceless, artist. That such a view is a grotesque misunderstanding, and misrepresentation, of this book should be apparent to any attentive reader. How could such a misconception arise? By applying to Brecht a system of ethics to which he himself never subscribed. It has, for example, been suggested that I have cast doubt on his honour by reporting that, after his exile in 1933, Brecht did not accept an invitation to work in the Soviet Union and even emigrated to America in 1941 by crossing its whole territory from Finland to Vladivostok. Did this not imply that he betrayed his faith for the sake of the fleshpots of Hollywood? I am accused of having presented Brecht as a coward and opportunist because I did nothing to explain away, or minimize, the otherwise undoubted and unquestionable facts that, before deciding to go back to East Germany, Brecht applied for an Austrian passport and secured a West German publisher and a Swiss bank account, and that in making this decision the prospect of at last obtaining control of a richly subsidized theatre was at least as important as his devotion to the interests of the party. Did this not ascribe the basest motives to a pure believer in the cause? I am attacked for trying to find an explanation for the paradox that Brecht *was* a Communist, but that much of his work was unacceptable to the party as Communist propaganda; for searching to establish the connection between Brecht's political convictions and the structure of his mind revealed in the imagery of his poetry. Is this not tantamount to questioning the purity of his motives?

'The fallacy of this approach lies in the naïveté of its underlying, but never openly acknowledged, assumptions. It presupposes that there could not possibly be a moral or ethical dilemma in being a Communist, even for a man of Brecht's deep sensitivity and penetrating intellect; that for a Communist all decisions would automatically flow from the basic equation that everything that is good for the party is good for all its believers, and that thus, for example, a Communist could not possibly hesitate before deciding to settle in East Germany, or make some arrangements to safeguard his political independence; and that it is sacrilege to suggest that there may be a conflict between the poet's instinct for truth and the party's propaganda requirements. These, however, are the basic assumptions of the most puerile level of Communist hagiography which, admittedly, form the foundation of the terrifyingly simple-minded picture of Brecht as a latter-day Communist classic painted by the same East German propagandists who attacked him in his lifetime as a dangerous formalist and revisionist. To turn a complexly motivated human being into a cardboard poster seems to me a far more reprehensible and repulsive act of denigration than an honest and objective assessment of his personality. I admire Brecht for being a shrewd and realistic person who pursued a policy of enlightened self-interest, because he felt that he had something important to say and therefore ought to do his best to survive in his troubled times rather than indulge in empty heroic gestures. He never tires of praising the unheroic heroes like Schweik or Azdak who manage to achieve what they set out to do even at the cost of occasionally appearing less than brave, virtuous, or truthful. This was the system of ethics taught by Brecht's alter ego, the charming and wordly wise Mr Keuner:

"The bearer of knowledge must not get involved in fights; nor speak the truth; nor fail to eat; nor refuse honours; nor be recognizable. The bearer of truth has, of all virtues only one: that he carries the truth within him," said Mr Keuner.[1]

And Brecht certainly regarded himself as the bearer of an important truth. Is it really an insult to suggest that for its sake he sometimes did not refuse honours like the Stalin Prize, that sometimes he tried to make his real motives unrecognizable, that for its sake he refused to starve, that for its sake he sometimes retreated when challenged to a fight? Those who throw up their hands in horror when confronted with the image of Brecht as a complex, contradictory, modern, and therefore far from guiltless, human being, instead of their own over-simplified comic-strip conception of a superman hero, do in fact betray an amazing insensitivity toward the truly heroic, because tragically

[1] 'Von den Traegern des Wissens,' Versuche 1.

ambivalent, aspect of their idol. It is, of course, fully understandable that the family and immediate circle of a great man would rather see some aspects of his character, his meanness in money matters perhaps, or the multiplicity of his love affairs, glossed over. But, in the long run, the "official, authorized" biographies of great men usually do more harm to their memories than the most irreverent. Even the failings of a great poet are valuable: they may reveal the sources of his poetry.

'There is only one other misunderstanding I should like to clear up. It concerns my method. In his brilliant, and deeply perceptive, essay,[1] Ernest Borneman criticizes me for – or compliments me on? – the fact that the way I build up my picture of Brecht from his biography and background toward a psychological and critical appreciation of the man and artist amounts to my using a Marxist, or crypto-Marxist, approach. This is a very penetrating observation, but it is valid only if the term "Marxist" is taken in its very widest sense, if, in fact, Marx could claim to be the only philosopher who insisted that all arguments should proceed from a foundation of solid fact. Marx may have been convinced that he had discovered the application of the scientific method to social (and perhaps also literary) analysis, but that does not mean that the scientific method was discovered by Marx. It is quite true that the argument of this book does proceed in a somewhat dialectical fashion. But this is inherent in the character of Brecht, who was a personality of contradictions and paradoxes, rather than in the method of the argument. In fact, Brecht's divided nature, in its alternation between anarchy and discipline, is the key to his deeply felt affinity to the Hegelian and Marxist dialectic. Moreover, as Borneman rightly points out, my book also relies on the use of modern psychological concepts and employs a system of philosophical and literary categories and values that would be anathema to Marx himself, let alone the scholastic dogmatists who claim to be the champions of Marxism today. Although I start from the facts of Brecht's life and background, my concern is to explain the relationship between Brecht's poetic genius and political convictions through an analysis of the psychological foundations of his personality revealed in the imagery of his poetry; a genuinely Marxist approach would be in the diametrically opposite direction: from his social and class background toward his psychology. Nor is my final conclusion, as Borneman

[1] Two Brechtians,' *The Kenyon Review*, Summer 1960.

would have it, that "the sole therapy for creative artists of Brecht's stamp . . . is to submit to Communist discipline," but, on the contrary, that conversion to Communism may often be the symptom of that profound psychological disturbance, the wound of the poet, for which his *creative genius* provides the therapy.'

So much for what I wrote in answer to criticism of this book in 1960. I stand by it today.

This new edition thus presents the same point of view as the first version of the book; but I have added a good deal of detail to my arguments from the material now available.

The *catalogue raisonné* of Brecht's writings as well as the bibliography of his collected works and their translations into English have been brought up to date; but the bibliography of books about Brecht has been restricted to the more important and significant biographical and critical material.

My thanks are due to the numerous friends who drew my attention to errors and omissions, and especially to Eric Bentley, whose vast knowledge of Brecht was always at my disposal and whose enthusiasm and generosity played a vital part in getting this book – and its present edition – published.

M.E.

Winchelsea, Sussex, August 1979

INTRODUCTION

There can be little doubt that Bertolt Brecht is one of the most significant writers of this century.

German literature, unlike that of France, Italy, pre-revolutionary Russia, or Scandinavia, is on the whole so remote from the taste and aesthetic conventions of the English-speaking world that its influence does not often make itself felt. Yet occasionally an author writing in German imposes himself and leaves a lasting impression: Kafka was one of these, Brecht is another. His influence on the theatre may well prove as powerful as that of Kafka on the novel.

It is an influence which has already left its mark; it did so long before Brecht's name itself was ever mentioned. Auden's and Isherwood's early plays, and a good many of the poems of their left-wing phase, clearly owe a debt to the early Brecht. In an entirely different sphere, that of the musical stage, the contemporary American musical with its blending of serious purpose in the book with popular tunes certainly derives to some extent from Brecht's experiments in *The Threepenny Opera*.

This first, anonymous and unacknowledged, impact of Brecht's ideas was followed, at an interval, by a second, more direct wave of his influence. This spread from Brecht's own theatre at East Berlin which gave him an opportunity to demonstrate the full range of his powers. His fame as a reformer of the stage was carried to Western Europe by visitors to Berlin and led to triumphant appearances of Brecht's Berliner Ensemble in Paris and London. Brecht's name became a household word, the daily coinage of dramatic critics. His theories were quoted in support of a multitude of contradictory causes. And his adherence to the East German Communist régime further confused the issue. Some argued that his greatness as a producer, backed by subsidies received from a Communist government, proved the cultural superiority of the Eastern camp, while others condemned him on the ground that he was a Communist propagandist and therefore could not be a great artist.

But Brecht's case defies such simplifications. It is far more complex and constitutes a curious paradox: Brecht was a Communist, he was also a great poet. But while the West liked his poetry and distrusted his Communism, the Communists exploited his political convictions while they regarded his artistic aims and achievements with suspicion. To understand this paradox it is necessary to examine not only Brecht's professed opinions, his background and his works, but also to subject them to an objective, critical analysis.

This book attempts to put such a factual, yet critical, study of Brecht's artistic personality before an English-speaking public. It is not primarily a biography, although its critical assessment of Brecht and its discussion of the more general problem of the politically committed poet of genius, takes an account of Brecht's life as its starting point. There may be writers whose work can be discussed without reference to their life; it may even be possible to deal with Brecht's *œuvre* in this way, if, that is, one were merely concerned with its aesthetic qualities. But this is not the concern of this book: Brecht was not only a political poet, he also claimed that his writings were weapons in a political struggle, that they were based on a correct assessment of the world around him, of society. Moreover he himself and his works have become the centre of a political and ideological debate: was Brecht's aesthetic theory truly Marxist? Was his assessment of the social forces of his time as correct as he claimed? What was the social and psychological basis for his conversion to Marxism? All these and a host of other questions are relevant to a true assessment of Brecht's impact and importance; and they cannot be answered without reference to the salient facts of his biography. After Brecht's death his patrons elevated him into the position of a saint in the Byzantine pantheon of Communist hagiography – and in order to do so had to suppress or embellish some essential features of both his life and his work: it is they who have made it necessary to start out from a biographical basis in discussing him as an artist and a political figure.

Brecht's importance, moreover, transcends his significance as a dramatist, poet, or amusing personality. He is above all an epitome of his times: most of the cross-currents and contradictions, moral and political dilemmas, artistic and literary trends of our time are focused and exemplified in Brecht's life and its vicissitudes. Through his commitment to a political cause, through his participation in the struggles of pre-Hitler Germany, his experience as an exiled writer in Europe and America, his plunge back into the drab but fascinating half-light of East Berlin, Brecht was more deeply involved in the conflicts of his age than most of his contemporaries. His experiences concentrate and distil its basic issues: the reaction of the generation of the First World War to the collapse of their entire civilization; the dilemmas facing a sensitive and passionate personality in an age of declining faith; the dangers that beset an artist whose indignation about the social evils of his society drives him into the arms of totalitarian forces; the theoretical and practical difficulties encountered by a writer of genius in a rigidly authoritarian society; the choice between lavishly subsidized but severely restricted working conditions in a Communist state on the one hand, and the limitations on the artist imposed upon him by a free, but commercial society. Brecht's experience exemplifies and sheds a light on all these problems.

The most intriguing question, however, posed – and largely answered – by Brecht's experience is: how far is it possible for a great writer to adhere to a creed so rigidly dogmatic, so far divorced from the reality of human experience as our latter-day brand of Communism without doing violence to his talent?

An analysis of Brecht's case will, I believe, put this problem into a new light by presenting the factual evidence of a concrete case of a committed major writer. It should help to explain the paradox why the most important Communist writer of his time was virtually banned within the Communist orbit, while, at the same time, being used to impress Western intellectuals with the achievements of Marxist culture.

And finally, although the main strength of Brecht's poetic power derives from his highly individual use of the German language, an attempt can be made at a critical survey of his work: his theory of the 'epic theatre' which he himself expounded in a most confusing manner and which has since then been further confounded by commentators hypnotized by the intriguing technical terms he invented, can be summarized in simple language and its real content and significance assessed. The real themes of his writing, which lie behind the surface of commitment and social purpose, can be laid bare and traced through the bewildering changes of style and tone of Brecht's Protean *œuvre*. This in turn will shed some further light on Brecht's personality and will help to explain the motives which made him an anarchist, nihilist, and cynic on the one hand, and a fervent believer in the collective virtues of discipline embodied in Marxist Communism on the other.

To avoid the need of wearying the reader with lengthy summaries of plays, novels, short stories, and poems which would interrupt the argument if they had to be inserted into the critical assessment of Brecht's work, a descriptive list of his writings is included in the reference section at the end of the book. This can be consulted as the need arises or studied separately at leisure. A short chronology of the main events of Brecht's career is also provided.

References to books and articles in periodicals and newspapers quoted are given in the footnotes, but in some cases titles have been abbreviated: e.g. Ernst Schumacher's massive study *Die dramatischen Versuche Bertolt Brechts 1918–1933* is referred to as 'Schumacher'. Full details of the more important sources used are given in the bibliography at the end of the book.

It is impossible to discuss a major writer without quoting from his works. To have given the quotations in the original German only would have been both pedantic and discourteous to the general reader. Brecht's poetry is peculiarly difficult to translate, but the quotations are nevertheless given in translated form. The translations are my own throughout the book (even in some cases of titles of works, where the existing form does not fully convey the intended meaning). They make no pretence at giving more than a suggestion of the meaning and the mood of the passages in question. Readers who know German are referred to the original; exact references to the passages concerned are provided.

As the book was designed to be a *critical* study of Brecht, and an objective account of his political convictions and the resulting tangled relations with the Communist party and authorities in Eastern Germany, it was impossible to approach his family and collaborators there without running the risk of later involving them in all kinds of embarrassments – and worse. Fortunately this was not necessary, as the whole story can be told by studying the ample material contained in newspapers and publications originating in East Germany and presenting the story in irreproachable 'official' form. Where personal accounts of events have been used, they were never accepted without rigorous cross-checking against the published facts and other independent sources.

For personal reminiscences of Brecht I am greatly indebted to Prof. Alfred Kantorowicz, Mr Ernest Borneman, Mr R. A. Harrison, Mr Melvin J. Lasky, Dr F. Wendhousen, and many others. I am particularly grateful to Mr Eric Bentley for his help with information about Brecht's stay in America.

Rare books, and other valuable material, were kindly put at my disposal by Frau M. Dobrozemsky of the National Library, Vienna; Mr Clemens Heller, Dr C. Brinitzer, Dr R. Weil, and others.

Miss A. Scherman helped me in finding my way through the East German Press, and I am most grateful to the Wiener Library, London, who gave me access to their files of newspaper cuttings, their collection of periodicals of the German emigration between 1933 and 1945, and also obtained for me material from Germany on microfilm.

I am grateful to Messrs Suhrkamp of Frankfurt on Main for permission to include quotations from Max Frisch's *Tagebuch 1946–1949*.

Part One: The Man

Chapter I

FROM AUGSBURG TO BERLIN
(1898–1924)

> I, Bertolt Brecht, am from the black forests.
> My mother carried me, as in her womb I lay,
> Into the cities. And the chill of the forests
> Will stay within me to my dying day.
>
> BRECHT, *Of poor B.B.*

Throughout his life Brecht loved to picture himself as representative of tormented twentieth-century man – a child of nature exiled to the barren asphalt and concrete cities of the industrial age. Yet the place where he was born and grew up was far from being such a monstrous megalopolis.

The city of Augsburg – *Augusta Vindelicorum* – had indeed once been one of the centres of European trade. But that was a long time ago: when the great merchant princes of the Renaissance, the Fuggers and the Welsers who vied with the Medici in splendour and acted as bankers to emperors and kings, had their headquarters there. By the time Brecht was born in Augsburg on 10 February 1898, it had long lost its position as one of the dominant centres of the German-speaking world and had become a provincial Bavarian backwater, a sleepy place with some 90,000 inhabitants, a sizeable textile manufacture, some paper mills, and a small but rapidly expanding engineering industry. But it had also remained a market town to which the farmers of the surrounding countryside brought their produce.

It was all very quiet and idyllic. Brecht says:

> Past my father's house there ran an avenue of chestnut trees along the old city moat; on the other side there lay the city wall with the remnants of ancient fortifications. Swans swam in the water that was like a pond. The chestnuts shed their yellow leaves. . . .[1]

[1] Brecht, 'Bei Durchsicht meiner ersten Stuecke', *Stuecke I* (Aufbau Verlag), pp. 12, 13.

3

Once a year the farmers came to amuse themselves and the town put on a show for them:

> I often visited the Herbstplaerrer ('autumn barker'), an annual fair of booths on the 'little drill ground' with the music of many merry-go-rounds, and 'panoramas' that displayed crude pictures of historical events, like 'The Shooting of the Anarchist Ferrer at Madrid' or 'Nero Surveys the Fire of Rome' or 'The Bavarian Lions Storm the Defences at Dueppel' or 'The Flight of Charles the Bold after the Battle of Murten'. I remember the horse of Charles the Bold. It had enormous frightened eyes, as though it felt the horror of the historical situation.[1]

Brecht's father was a respected and well-to-do citizen, the managing director of a paper mill, his mother the daughter of a civil servant from the Black Forest. Theirs was a mixed Catholic-Protestant marriage, and young *Eugen Berthold Friedrich* Brecht was christened in the Protestant faith of his mother. It would be easy to speculate on the influence of the conflict of faiths in his family on Brecht's ambivalent and self-contradictory character, but there is no evidence to support such an assumption, beyond the fact that his Protestant upbringing accounts for the strong influence the language of Luther's Bible exercised on him. As to the three names he had been given, he later rejected them all, avoiding Eugen and Friedrich with their patriotic overtones, and amending Berthold as the mood took him by shortening it to Bert or hardening the rather sentimental syllable '-hold' (which can mean 'lovely') into Bertolt.

He was a sensitive and taciturn child, non-conformist and rebellious in a quiet, negative way. It may be of some significance that his younger brother was the one who followed closely in his father's footsteps, and showed such interest in the problems of paper-making that he later became Professor of Paper Manufacture at the Technical University of Darmstadt. Be that as it may, Brecht himself always saw himself as a rebel and a traitor to his bourgeois background:

> *I grew up as the son*
> *Of well-to-do people. My parents*
> *Put a collar round my neck and taught me*
> *The habit of being waited on*

[1] Brecht, 'Bei Durchsicht meiner ersten Stuecke', *Stuecke I* (Aufbau Verlag), pp. 12, 13.

> *And the art of giving orders. But*
> *When I had grown up and looked around me*
> *I did not like the people of my own class*
>
> .   .   .   .   .
>
> *And I left my own class and joined*
> *The common people. . . .*[1]

There is a hint in one of Brecht's later short stories[2] that his revolt against the respectability of his parents may have been inspired by the example of his grandmother: at the age of seventy-two, when her husband died, this old lady had suddenly shocked the family by abandoning the dull, cramped conventions of petty bourgeois gentility and consorting with all sorts of queer and not quite respectable people. Contempt for respectability in any shape or form, and a strong and largely unfulfilled yearning for the company of 'plebeian' people, certainly became one of the dominant features of Brecht's whole life and character.

Both on his father's and his mother's side his ancestors had been shrewd, hard-headed peasants from Baden. His friends have often attributed his calculated, cunning and indirect approach to intellectual as well as business matters to his descent from a long line of sly, suspicious country people with their ingrained distrust of city slickers, their scepticism about anything that sounds high-flown or pompous. Brecht's horror of all sentiment and phrase-making, his love of irony and parody, and his often proclaimed faith in the wisdom of cowardice may well have had its origins in his canny peasant blood. That he was already master of this oblique, 'dialectical' approach in his early years is shown by an often quoted story for which we have the authority of one of his schoolfellows:

For Brecht and one of his classmates a great deal depended on their success in the end-of-term test papers in French and Latin respectively. But Brecht's French was as weak as his friend's Latin, and both papers came back with numerous corrections in red ink – and bad marks. Brecht's friend tried to retrieve the situation by erasing some of the corrected mistakes, substituting the correct versions

---

[1] Brecht, 'Verjagt mit gutem Grund', *Hundert Gedichte*, East Berlin, 1951, p. 298.

[2] Brecht, 'Die Unwuerdige Greisin' ('The Unworthy Old Woman'), in *Kalendergeschichten*.

and complaining to the Latin master that his paper had received too low a marking. But the Latin master held the paper up against the light, immediately saw that it had been tampered with, and the boy's stratagem proved a miserable failure. Brecht himself had a far subtler plan: he liberally inserted additional red marks in places where his translation had been quite correct, then went to his French master and very tactfully and humbly queried some of these corrections. The master was highly embarrassed at having absent-mindedly faulted some perfectly correct phrases, apologized, and hastened to give Brecht's paper a much higher marking.[1]

Always a rebel, Brecht maintained that he had learned more from opposition than emulation in his schooldays. As he himself put it:

Elementary school bored me for four years. During my nine years at the Augsburg Realgymnasium (Grammar School) I did not succeed in imparting any worthwhile education to my teachers. My sense of leisure and independence was tirelessly fostered by them. . . . By indulgence in all kinds of sport I acquired some heart trouble which introduced me to the mysteries of metaphysics. . . .[2]

Brecht was sixteen when the First World War broke out, and he soon got into trouble with the authorities in his Realgymnasium by voicing violently pacifist views in an essay on the theme of '*Dulce et decorum est pro patria mori* . . .'. Only the intercession of one of his teachers who pleaded that the war must have completely upset the sensitive boy's mind saved him from being expelled. At this time he was already contributing occasional book reviews and poems to a local newspaper under the pen-name 'Berthold Eugen'. The journalist who helped him to get his first efforts printed later described him as 'a shy, reserved young man, only able to speak after the clockwork inside him had been wound up'.[3]

He can hardly have been as tongue-tied in the company of his schoolmates, for he became the centre of a circle of faithful friends who remained loyal to him all his life, chief among them Caspar

[1] Told by Herbert Ihering in 'Der Volksdramatiker', *Sinn und Form*, First Special Brecht Issue, 1949, p. 5.

[2] Brecht in a letter to Herbert Ihering (1922), published in *Sinn und Form*, 1958 I, p. 31.

[3] Wilhelm Bruestle, 'Wie ich Brecht entdeckte', *Neue Zeitung*, Munich, 27.11.1948. Quoted by Schumacher, p. 26.

Neher, the eminent painter and stage designer whose work was always closely linked with Brecht's.

In 1916 he left school and moved to Munich, where he began to read medicine and science at the university. But after a few terms he had to interrupt his studies. It was war-time. He was called up. And being a medical student, he became a medical orderly in a military hospital.

There can be no doubt that this was one of the decisive events of his life.

> I was mobilized in the war [he told Sergei Tretyakov] and placed in a hospital. I dressed wounds, applied iodine, gave enemas, performed blood-transfusions. If the doctor ordered me: 'Amputate a leg, Brecht!' I would answer: 'Yes, Your Excellency!' and cut off the leg. If I was told: 'Make a trepanning!' I opened the man's skull and tinkered with his brains. I saw how they patched people up in order to ship them back to the front as soon as possible.[1]

Seeing human beings cut up in this way and having to do this gruesome work himself was a traumatic experience that left lasting traces in Brecht's character and work: his poetry is haunted by images of dismembered bodies; a fanatical pacifism became the basis of all his political thought, and his implacably violent attitude clearly springs from the impotent rage of the helpless bystander, yearning to inflict the same cruel treatment upon all those he felt responsible for such senseless mutilation; even Brecht's ostentatious display of defiant toughness in later life, the disgusted rejection of anything even remotely smacking of high-minded sentiment, whether religious or patriotic, can be seen as the reaction of a basically tender mind, shaken to its core by the sheer horror of existence in a world where such suffering was allowed to happen. Whether he had been religious or not in any conventional sense, the blatant cynicism of his public *persona* in later life is all too obviously the mask of one whose faith has been shattered and who has decided to meet the world on its own inhuman terms.

This is the experience behind Brecht's first characteristically Brechtian poem, *The Legend of the Dead Soldier*, a ballad about a dead body, which is dug up and solemnly pronounced fit for military service

[1] Sergei Tretyakov, 'Bert Brecht', *International Literature*, Moscow, May 1937.

in the fifth year of the war, because the Kaiser needs more cannon-fodder:

> They poured some brandy down his throat
> The rotten corpse to rouse.
> Two hefty nurses grabbed his arms,
> And his half-naked spouse.
>
> Because the rotten body stank,
> A parson limped ahead
> And over him his incense swung
> To cover the stench of the dead.[1]

And so the dead soldier is paraded through the streets in solemn procession:

> The band in the van with rum-tum-tum
> Played him a rousing march.
> The soldier as he had been drilled
> Kicked his legs high from his arse.[1]

The determination to shock, to be as coarse and crass as possible, is only too clear. But so is the shattered faith behind the defiance and despair:

> You could not see him for the crowd
> Thronging round him with hurrahs!
> One might have seen him from on high:
> But nothing was there – but the stars.[2]

When the revolution came in November 1918 and was followed by a brief spell of Communism in Bavaria, Brecht was whole-heartedly on the side of the revolutionaries; as he told the audience in the Kremlin when he was given the Stalin Peace Prize:

I was . . . twenty when I saw the reflection of the great fire (of the Russian Revolution) in my own home town. I was a medical orderly in an Augsburg military hospital. The barracks and even the military hospitals emptied, the ancient city suddenly filled up with new people, who came in large numbers from the outskirts. . . .[3]

[1] Brecht, 'Legende vom Toten Soldaten', *Hauspostille*, Berlin, 1927, p. 127.
[2] ibid., p. 129.
[3] Brecht, Speech on receiving the Stalin (later Lenin) Peace Prize, Moscow, 1955, *Versuche 15*, p. 146.

Twenty years earlier he had related the same episode in somewhat less idealized terms to Sergei Tretyakov:

> I was a member of the Augsburg Revolutionary Committee. The hospital was the only military unit in the town. It elected me. . . . We did not boast a single Red Guardsman. We didn't have time to issue a single decree or to nationalize a single bank or to close a single church. After two days General Epp's troops came to town on their way to Munich. One of the members of the revolutionary committee hid at my house until he managed to escape.[1]

Soon the whole revolutionary episode was forgotten. Brecht returned to the Bohemian life of a medical student in Munich. He had started to write plays. Characteristically his very first effort originated in his fury about an existing play, *Der Einsame* by Hanns Johst (later the leading poet of Nazi Germany), which had been published in 1917. This is a dramatic biography of the German poet Grabbe, who was an outsider and drunkard but a genius. Brecht, discussing this play with his school friend George Pfanzelt, criticized the false idealism and sentimentality with which Johst had presented the life of a dissolute character. When challenged to do better, he wagered with Pfanzelt that he would write a better play on a similar theme in four days. And he did. His play, *Baal*, also tells the story of a poet, an anti-social outsider who seduces women, throws them to the dogs afterwards, and finally murders his best friend in a fit of homosexual jealousy reminiscent of Verlaine's attack on Rimbaud. The play is preceded by an orgiastic ballad in the style of *The Legend of the Dead Soldier*. *Baal* is a wild and extravagant effusion in the tradition of Buechner's *Woyzeck*, episodic and disjointed but carried along by a torrent of powerful images that unmistakably bear the marks of genius.

Brecht knew that *Baal* had little chance of being performed. So he wrote another play, with an eye to the requirements of the moment. Lion Feuchtwanger, the novelist, playwright and man of letters, thirty-five and already an established author at that time, has described how Brecht came to see him with this play:

> At the turn of the year 1918, shortly after the outbreak of the so-called German Revolution, a very young man came to my Munich

---

[1] Sergei Tretyakov 'Bert Brecht', *International Literature*, Moscow, May 1937.

apartment, thin, badly shaved, and unkempt in appearance. He slunk around the walls, spoke Swabian dialect, had written a play, and was called Bertolt Brecht. The play was called *Spartakus*. Unlike most young authors, who on handing over their manuscripts have a habit of pointing to their bleeding hearts from which their work has been torn, this young man stressed that he had written his play *Spartakus* exclusively to make money.[1]

Feuchtwanger read the play. It was about a soldier who had come back from the war and was drawn into the revolutionary troubles of the 'Spartakus' rising in Berlin. He was impressed.

I . . . telephoned the unkempt young man and asked him why he had lied to me; he could not possibly have written this play merely out of material necessity. At this the young author became very violent and dialectical almost to the point of incoherence and declared that he had indeed written this play for money's sake only; but that he had another play as well, which was really good and he would bring it to me. He brought it. It was called *Baal* . . . and turned out to be an even wilder, even more extravagant and very splendid piece of work.[1]

Feuchtwanger, who was fourteen years older than Brecht, helped him with his plays and *Spartakus*, renamed *Trommeln in der Nacht* (*Drums in the Night*), later became Brecht's first stage success.

But that was almost four years later. In the meantime Brecht led the life of a student who was gradually drifting into the world of the theatre and literature, a world of smoke-filled cafés and taverns, endless discussions, and a great deal of dissipation. Brecht would sing the *Ballad of Baal* and *The Legend of the Dead Soldier* in taverns and coffee houses, accompanying himself on the guitar or banjo and bawling out the verse in his high-pitched voice. Often some living ex-soldiers with patriotic sympathies would take exception at the sentiments expressed in the ballad about the dead soldier and give the young bard a good hiding.

But he also made interesting acquaintances in this way. Peter Suhrkamp, who became his firm friend and later his publisher, has

[1] L. Feuchtwanger, 'Bertolt Brecht, dargestellt fuer Englaender', *Die Weltbuehne*, Berlin, 4.9.1928.

described how he met him in some rural Bavarian tavern, singing his ballads to a group of coachmen and carters.[1] And the strange young vagabond poet also had a fascination for women when he sang his ballads. In his novel *Erfolg*, Feuchtwanger describes young Brecht, thinly disguised as Kaspar Proeckl, a motor-car designer, as casting a peculiar spell on women:

> Of course, this fellow was always unshaven. But the way he made his hair grow over his forehead had a kind of naïve coquettishness. He smelt like soldiers on the march. Nor did his angular, malicious sense of humour seem the right thing for the ladies. There was an unmistakable odour of revolution about him. Clearly it was his way of singing his crude ballads that did it. When he sang them with his shrill voice women swooned. . . .[2]

And Brecht's schoolmate and fellow medical student, Otto Muellereisert, later said about Brecht's singing: 'He got ninety per cent of his women that way.'[3]

The times were troubled and manners rough. In the ups and downs of revolution and counter-revolution politics often came between friends. A story, later told by Muellereisert, shows that in spite of his violently left-wing views Brecht retained his own special sardonic sense of humour: one day Muellereisert decided to join one of those bands of right-wing irregulars, the *Freikorps*, that harassed the allied armies in Germany at the time. He wrote Brecht about it. Brecht angrily replied that their friendship was at an end and that he would not even come to his funeral if Muellereisert were killed. But a week later he wrote another letter: he had changed his mind. Stupidity, after all, was not a ground for divorce. He had reached the conclusion that he would attend his funeral after all. Muellereisert never joined the *Freikorps*.

In October 1919, while continuing his studies and his Bohemian existence in Munich, Brecht began to commute to Augsburg to act as theatre critic for *Der Volkswille*, the local organ of the extreme

[1] Peter Suhrkamp, 'Introduction to Brecht, *Gedichte und Lieder*', Berlin and Frankfurt, 1956, p.5.
[2] L. Feuchtwanger, *Erfolg*, Berlin, 1930, vol. I, p. 179.
[3] *Der Spiegel*, Hamburg, 13.9.1950.

left-wing Independent Socialist Party. His notices are distinguished mainly by their rudeness:

> The man who has leased the Augsburg Municipal Theatre as his milch-cow knows today, after so many years, about as much about literature as an engine driver knows about geography . . .[1]

is a fair sample of his rough-and-ready kind of wit. The personnel of the theatre protested in an open letter against the tone of these criticisms – only to be rebuked in even ruder terms. Brecht continued to belabour the management and actors of this no doubt miserable provincial company until the beginning of 1921.

By this time his medical studies had lapsed. Brecht had finally entered the world of the stage, in the capacity in which most young dramatists in the German-speaking theatre begin to make their living: as a 'Dramaturg'. This post, non-existent in the Anglo-Saxon theatre, combines the position of a resident playwright and play-adaptor with that of a reader and literary adviser of the management, editor of the programme brochure, and public relations officer. Brecht became one of the Dramaturgen of the Munich Kammerspiele, whose manager Otto Falckenberg had been impressed by his manuscript plays and was planning to put on *Trommeln in der Nacht*. But while doing a certain amount of work for Falckenberg, Brecht also tried to place his plays elsewhere, to find a publisher and perhaps to gain a foothold in the capital city of the German theatre – Berlin.

In the course of the year 1921 he went to Berlin several times for this purpose. And there, early in 1922, he met Arnolt Bronnen.

Bronnen is one of the most extraordinary, and most controversial, figures of contemporary German literature: the son of a Jewish-Austrian schoolmaster called Bronner, he rose to fame as one of the leaders of the Expressionist movement, but later abandoned his left-wing friends and put his very considerable talents at the service of the Nazis – having established his racial purity by making his mother testify in court that he was not her husband's son. Towards the end of the Second World War he joined the anti-Nazi underground movement, became a Communist, was burgomaster of a mountain village

---

[1] Brecht writing in *Volkswille*, Augsburg, 13.10.1920. Reprinted in *Sinn und Form*, Second Special Brecht Issue, 1957, p. 220.

for a time, and moved to East Germany after the Soviet troops left Austria.

In 1922 Bronnen was trying to make his way as an author while working as a clerk in a Berlin department store. He has described how one afternoon, in the apartment of Otto Zarek, the writer and journalist, who had invited him to tea to meet some literary friends, he had left the drawing-room and was exploring the large flat:

> From one of the rooms I could hear guitar music. . . . I went in. It was rather dark there; at first I could only hear a croaking voice. . . . Then I saw the singer: an emaciated young man of twenty-four with steel-rimmed glasses and untidy dark hair that fell over his forehead. I stared at him. I was as if under a spell. I experienced a sensation which perhaps is only given to very lonely human beings: to be suddenly confronted with man in all the richness of his being. He sang, he spoke, he read aloud, there were four other young people in the room; I did not see them. I only stared at this one young man. Later Otto Zarek told me that his name was Bert Brecht.[1]

Soon Brecht and Bronnen were firm friends. Bronnen's play *Vatermord* (*Parricide* – what else could Bronnen's first play be called?) had just been accepted by Moritz Seeler, the pioneer of Expressionist drama who ran an experimental matinée theatre, Junge Buehne. Brecht insisted that he was the only person who could produce Bronnen's play. Bronnen agreed. But Brecht was so undernourished that he fell seriously ill and had to be taken to hospital. Bronnen tried to help him financially as far as his own meagre means permitted and impatiently waited for him to be well enough to start rehearsals.

Seeler had secured two very distinguished artists for the main parts of the play – Heinrich George and Agnes Straub. These already famous actors were horrified when the young unknown producer with his marked Bavarian accent hurled strings of obscene invective at them. Bronnen's play was written in the explosive, declamatory style of the Expressionists. But Brecht wanted to produce it quietly and realistically. Already at this early stage he hated noisy, emotional tantrums in the theatre. The stars insisted that the text demanded such outbursts. And so the day came when Heinrich George threw his part away with

[1] *Arnolt Bronnen gibt zu Protokoll*, Hamburg, 1954, pp. 97–8.

such force that it landed in the fifteenth row of the stalls and Agnes Straub had to be taken away in convulsions. The world première of *Vatermord* was off. Brecht congratulated Bronnen: 'It would not have been a success with these actors.'

Brecht returned to Munich, having as Bronnen claims plagiarized part of his name: Bronnen had hardened his Christian name Arnold into the more archaic-looking and more original Arnol*t*, and this, he claims, gave Brecht the idea of turning his own first name Berthold into Bertol*t*. While Bronnen's play was being performed in Frankfurt and produced by another and more diplomatic producer in Berlin as well, Brecht's *Drums in the Night* was also to have its world première. In a letter dated 22 September 1922 Brecht asked the influential Berlin critic Herbert Ihering to come to Munich for the first night

> which will be on 29 September (Friday). I know exactly how much I am asking, but very much indeed depends on it for me. Since Berlin has ceased to make experiments, it has become extremely difficult to obtain decent criticism at a time when one needs it most.[1]

The first night at the Kammerspiele was a great success. The audience had been greeted by streamers with inscriptions like 'DON'T STARE SO ROMANTICALLY' and 'EVERY MAN FEELS BEST INSIDE HIS OWN SKIN'. They saw the action taking place in a non-realistic setting with the picture of the city rising up behind the screens that suggested the walls of the rooms, where the soldier Kragler made his decision to marry his shop-soiled bride and turn his back on the revolution, while a red moon hung above like a Chinese lantern.

Ihering *had* gone to Munich. His review in the *Berliner Boersen-Courier* was enthusiastic and brilliantly perceptive:

> The twenty-four-year-old poet Bert Brecht has changed the literary physiognomy of Germany overnight. With Bert Brecht a new tone, a new melody, a new vision has entered our time. . . . Brecht is impregnated with the horror of this age in his nerves, in his blood. This horror creates a pallid atmosphere, a half-light round men and things. . . . Brecht physically feels the chaos and putrid decay of the times. Hence the unparalleled force of his images. This language can be felt on the tongue, on the palate, in one's ears, in one's spine. . . . It is brutally sensuous and melancholically tender. It

[1] Letter from Brecht to Ihering, *Sinn und Form*, 1958/I, p. 29.

contains malice and bottomless sadness, grim wit and plaintive lyricism. . . .[1]

As it happened Ihering acted as adjudicator for the Kleist Prize, an annual award to the best young dramatic talent, for the year 1922. Originally he had intended to share the prize between Bronnen and Brecht. But in the end he gave it to Brecht alone. Brecht's reputation as a rising dramatist was established.

But the road to success was far from smooth. Germany's leading theatre, Reinhardt's Deutsches Theater, was planning to produce *Drums in the Night* in December 1922. Brecht returned to Berlin and filled himself up with the unlimited number of rolls served free with even the cheapest dish in the Aschinger chain of restaurants. He was so careful with his money that Bronnen had great difficulty in persuading him to take an occasional tram. He resisted these seductions by pointing out that extravagance usually leads to ruin: 'The tram-ride will end in a pauper's grave,' he said.[2]

The great Max Reinhardt himself was so fascinated by Brecht's play that he attended the rehearsals of *Drums in the Night* every day for three weeks, quietly sitting in the back of the theatre. But there were difficulties about the casting and décor, and Brecht greatly disagreed with Felix Hollaender, who was managing the Deutsches Theater for Reinhardt at the time. Eventually *Drums in the Night* was a failure in Berlin. Brecht wrote to Ihering from Munich:

So Hollaender has murdered the *Drums*. What a black heart that man has in his chest. God will sit in judgment over him. That will be unpleasant for him. But I too shall sit in judgment over him. And that will be even more unpleasant.[3]

In Munich the State Theatre was about to produce another new play by Brecht: *Im Dickicht* (later renamed *Im Dickicht der Staedte – In the Jungle of the Cities*). This curious play with its 'motiveless action' which foreshadows Beckett, Ionesco or Adamov puzzled the audience

[1] Herbert Ihering, 'Der Dramatiker Bert Brecht', *Berliner Boersen-Courier*, 5.10.1922. Reprinted in *Sinn und Form*, Second Special Brecht Issue, 1957, pp. 230–1.

[2] Bronnen, op. cit., p. 110.

[3] Letter from Brecht to Ihering dated February 1923, *Sinn und Form*, 1958/I, p. 32.

when it was performed in May 1923. And Brecht's earliest effort, *Baal*, which had its first stage performance in Leipzig in December, caused a veritable scandal. One critic called the play a 'mud-bath' and added: 'It would have been wiser and in better taste if the municipal theatre had left this 'boy's *tour-de-force*' to people who like to read this kind of thing and had spared us, Brecht, and itself this wild evening.'[1]

Undaunted, Brecht was already working on a new play. His contract with the Munich Kammerspiele also required him to produce. He was asked to tackle *Macbeth*, but felt that such a task would be beyond him. So he decided to try his hand on a lesser Elizabethan dramatist, and chose Marlowe's *Edward II*. But as he did not like the existing translation he began to make an adaptation of his own. Lion Feuchtwanger helped him with this work: Brecht would bring him his version, and Feuchtwanger would tighten the construction and roughen the verse when it ran too smoothly. In the end, the play, while following Marlowe's plot fairly closely, had become an entirely original work through its unusual form and language: a balladesque chronicle play in the naïve style of the historical paintings Brecht had seen in the 'panoramas' of the Augsburg fair-ground. Brecht himself produced *Edward II*, which was first performed in March 1924. In many ways this was the début of Brecht's 'epic theatre': a production naïvely sophisticated, yet highly stylized. In later years Brecht used to tell the story of how he had been in difficulties with a battle scene. He had asked everyone for advice and finally come to Karl Valentin, the famous clown of the Munich beer halls, whom he greatly admired as a folk artist of naïve profundity. 'What do soldiers do in a battle?' Brecht asked the lanky, quixotic comedian. Valentin replied: 'They are afraid.' And so Brecht made his soldiers appear in the battle with their faces made up chalk-white. The scene produced an unforgettable effect.

Brecht's artistic personality was already clearly formed in these early days in Munich and Berlin: he was the exact opposite of the conventional German idea of a poet – anything but a withdrawn individualist who spins the sacred essence of his personality out of himself in the secrecy of some lonely garret, but a collective being, always the centre of a crowd of collaborators, asking advice and accepting it from anyone who cared to offer it. Even while lying in a state of collapse in the Berlin Charité Hospital, Brecht, as Bronnen reports, was never alone,

[1] *Leipziger Neueste Nachrichten*, 10.12.1923. Quoted by Schumacher, p. 42.

but 'always in a whirl of heads, from which his own head stood out. . . .'[1] Bronnen describes Brecht's method of work as based on complete relaxation:

> comfortably puffing his cigar Brecht stalked through the room listening to arguments and counter-arguments from dozens of people, cracked jokes, but stuck unshakeably to his main line of work. He rode his thought until, magnificently formulated, he could dictate it to the miniature audience of his ever-present aides.[2]

As he regarded his work not as the emanation of some metaphysical experience but as the product of trial and error, Brecht was always ready to change and amend his writings. According to Feuchtwanger

> he rewrites his work countless times, in twenty, thirty different versions to suit the needs of any insignificant provincial theatre. He attaches no importance whatever to the fact that a piece of work is finished. Even if it has been printed ten times, the last version always turns out to have been the last but one. He is the despair of publishers and producers. If his attention is drawn to some inner inconsistency, he does not hesitate to throw out the work of a whole year; but he would not devote a minute to the correction of some blatant error in external probability. He leaves that to the producer, or to his secretary, or to Mr X.[3]

Bernhard Reich, who worked with Brecht at the Munich Kammerspiele, confirms that this attitude extended to his own work as a producer:

> If the producer Brecht liked an actor, the actor had to be shown to greater advantage. The poet Brecht immediately took a piece of paper from his pocket and wrote new text for the actor. The producer Brecht discovered that the author's intention could not in practice be realized on the stage. So the poet Brecht arrived the next morning with a rewritten and changed text. As the dress rehearsal approached, Brecht became more and more busy, handing up whole reams of new text to the actors from the auditorium. . . .[4]

[1] Bronnen, op. cit., p. 98. [2] ibid., p. 109.
[3] L. Feuchtwanger, 'Bertolt Brecht, dargestellt fuer Englaender', *Die Weltbuehne*, Berlin, 4.9.1928.
[4] Bernhard Reich, 'Erinnerungen an den jungen Brecht', *Sinn und Form*, Second Special Brecht Issue, 1957, p. 432.

The power to gather a circle around him testifies to Brecht's genius for friendship: it is remarkable how starting from his schoolmates at Augsburg all those to whom he had given his friendship remained his firm friends to the end, often in spite of political disagreement and across the East–West barrier. And yet the same slight, thin young man, unkempt and unshaven, with his cheap steel-rimmed glasses, his leather coat and leather cap, and his rudeness, terrified other people out of their wits as a sinister individual, sullen, hard, and disgusting. This dual nature of Brecht's character was apparent even to his friends. The first edition of *Hauspostille* contains a drawing of Brecht by his friend Caspar Neher. Underneath it is a revealing inscription in schoolboy's dog-Latin:

Iste erat Hydatopyranthropos/ vivens Augustis Vindelicorum/ per unum saeculum/ 1898–1998/ . . ./ major nisi Himalaya tamen certe Monte Blanco/ Caput Benevolentiae Integritatis/ semper aequam servans mentem/ pueris puellisque amicus/ inimicis terror. . . .

This touching tribute with its wish that he might live a hundred years and its insistence on Brecht's friendliness and integrity and his friendship for boys and girls recognizes the inner contradiction of his character by labelling him *Hydatopyranthropos* – a man compounded of fire and water – and a terror to his enemies.

Feuchtwanger, who was his great friend and had worked with him, modelled the character of the motor-car designer Kaspar Proeckl in his long novel *Erfolg* on Brecht. This portrait reveals the deeper layers of Brecht's personality that had been so terribly hurt by his war-time experience.

That Brecht had stood model for Proeckl was publicly acknowledged by all concerned when passages from the novel were linked in a radio portrait of Brecht, broadcast in December 1930. It is significant that Feuchtwanger has made Proeckl not a poet but an engineer, the designer of a people's car: an expression of Brecht's attitude to art as a kind of mental engineering. Proeckl, like Brecht, is talkative, yet reticent about his own personality and thoughts.

. . . he had made up a theory for himself, according to which he only spoke with people he met about *their* affairs, never about his own or about general topics. For people usually are well informed only about their own affairs, and only on those matters can you learn anything worth while from them. . . .[1]

But behind this severely rational attitude of Proeckl/Brecht there lies a substratum of sentiment. People do not know, Proeckl tells himself in a moment of emotional tension, 'how much it costs him to suppress sentiment by clear, hard rationality'.[2] And another character in the book insists that Proeckl/Brecht is driven into a collective, social frame of mind by certain deep deficiencies within him:

> That you have been taken in by Communism . . . is due to the fact that from birth you have been singularly deficient in social instincts. What for others is a matter of course, instinct . . . overwhelms you by its novelty, by its scientific façade. You are a poor creature. You are unable to feel yourself into other people. You cannot have sympathy with others; that is why you are trying to get things by artificial means. . . . And on top of that – you are a puritan. You lack the most important human organs: senses capable of pleasure and a charitable heart.[3]

This view – in the novel it comes from a character with a strong emotional bias – may be unjust to Proeckl/Brecht, but it shows one side of his nature: a person basically tender, driven to suppress his emotion, to appear hard and rational, a human being so deeply hurt that he has become afraid of being involved in the feelings of others, and therefore appears incapable of sympathy – and empathy. All this is highly relevant to the complex character of the young Brecht: after all, the whole theory of the 'epic theatre' is based on the rejection of empathy and the emotional involvement of the audience with the characters on the stage.

Young Brecht was indeed 'compounded of fire and water', a bundle of apparent contradictions: he was a sensualist and Don Juan, whose relations with women were highly complex: his first illegitimate child, Frank (named after Wedekind) was born to one of his school sweethearts, Paula (Bie) Banholzer when Brecht was twenty-one. (He grew up with foster parents and was killed as a soldier in Russia in 1943.) Another child, by Otto Zoff's sister, the singer Marianne Zoff was aborted; when Marianne became pregnant again Brecht married her

[1] Feuchtwanger, *Erfolg*, Berlin, 1930, vol. I, p. 170.
[2] ibid., vol. II, p. 266.   [3] ibid., vol. I, pp. 422-3.

(in November 1922). His daughter Hanne was born in March 1923. A year later, Brecht had a son – Stefan Brecht, born 6 March 1924 – by Helene Weigel whom he married, after his divorce from Marianne Zoff, in April 1929. Yet, in spite of his lifelong amorous involvements, often with three or four women at the same time, Brecht was emotionally more attached to male friends. On 16 July 1920 he noted in his diary: 'It is better with a friend than with a girl'.[1] His first plays again and again return to the theme of homosexuality (*Baal, Edward II, In the Jungle of the Cities*). There can be little doubt that his Don Juan complex and his suppressed homosexuality are closely connected. Was this the reason why Feuchtwanger portrayed him as a man unable to achieve lasting human attachments? Gregarious and lonely, sensualist and puritan, repulsively unkempt in the eyes of some, highly attractive to others, Brecht appeared as the soul of tact and friendliness to those he wanted to impress, intolerably rude and repulsive to those he wanted to shock.

In Feuchtwanger's novel, which presents a wide canvas of Munich life and society at the time of the first Hitler *putsch* of November 1923, the young motor engineer Proeckl finally leaves Munich – for Moscow. In real life Brecht also left Munich after the beer-cellar *putsch*. But *he* went to Berlin.

[1] Brecht, *Tagebuecher 1920–1922. Autobiographische Aufzeichnungen 1920–1954*. Frankfurt, Suhrkamp, 1975, p. 20.

Chapter II

BERLIN
(1924-1933)

Into the cities I came in the time of disorder. . . .
BRECHT, *An die Nachgeborenen*

Berlin had always attracted Brecht: it really was the modern megalopolis he so loved to hate; the vast pile of stone, concrete, and asphalt so many of his poems speak of, where man is lost in a jungle; the seething cauldron of lust, greed, and corruption that for him summed up the twentieth-century world: dreadful, doomed – and magnificent. As one of his letters to Bronnen, written around 1923[1] shows, Brecht had nicknamed Berlin 'Mahagonny', and so it is clear that Mahagonny, the town whose rise and fall he made the subject of an opera, stands for Berlin. And in fact that mythical pioneer city of Mahagonny, a jerry-built jumble of brothels and saloons somewhere between the California of the forty-niners and the Alaska of the Klondike goldrush, where everything is to be had for money and the only capital crime is lack of cash, seems a very apt symbol for the Berlin of the middle twenties and early thirties.

Berlin was the place where a young man of Brecht's boundless ambition had to make his way to become famous and to acquire influence. And Brecht wanted to have influence. According to Bernhard Reich, Brecht at that time

> believed that he would have to create for himself a network of
> followers and believers that would cover the whole of Germany,
> people who would work for a new art of the theatre from key
> positions – in theatres, publishing houses, and newspapers. He saw
> himself as the chieftain of this band.[2]

The German theatre could only be transformed and renewed from

[1] *Arnolt Bronnen gibt zu Protokoll*, Hamburg, 1954, p. 117.

[2] Bernhard Reich, 'Erinnerungen an den jungen Brecht', *Sinn und Form*, Second Special Brecht Issue, 1957, p. 434.

the centre – and the centre of the German theatre was undoubtedly Berlin.

Brecht moved to Berlin late in 1924. His play *Im Dickicht* was due to be performed at the Deutsches Theater in October of that year, and *Edward II* was to follow at the Prussian State Theatre in December. Moreover, he had landed a job as 'Dramaturg' of the Deutsches Theater which could afford a number of such literary editors and advisers. Carl Zuckmayer, who was one of Brecht's colleagues in this office, has described how in that dismal and hungry post-inflation winter he himself would come to his office every morning, merely to collect the pile of coal briquettes that had been put in readiness by the stove, pack them in his brief-case and leave again, accompanied by the approving nods of the porter, who was duly impressed by the amount of work the 'Herr Dramaturg' had taken home again in his bulging brief-case. As to Brecht –

> he only rarely put in an appearance in his loose leather jacket that made him look like a cross between a truck driver and a Jesuit seminarist. He demanded that full powers be transferred to himself so that he could mould the repertoire entirely according to his own ideas and rename the Reinhardt theatres 'epic smoking theatres'; for he was of the opinion that people might be more inclined to think if they were allowed to smoke in the theatre. As these demands were rejected, he confined his activity to occasional appearances to collect his salary.[1]

All the more energetically he plunged into the bustling activity of projects and counter-projects, endless discussions, plots and counter-plots of the life of the Berlin theatrical and literary world.

The Berlin theatre at that time was dominated by three great producers: Reinhardt who had created a colourful style of his own, a cross between realism and romanticism, but who, at that time, was looking for new worlds to conquer: vast spectacles in circuses and giant halls or open-air productions involving whole towns, like his *Everyman* at the Salzburg Festival. Leopold Jessner at the Staatstheater (Prussian State Theatre) was the exponent of Expressionism as applied to the classics: highly stylized productions built around huge staircases. And finally there was the radically left-wing Agitprop

[1] C. Zuckmayer, 'Drei Jahre' in *Theaterstadt Berlin, Ein Almanach*, ed. Herbert Ihering, Berlin, 1948, pp. 87–9.

theatre of Erwin Piscator, who regarded the stage above all as an instrument for mobilizing the masses. Piscator sought a topical, highly political theatre. He relegated the author to a relatively minor position, and was often content to compile his productions out of newspaper reports or documentary material. Piscator put these spectacles on to a constructivist stage and used graphs of statistics, explanatory captions, lantern slides of photographs or documents, newsreels, and documentary film sequences to convey the political or sociological background of the play, while the propaganda lesson was drawn by choruses, spoken or sung, on stage or in the auditorium, so that the spectators were inevitably drawn into the action. His aim was a theatre that would be political, technological – and *epic*. By the latter term he meant a drama which would be utterly different from the conventional 'well-made' play: a kind of illustrated lecture or newspaper report on a political or social theme, loosely constructed in the shape of a serious *revue*: a sequence of musical numbers, sketches, film, declamation, sometimes linked by one or several narrators.

Piscator produced the first play billed as an 'epic drama': *Fahnen* (*Flags*) by Alfons Paquet, a dramatization of the Chicago anarchists' trial of 1886. In this production, which opened Piscator's tenure of the Volksbuehne in 1924, photographs of the historical figures appearing in the play were projected on to a screen during the prologue, and after each scene a written commentary on the action appeared on two boards on either side of the stage. Piscator claimed that 'in a certain sense *Fahnen* represented the first Marxist drama and the production the first attempt at laying bare the materialist motive forces of the action. . . .'[1]

There can be no doubt that Brecht's later theories of the 'epic theatre' were greatly influenced by Piscator's conception. Brecht also wanted a scientific, Marxist drama, loosely constructed so as to make it possible to explain the wider social and historical background of the play – and 'he grew very angry if this invention of his was explained by his lack of sense for dramatic construction'[2] – he too used posters and placards, songs, and choruses. But while Piscator attached little importance to purely literary values, Brecht laid great stress on the poetic aspects of such a drama. And so, although Brecht became a close

[1] E. Piscator, *Das politische Theater*, Berlin, 1929, p. 57.
[2] Feuchtwanger, 'Bertolt Brecht, dargestellt fuer Englaender', *Die Weltbuehne*, 4.9.1928.

collaborator of Piscator's, although he worked on many adaptations of plays for his theatre and they discussed several joint projects, Piscator never tackled one of Brecht's own plays.

Both Brecht's and Piscator's efforts on behalf of a modern, Marxist theatre were, incidentally, viewed with suspicion by the Communist party, whose interests they were intended to serve. Brecht had his own difficulties with the party, which are dealt with elsewhere in this book.[1] As to Piscator – when 'socialist realism' became the ruling aesthetic creed in Russia, his theory and practice were rejected by the Communists, and classed as formalist aberrations no less heinous than those of Kerzhentsev's Proletkult theatre in the Soviet Union.

If Reinhardt, Jessner, and Piscator formed the hard artistic core of the Berlin theatre of that period, around them there revolved a kaleidoscope of lesser lights, ranging from the vulgarly commercial boulevardiers who produced cheap farces, drawing-room comedies, or musical shows – the operetta merchants, as Brecht called them with contempt – to the young and struggling *avant-gardists*, talented and untalented, backed and without backing, who were trying to come to the fore. Competition was intense and the tone was decidedly rough. Rows and scandals, angry accusations and counter-accusations were the order of the day. In the autumn of 1924 Brecht was accused of plagiarism. Somebody had discovered that a number of lines in *Dickicht* were taken from a German translation of Rimbaud's *Une saison en enfer*. Brecht cleared himself by pointing out that these lines appeared in quotation marks in the text and were in fact being quoted by the character. It was not the last accusation of plagiarism he had to rebut. At another time right-wing circles tried to have an action for blasphemy brought against him for a Christmas poem of his, which cast doubt on the divinity of Jesus. The public prosecutor was reported as having the matter on his agenda. While Brecht's friend, the painter and cartoonist George Grosz, who had shown Christ crucified wearing a gas-mask, was brought to trial, the matter did not reach the courts in Brecht's case. But Brecht gave as good as he got. He and Bronnen vigorously hit back at their main critical opponent: Alfred Kerr, the doyen of Berlin critics who wrote his exquisite notices in the *Berliner Tageblatt*. Kerr, himself a poet, was a great believer in the 'beautiful', a category wholly rejected and detested by

[1] See Chapter VII.

24

Brecht, and never missed an opportunity for voicing his dislike of such dramatic iconoclasts and vulgar exhibitionists as Brecht and Bronnen. When Bronnen's play *Die Katalaunische Schlacht* was badly reviewed by Kerr, Brecht replied in a poem which compared Kerr to the opponents of railways at the time of their invention who had objected to them on the grounds that 'they had no tails and ate no oats. . . . Who had ever seen a locomotive producing horses' droppings?' But if Kerr was stubbornly against Brecht, the other leading Berlin critic, Herbert Ihering, his discoverer, staunchly supported him in the *Berliner Boersen-Courier*.

These rows and scandals were by no means confined to the columns of the newspapers. When Brecht's *Baal* reached the Berlin stage early in 1926, the audience of the first night, aware of the reputation of this play as strong, scandalous stuff, was tense with expectation. An eyewitness has described how suddenly the storm broke loose:

> People whistled, shrieked, booed, applauded. The actress who happened to be on stage by herself, jumped on to the piano and began to bang the keys with her feet, singing: 'Allons enfants de la patrie!' The noise grew deafening . . . and was kept up until the instigators of the scandal were utterly exhausted. Suddenly everything was quiet again. Only from one of the galleries one could hear the words 'You aren't *really* shocked, you are only pretending . . .' followed by the loud noise of a face being slapped. Then applause started, rose to a climax and the performance went on. . . .[1]

A few weeks later Brecht was in the centre of another scandal. The Dresden State Opera was producing Verdi's *Forza del Destino* with an entirely new libretto by the poet Franz Werfel. This was considered to be an event in the history of opera, and to mark it, it was decided to invite representatives of the new generation of German literature. Brecht, Bronnen, and the novelist Alfred Doeblin were chosen for this honour, and very proudly they travelled down to Dresden in March 1926, to bask in the sun of public recognition and to read from their own works at a special Sunday matinée arranged for them at the Dresden State Theatre on the morning after the first night of *Forza del Destino*. But when the three emissaries of the new generation arrived in the offices of the Saxon State Theatres the bureaucrats

[1] Hans Henny Jahnn, 'Vom armen B.B.', *Sinn und Form*, Second Special Brecht Issue, 1957, p. 425.

there treated them rather haughtily and handed them three seats somewhere on the side in the upper gallery. And there was no invitation to the official reception after the performance. The three young authors were speechless. Solemnly they tore up the gallery tickets and placed them in an envelope to be handed back to the 'Herr General-intendant' of the Saxon State Theatres. Then they left and were not seen again all evening. On the next morning they were just about to leave their hotel to take the train to Berlin when the envoys of the authorities came dancing in, apologizing for the mistake that had been made and begging them not to leave them in the lurch with the public already eagerly awaiting their appearance in the sold-out State theatre.

> Gentle, kind-hearted Alfred Doeblin [Bronnen reports in his memoirs] was immediately moved to pity for these eunuchs . . . Brecht had already got rid of his fury in a little allegorical ballad he had composed and looked upon the proceedings with sovereign disdain. Only I was boiling, and I continued to boil while we were being escorted in triumph to the theatre. . . .[1]

The matinée started well enough. Doeblin read from his works quietly and at great length. Brecht recited his ballad on the incident: it was about three gods who had been invited to the city of Alibi on the River Alibe (Elbe) to honour the great Alea (alea means dice, and dice in German is Wuerfel, which suggests Werfel), but

> *when they arrived, only the rain had come*
> *To receive them. . . .*[2]

and when they came into the great hall of the city

> *They saw their chairs standing*
> *Where coats are hung up and rotten eggs are boiled.*[2]

And not a crumb fell for them from the table of great Alea. Finally the gods had to be prevailed upon not to drown the city in a great flood. This poem too was received in silence as the audience did not understand its allusions, and Brecht proceeded to read some of his other works. Then it was Bronnen's turn, and Bronnen was known for his

[1] *Arnolt Bronnen gibt zu Protokoll*, Hamburg, 1954, pp. 158–9.
[2] Brecht, 'Matinée in Dresden', *Berliner Boersen-Courier*, 23.3.1926. Reprinted in Hans Meyer, 'Gelegenheitsdichtung des jungen Brecht', *Sinn und Form*, 1958/II, p. 287.

hot temper. One of the Saxon bureaucrats was so terrified at what would happen that he whispered in his ear: 'If you keep quiet we'll put on your next play!' This attempt to bribe him so enraged Bronnen that he launched into a violent and obscene diatribe against the shameful way he had been treated. The uproar that followed is said to have been beyond description.

Brecht's poem about the three gods became the germ which, at a much later date, burgeoned into the three gods of *The Good Soul of Setzuan*.

There can be no doubt that Brecht greatly enjoyed these scandals. He disliked the polite aesthetic atmosphere of educated and respectable society and wanted the theatre to become more like a sports arena. He elaborated this idea in a number of articles and favourably compared the genuine enthusiasm and technical expertise to be found on the sports ground with the pallid and inexpert reactions of audiences in the theatre. But, of course, a new kind of theatre needed a new kind of play and a new kind of building.

In the old kind of theatre [Brecht said in 1926] we are as out of place with our plays as Jack Dempsey would be unable to show his skill in a tavern brawl, where someone could knock him out by hitting him over the head with a chair. . . . [1]

To show his disdain for the effete world of the intellectuals Brecht sought the company of boxers and racing cyclists. Paul Samson-Koerner, the German light-heavyweight champion, became his friend and constant companion. In July 1926 Brecht announced that he was writing Samson-Koerner's biography. And when the film of the Dempsey-Tunney fight of 1926 was shown at a Berlin cinema, the performance was preceded by a poem by Brecht, recited by the well-known actor, Fritz Kortner.[2]

Brecht's rejection of the over-refined attitude of the aesthete in preference for a boisterous sportsmanlike approach led to another notable scandal of which he became the protagonist. In the autumn of 1926 a leading literary review asked Brecht to act as judge in a competition for a poetry prize it was organizing. Brecht accepted and four hundred young poets sent in their work. In February 1927 Brecht

[1] Elisabeth Hauptmann, 'Notizen ueber Brechts Arbeit 1926', *Sinn und Form*, Second Special Brecht Issue, 1957, p. 241.
[2] PEM, *Heimweh nach dem Kurfuerstendamm*, Berlin, 1952, p. 205.

published the result. He declared himself unable to award any prize at all: none of the poems received struck him as serving any useful purpose whatever – and in his view poetry had to be of some practical use.

> Poetry [he said in his report on the competition] must surely be capable of being examined from the point of view of its practical value. . . . All great poems have the value of documents. They show how their author, a significant human being, expressed himself.[1]

The young poets who had taken part in the contest, however, had shown themselves as nothing but decadent and uninteresting specimens of contemporary youth

> whose acquaintance [Brecht rudely declared], I should much more profitably have been without. . . . Here we have them once more, those quiet, gentle, dreamy creatures, the sensitive section of used-up *bourgeoisie*, with whom I do not want to have anything to do. . . .[1]

And so having refused to award a prize to, or even print, any of the exquisitely sensitive poems that had been submitted, to indicate what he meant by poetry that *was* of some practical use Brecht printed a poem, which had not been entered in the competition at all: a very naïve and crude piece of doggerel in praise of a six-day cycle racing hero of the time, Reggie MacNamara, that he had found in a cycling paper. It has the title (in English): *He! He! The Iron Man!*

The uproar created by this decision, and the calculated insult implied by the choice of this poem, can be imagined. He was accused of various base motives; above all, envy and jealousy of the superior talent of the poets he was to have judged. High-minded defenders of the most sacred values of German literature reproached him with deliberately wanting to debase the refined and respectable traditions of the nation's poetic patrimony and dragging it down to the level of vulgar fair-ground jingles. This, of course, was precisely the reaction Brecht had intended. To destroy the existing values of ossified sentiment was his aim and *Epatez les Bourgeois!* his slogan.

And yet representatives of an older and more gracious tradition of letters – and manners – recognized Brecht's importance from the very beginning. One of his earliest supporters among these was Hugo von

[1] Brecht, 'Kurzer Bericht ueber 400 (Vierhundert) Junge Lyriker, *Die Literarische Welt*, Berlin, 4.2.1927.

Hofmannsthal, the gentle and aristocratic writer of exquisitely melancholy verse, author of *Der Rosenkavalier* and other delicately constructed Viennese comedies. 'He had a high opinion of Brecht and even admired him in a certain sense, but spoke of him . . . as of a somewhat sinister person. . . .'[1]

Hofmannsthal even wrote a dramatic prologue to the performance of *Baal* by the experimental studio of the Theater in der Josephstadt in Vienna on 21 March 1926. This charming little piece, which has become a bibliographical rarity, shows members of the company discussing the strange new play they are about to perform. Each of the actors appears as himself. Oscar Homolka, well known in later years in Hollywood and London, who played Baal in the performance, is made the spokesman of the new drama:

> A play like this represents the ultimate in dramatic unity. These are not just cleverly thought-out words pasted on to a cleverly thought-out plot. Gesture and word have become one. Pent-up forces of the soul break forth and create a new kind of living-space which they fill with themselves.[2]

Behind his gentle mockery of the grandiloquence and exuberant language of Brecht's *Baal*, Hofmannsthal admits, with a gesture of amused resignation, that in the new era that is about to dawn the whole concept of character and of the sacred integrity and unity of human personality will have to be abandoned – on the stage as in life:

> Our time is unredeemed; and do you know what it wants to be redeemed from? . . . The individual. . . . Our age groans too heavily under the weight of this child of the sixteenth century that the nineteenth fed to monstrous size. . . . We are anonymous forces. Potentialities of the soul. Individuality is an arabesque we have discarded. . . . I should go so far as to assert that all the ominous events we have been witnessing in the last twelve years are nothing but a very awkward and long-winded way of burying the concept of the European individual in the grave it has dug for itself. . . .[2]

And so with a gesture, deprecating yet politely acknowledging his importance, ironical, sardonic yet with a tinge of horror in his smile,

[1] Willy Haas, *Bert Brecht*, Berlin, 1958, p. 11.

[2] Hugo von Hofmannsthal, *Das Theater des Neuen*, Vienna, 1947.

Hofmannsthal introduced the playwright of the violent new age of impersonal collective forces to the Viennese public.

In spite of rows and scandals and other time-wasting activities, Brecht worked with astounding energy in those years. He had acquired a secretary, who became far more than a secretary to him: Elisabeth Hauptmann, co-author of many of his plays and a loyal friend beyond the grave. Some notes from her diary for 1926 that have been published show Brecht not only writing short stories – mainly to make money – but also putting the finishing touches to his comedy *Mann ist Mann* (*Man equals Man*) prior to its first performance in Darmstadt, attending the rehearsals for the production of *Baal* that caused the Berlin theatre scandal we have mentioned and pursuing a remarkable number of projects which were to remain unfinished: a comedy about juvenile delinquents, a play on *Charles the Bold* whose picture he had seen in the 'panoramas' of the Augsburg fair-grounds of his youth, a revue for Reinhardt, a novel, a play on *Dan Drew and the Erie Railroad*, and another on the machinations of wheat speculators on the Chicago stock-market, which later developed into *St Joan of the Stockyards*. Over and above all this, Brecht was assembling his first major collection of poems, which was published in the course of 1926 in an edition limited to only twenty-five copies under the title *Taschenpostille* (*Pocket Breviary*). This book which contains some pretty scandalous poems was made up to look exactly like a prayer-book: bound in flexible black leather and printed on Bible paper in two columns with titles in red and the lines of the poems running on like Bible verses. The ordinary edition of this book was published in 1927 under the title *Hauspostille* (*Domestic Breviary*), looking like a conventional volume of poems.

Apart from all this literary activity Brecht continued to work on his own education. His project of a play about grain speculators had led him to study economics. It also brought him face to face with the problem of how the theatre could deal with the workings of high finance and commerce. Elisabeth Hauptmann notes in her diary that he began to think

> that the forms of drama as they had existed hitherto were not suitable for the exposition of such modern processes as the world distribution of wheat, nor for the presentation of the life story of present-day human beings. 'These things,' he said, 'are not dramatic

in the accepted sense and if you try to translate them into poetic terms they are no longer true. . . . But if it is realized that the present-day world does not fit the established dramatic form, then that dramatic form is no longer suitable for our world.'[1]

After the first night of *Mann ist Mann* Brecht took a holiday which he spent studying *Das Kapital*. The man who played the most important part in Brecht's development as a Marxist and to whom Brecht himself used to refer as his 'teacher' was Karl Korsch, who, ironically and significantly, had been expelled from the German Communist Party as early as 1926. Korsch (1886–1961) was undoubtedly one of the most important Marxist thinkers and theoreticians of his generation. He had been a university teacher, member of the Reichstag, Minister of Justice in the socialist state government in Thuringia, and had written important books on Marxist theory. It was to Korsch, who had remained a Marxist but was in bitter opposition to the German Communist Party's line, and later to Stalin, that Brecht turned, throughout his later life, when grappling with problems of Marxist theory.

As important for Brecht's subsequent development as his encounter with *Das Kapital*, Karl Marx and Karl Korsch was the beginning of his collaboration with the composer Kurt Weill (1900–50) which dates from this time.

Brecht had always sung his own ballads to the guitar: he composed the music with the words. Later he also made up his own music for any songs or ballads that occurred in his plays. In 1926 he and Elisabeth Hauptmann still improvised the music for the production of *Mann ist Mann*, basing the theme song on *Madame Butterfly*.[2] However amateurish and primitive this Brechtian music may have been, it had an unmistakable personal touch, which shines through the musical treatment of his poetry by composers as individually different and original as Weill, Hanns Eisler, and Paul Dessau, and which springs from the highly personal music of Brechtian verse as well as from the more direct effect of Brecht's assistance and advice in working with the composer.

Brecht's attitude to music was highly idiosyncratic: he hated Beethoven and the sound of violins, but liked Bach and Mozart. But

[1] Elisabeth Hauptmann, 'Notizen ueber Brechts Arbeit 1926', *Sinn und Form*, Second Special Brecht Issue, 1957, p. 243.
[2] Schumacher, p. 117.

above all he disliked the atmosphere of concerts: the spectacle of
frock-coated gentlemen sawing away at their instruments, of polite
and educated people gently bored and pretending to be moved. So
great was Brecht's contempt for this kind of music that he rejected
the term itself and designated the music he liked by a new generic term
he had invented for himself: *misuk*. Brecht's composer friend Hanns
Eisler finds it difficult to define *misuk*. 'It is above all popular,' he says,
'and it is best described as reminiscent of the singing of working
women in the backyards of tenements on Sunday afternoons.. . .'[1]

Brecht had known Kurt Weill since the early twenties. Nicolas
Nabokov has described how he, together with Isadora Duncan, the
Russian poet Essenin, Brecht, and Weill, had 'sniggered indecently'
at the old-fashioned Russian world presented to them by Stanislavsky's Moscow Art Theatre at a performance of *The Three Sisters* during
its appearance in Berlin in 1922 or 1923.[2]

Weill, a pupil of Busoni, shared Brecht's contempt for the polite
neo-Romanticism of the still dominant style of music in Germany. He
too wanted to return to a popular, modern, form of musical expression
that would be free from the over-elaboration of the large orchestra
wallowing in beautiful sound, and be harsh, topical in catching the
mood of its time, and serve a purpose in fitting into the everyday life
of the people.

The sequence of 'Mahagonny Songs' in *Hauspostille* gave Weill an
opportunity to try out his ideas. His operatic cantata *Mahagonny* was
performed at the Baden-Baden festival of modern music in 1927. This
short work formed the germ of the full-length opera *Rise and Fall of
the City of Mahagonny* and was the beginning of an association which
produced Brecht's –and Weill's – greatest success: *The Threepenny
Opera*. In the course of their co-operation in this and a great many
other projects Brecht and Weill mutually influenced each other.
Brecht's theory of the function of opera and of the 'epic' theatre in
general owes a great deal to Weill's ideas.

Another influence, entirely different in kind but no less important,
which Brecht encountered at this time, was that of a great character
of fiction: Jaroslav Hašek's *Good Soldier Schweik*.

---

[1] Hanns Eisler, 'Bertolt Brecht und die Musik', *Sinn und Form*, Second
Special Brecht Issue, 1957, pp. 440–1.

[2] Nicolas Nabokov, 'Time in Reverse'. Talk in BBC Third Programme,
broadcast 11.6.1958.

Piscator planned a production of this great comic novel of the First World War, but the only authorized adaptation did not meet his requirements. So he called in a team of new adaptors, the Communist playwright Gasbarra, Leo Lania, and Brecht to make a new version, while the names of the authorized adaptors remained on the programme for reasons of copyright.

Piscator's production of the *Good Soldier Schweik*, which opened in January 1928, was one of his most notable achievements. The great Austrian comedian Max Pallenberg, one of the outstanding comic actors of his day, played Schweik: round-faced, genial in his simulated simplicity, coarse and gentle at the same time. This great character moved through a brilliantly conceived comic world, designed by the most bitter of German post-war satirical artists, George Grosz. Or, rather, the scenery moved round Schweik. As the good soldier's 'anabasis' proceeded, the backdrop behind him showed the landscape passing as he marched and the houses, sheds, privies, railway stations, taverns, and trees he encountered came rolling on to the stage as he approached them.

Schweik is more than a mere character: he represents a basic human attitude. Schweik defeats the powers that be, the whole universe in all its absurdity, not by opposing but by complying with them. He is so servile, so eager to please and to carry out the letter of any regulation or command that in the end the stupidity of the authorities, the idiocy of the law is ruthlessly exposed. Brecht not only entered into the ways of thought of Hašek's immortal character so completely that twenty years later he could reproduce the authentic accents of the little soldier in his own play on *Schweik in the Second World War*; he also made the Schweikian attitude his own. Many of the characters in his later plays show features of this ironic servility: the hired man Matti in Puntila, the rascally judge Azdak in *The Caucasian Chalk Circle*, the great Galileo himself. And these characters are all, in some way, self-portraits of Brecht. So also is Brecht's perhaps most completely Schweikian character, an unmistakable likeness of his author: Herr Keuner, the hero of a collection of short anecdotes Brecht started to write in the late twenties to illustrate his attitude to issues of conduct and ethics. These Keuner stories provide a key to Brecht's character. Many of his later actions that have puzzled and antagonized public opinion become intelligible if seen in the light of Keuner's, and Brecht's, Schweikian philosophy, based as it is on the idea that it is often wisest to purchase one's peace and quiet by a show of compliance and even cheerful servility towards even the most absurd authorities, regardless whether they are the U.S. 'Committee on Un-American Activities' or the Communist bureaucrats of Eastern Germany.

Brecht's own basic attitude had always contained Schweikian elements, inherited from the Black Forest peasantry to which his ancestors belonged. But there can be no doubt that his work on Schweik helped him to crystallize these instinctive features of his nature into a coherent and conscious philosophy – a philosophy of enlightened self-interest based on the conviction that survival – and success – is more important than the striking of heroic attitudes. Long before this philosophy was put to the test in Brecht's dealings with Nazis and Communists he summed it up in one of his most revealing Keuner stories: *Measures Against Violence*.

In this story Keuner behaves in a rather cowardly manner when faced with the threat of violence. His disciples ask him if he has no backbone. He replies: 'I have no backbone to be smashed. I, of all people, must outlive violence.'[1] And to show what he means by tnis reply, Keuner tells the story of a man whose home was invaded by an agent of authority who asked him: 'Will you serve me?' Without saying a word the man served the agent of violence for seven years until the intruder finally got so fat that he died. The man wrapped his body in an old blanket and threw it out of the house. 'Then he washed the bedstead, whitewashed the walls, breathed a sigh of relief and answered: "No."'[1]

The year 1928, which had started with Piscator's triumphant *Good Soldier Schweik*, was Brecht's *annus mirabilis*. In December he won the first prize in a short-story competition organized by the *Berliner Illustrirte Zeitung* – 3,000 marks, at that time a very considerable sum. But by that time he was no longer impressed by such amounts of money. For in the summer he had scored his greatest success: *The Threepenny Opera* had had its first night on 31 August and had made Brecht and Weill famous.

The tremendous success of Nigel Playfair's London revival of Gay's *Beggar's Opera* had drawn the attention of stage circles throughout Europe to this evergreen work. Brecht's secretary and collaborator

[1] Brecht, 'Massnahmen gegen die Gewalt', *Versuche 1*, pp. 22–3.

Elisabeth Hauptmann made a translation of the *Beggar's Opera* which so fascinated Brecht that he began to adapt it. In the end the adaptation bore very little resemblance to the original. He transposed the action into seedy Edwardian costume, added songs and ballads based on Villon and Kipling, and made the play into a bitter satire on the bourgeois society of post-war Germany. Weill wrote a brilliant musical score, one of the first attempts to make jazz into an idiom for a serious composer.

The Theater am Schiffbauerdamm decided to take the risk of putting on a play so novel and unusual, but in the course of the rehearsals, which were beset by all kinds of misfortune, leading members of the cast falling ill and having to be replaced at short notice, the management developed serious doubts about the whole venture and was inclined to call it all off at the last moment. Eventually the first night did take place on 31 August 1928 and *The Threepenny Opera* was an immediate success, even if only a *succès de scandale* for some sections of the Press and public. It became one of the longest runs in the history of the Berlin theatre, the rare case of a play intended as a work of serious *avant-garde* art achieving genuine popular success. Performances throughout the world, including the phenomenally successful New York revival of the fifties – although Marc Blitzstein's adaptation differed considerably from the original – have proved its immense vitality.

Brecht would not have been Brecht and Berlin not Berlin if the success of *The Threepenny Opera* had not brought its own quota of scandals in its wake. His sudden success certainly made Brecht cocky. He began to suspect the motives of critics who failed to join in the general chorus of praise, particularly if they belonged to the left, whom he regarded as natural allies. The critic of the intellectual progressive weekly *Die Weltbuehne* (the nearest thing to a *New Statesman* in pre-war Berlin), Harry Kahn, had found *The Threepenny Opera* disappointing . . . 'a green room rag put on with excellent and lavish means. . . .'[1] Brecht countered this with a characteristically mean letter addressed to the critic:

Dear sir, I am compelled to confess that I have made a mistake. When, before the twenty-fifth performance of *The Threepenny*

[1] Harry Kahn, 'Traum und Erwachen', *Die Weltbuehne*, 2.10.1928.

Opera . . . you rushed towards me with the request that I should get you a better seat, I should not have refused it. It was pure *hubris* on my part. Probably success had gone to my head: you said that in the interests of objective criticism it was important to get you a seat farther to the front. I thought at the time that your seat was not too far back for objective criticism. But I have been wrong. It was. . . .[1]

This foolish outburst exposed Brecht to a deserved rebuff. Kahn ironically remarked that of course he had only attacked Brecht's previous play *Mann ist Mann* (which in fact he had highly praised) because he had not received a free portion of sausages in the interval of the first night. . . .

But *The Threepenny Opera* caused more serious rows than that. On 3 May 1929 Brecht's old enemy, Alfred Kerr, the doyen of Berlin critics, attacked Brecht in the *Berliner Tageblatt* for having plagiarized an existing translation of Villon's ballads by using whole passages from it without acknowledgement in *The Threepenny Opera*. The translation in question was by K. L. Ammer and had been out of print since 1909. Kerr's discovery caused a storm: there were only too many people in literary circles who were delighted to see the successful young poet exposed as a thief of literary property. Brecht defended himself with studied nonchalance. He published a short statement which merely said:

A Berlin newspaper has somewhat belatedly noticed that in the Kiepenheuer edition of *Songs from the Threepenny Opera* the name of the translator Ammer has been omitted next to that of Villon, although in fact 25 out of my total of 625 lines are identical with Ammer's excellent version. I am asked for an explanation. I therefore truthfully declare that I have, alas, forgotten to mention Ammer's name. This in turn I explain by my basic laxity in matters of literary property.[2]

A chorus of indignation greeted this boastful admission of 'laxity'. A literary periodical pontificated: 'Basic laxity – that in fact means the

[1] Brecht, Letter to *Die Weltbuehne*, 20.11.1928.
[2] Brecht in *Berliner Boersen-Courier*, 6.5.1929. Quoted by Schumacher, p. 242.

most sinister determination to get rich at the expense of others. This is fully in accordance with the views of that section of the nation who allow themselves to be amused by Bert Brecht.'[1] Die Weltbuehne published one of Brecht's poems with a different author's name and added in a footnote: 'In spite of his basic laxity in matters of literary property the author of this poem does not lay claim to a fee. . . .'[2] On great Viennese satirist Karl Kraus, one of the most brilliant polemical great Viennese satirist Karl Kraus, one of the most brilliant polemical writers of his time, who had been waging an endless feud against Kerr, regarded all of Kerr's bêtes noires as his special friends. He came out with a withering attack on Kerr's pettiness in which he declared that in spite of his 'immoral sanity' Brecht had 'more in common with the real world of poetry and the stage than all the horrid ephemeral crew that have now started yapping round his heels'.[3]

All this scandal had an excellent effect on the run of The Threepenny Opera. K. L. Ammer's translation of Villon had become so famous that it was reprinted, preceded by a sonnet by Brecht in which he gaily confessed that he had 'helped himself' to some of it. And, of course, K. L. Ammer, an Austrian officer called Klammer, was given a share in the royalties. According to a recent newspaper account he was still drawing his share of the takings in 1958.[4]

The biggest row in the wake of The Threepenny Opera's success, however, concerned the film version.

A film company, Nero-Film, paid Brecht and Weill 40,000 marks for the film rights of The Threepenny Opera. But both the author and the composer insisted that they must retain control of the adaptation of book and music. For their work in this respect Brecht and Weill were to be paid separately. Brecht was to receive 14,000 marks for the screenplay. The film was to be directed by G. W. Pabst.

In June 1930 Pabst and the writer Leo Lania, who had worked with Brecht on the adaptation of Schweik for Piscator and was to collaborate with him on the screenplay, visited Brecht, who was on holiday in Le Lavandou, to discuss the film. But it soon became clear that Brecht's views differed so radically from Pabst's that collaboration

[1] Die schoene Literatur. Quoted by Schumacher, p. 242.

[2] Egon Jacobsohn, 'Kanonen-Song', Die Weltbuehne, 28.5.1929.

[3] Karl Kraus, 'Kerrs Enthuellung', Die Fackel, August 1929. Reprinted in Kraus, Widerschein der Fackel, Munich, 1956, p. 405.

[4] Manchester Guardian, 29.7.1958.

would be well-nigh impossible. Nevertheless on 3 August 1930 the film company agreed to Brecht's furnishing the story outline for the film and to his retaining a right to suggest reasonable alterations to the final screenplay. But in due course the company came to the conclusion that it could not follow Brecht's outline: since he had written the stage version of *The Threepenny Opera* Brecht had become much more radically Marxist in his views, and he insisted on giving the story a far more openly anti-capitalist twist, with Macheath ending up as the president of a bank. The company offered to pay Brecht his full fee for the story if he would consent to withdraw from the work of adaptation altogether. Brecht refused. In the meantime work on the film had already started and the company was investing the, at that time enormous, sum of 800,000 marks in the project.

While the film was being shot Brecht and Weill sued the company for breach of contract and demanded an injunction against its being shown. This was not only a sensational *coup de théâtre* but also aroused interest as involving the principle of how far the author of an original work could insist on its being filmed according to his views, rather than being treated like any other piece of goods, which passes into the hands of a buyer outright after he has paid the purchase price.

The hearings of the case on 17 and 20 October 1930 in Berlin were a social occasion: everyone wanted to see the famous author of *The Threepenny Opera* pleading his cause. And the sessions certainly were stormy. Brecht theatrically refused an offer by the company's lawyer to renounce all further rights for 25,000 marks. At one point he angrily left the courtroom. The opposing lawyers argued that Brecht himself had shown little regard for literary property in purloining Ammer's translations of Villon. Brecht retorted that in this matter he was not concerned with his own rights but the *rights of the public*, who were entitled to be shown a film version of a play faithful to the author's intentions rather than to be fobbed off with an inferior product bearing the name of a famous and respected literary work. The Schiffbauerdamm theatre, where the run of *The Threepenny Opera* had come to an end, dutifully revived the stage version to allow the court to judge the literary merits of the play for themselves.

But it was all in vain. Brecht's demand for an injunction against the company was rejected, largely on the grounds that he had never shown sufficient readiness to get down to serious work on the film version instead of merely criticizing the company's version. Weill, on the other hand, won his case: the company had to remove alterations of his score they had introduced and he was given the right to supervise the music of the film.

Nevertheless Brecht, with his native shrewdness, fared by no means badly in the end. The company were afraid that he might appeal against the decision of the lower court. To guard themselves against the complications any prolongation of the case might cause them after the completion of the film, they offered Brecht a settlement if he undertook not to appeal against the decision. In return for a payment of 16,000 marks (9,000 still owing to him for his story outline and 7,000 towards his costs), and the company's undertaking that the film rights would revert to him after only two years, he agreed.

The film was finished and was immensely successful: it incorporated a good deal of Brecht's new story line, but in Brecht's view in far too prettified a form. And the quarrel spread: Brecht's staunch friend and supporter, Herbert Ihering, bitterly attacked the well-known Communist script-writer Bela Balazs for having betrayed the left-wing cause in having gaily stepped into Brecht's shoes and helped to complete the emasculation of a left-wing work in the interests of the capitalists. Balazs countered by claiming that he had in fact saved a left-wing work of art from going by default, and that he had taken the job precisely because he wanted to preserve the message of the original. To which Ihering retorted by quoting a right-wing paper to the effect that the story of The Threepenny Opera film 'has such a fairy-tale-like effect and is told with such charm and humour that in the end one completely disregards the intended meaning and just enjoys the story. . . .'[1]

Brecht was accused of having once more caused a scandal for the sake of personal publicity and of having emerged from it both in a martyr's pose and considerably richer than before. To explain his own

---

[1] This account on the lawsuit about *The Threepenny Opera* film is based on:
   Archiv fuer Urheber – Film- und Theaterrecht, Berlin, vol. IV, no. 1, 14.2.1931, pp. 73 ff.
   Lotte H. Eisner, 'Sur le procès de l'Opéra de Quat' sous', *Europe*, Paris, January February, 1957, pp. 111 ff.
   Die Weltbuehne, 10.2.1931.
   ibid., 17.2.1931.   ibid., 24.2.1931.   ibid., 3.3.1931.
   Brecht, 'Der Dreigroschenprozess', *Versuche 3*, pp. 256–306.

case and to show why he had gone to law, Brecht not only published his own story outline under the title *Die Beule* (*The Boil*) but also wrote a long and pretentious essay in which the whole case was described as a valuable 'social experiment' designed to demonstrate the fact that in a capitalist society it was unthinkable that an industrial project, involving an investment of 800,000 marks, could ever be stopped just because the author's rights had been violated. In this experiment he claimed complete success. He had demonstrated that 'justice, freedom, character have all become conditional upon the process of production. . . .' As to the reproach that he had settled the action out of court rather than appealing, Brecht argued: 'The case aimed at publicly proving the impossibility of collaboration with the film industry, even with contractual guarantees. This aim has been fulfilled. . . .' And in any case he had acted not in his own interest, but in that of the public.

> The public was entitled to our trying to obtain justice: for we had the duty towards the public of making sure that the spiritual attitude of our work, which is an oppositional attitude, should be preserved in every shape or form this work might assume. . . .[1]

It will be noticed that in this case Brecht adopted his Schweikian attitude of pretended servility and ironical obsequiousness not towards the authorities but towards the public.

It is one of the ironies of Brecht's life that, having written this lengthy essay to prove that his difficulties in connexion with *The Threepenny Opera* film were due to the inherent evil of capitalist society, twenty-five years later he was involved in an equally acrimonious dispute about the filming of another work of his, *Mother Courage* – but this time with the State-controlled film production company of Communist East Germany. And in that case he had no opportunity to seek redress in the courts.

In the meantime, while the various disputes arising from *The Threepenny Opera* had run their course, Brecht had been exceedingly active. He had not only tried to repeat the success of *The Threepenny Opera* but had set out to conquer entirely new spheres.

The attempt to produce another Threepenny Opera proved a dismal failure. It took the form of a musical play, *Happy End*, billed as an

[1] Brecht, 'Der Dreigroschenprozess', *Versuche 3*, pp. 256–306.

adaptation by Elisabeth Hauptmann 'from a short story by Dorothy Lane published in the *J.L. Weekly*, Saint Louis', with lyrics by Brecht and music by Kurt Weill. The imitation of the pattern of *The Threepenny Opera* is only too obvious: an Anglo-Saxon original, adapted by Elisabeth Hauptmann with poetry by Brecht. The subject of *Happy End* concerns the efforts of a Salvation Army girl to save the souls of some Chicago gangsters. To win their confidence she has to become something like a gangster's moll herself. The American source was pure invention, intended to give the play the cachet of authenticity and the prestige of a transatlantic original.

Happy End opened the autumn season at the Schiffbauerdamm theatre in September 1929. The first night ended in a scandal and the play was immediately withdrawn.

Brecht has often been reproached with having launched this weak play under the name of his secretary. Brecht certainly never published *Happy End* in any of the collected editions he supervised. There can be little doubt that his share in it was greater than the mere writing of the lyrics. But, on the other hand, his method of work had always been a collective one, and no doubt in this case he had contributed somewhat less than in others. He certainly used some of the basic motives and situations of *Happy End* in one of his masterpieces, *St Joan of the Stockyards*, which is also laid in Chicago, and also has a Salvation Army girl as heroine.

While *Happy End* had obviously been put together with the left hand, very serious work went into a number of other joint efforts with Kurt Weill, which marked the beginning of a new phase in Brecht's development – the *Lehrstuecke* (didactic plays).

If Brecht had started in an exuberant, poetic vein, which expressed his anarchic nihilism in strings of extravagant and earthy images, his preoccupation with Marxism was changing his outlook to one of austerity, economy of expression, and strictly utilitarian aims. This was wholly in the spirit of the times. Functionalism, the admiration for the beauty of useful objects, the machinery, skyscrapers, and motor-cars of America, had produced the movement called 'Neue Sachlichkeit' (New Objectiveness). This opposed the functional beauty of machinery to the traditional romantic bombast of German literature. Poets were to become social engineers, their work was to be useful in a very practical and concrete sense by stimulating desirable social attitudes. This was the age of 'Gebrauchslyrik' (Utilitarian Poetry) as of 'Gebrauchsmusik' (Utilitarian Music). The functional ideal of 'Neue Sachlichkeit', combined with Marxism and Watson's Behaviourism, which rejected all introspective psychology and confined itself to the study of observable human reactions, led Brecht and Weill to formulate the theory of a new kind of musical drama. This new type of musical play, 'school opera' or 'didactic drama', would not even try to arouse emotion by depicting the fate of individuals: it would teach social attitudes by showing the highly formalized actions of abstract social types. And what is more, this kind of musical drama would aim not so much at educating an audience as at educating those participating in the performance itself. Such a musical drama would be a teaching aid rather than an entertainment; it would therefore have to go into the schools rather than the theatre, hence the idea to write *Schulopern* – school operas.

Brecht's first two attempts in this genre were brought before the public during the Baden-Baden Festival of Modern Music in 1929. *The Flight of the Lindberghs* was described as 'a didactic radio play for boys and girls'. To avoid even the suggestion of individual hero-worship the part of the heroic airman, Charles Lindbergh, was played by a whole choir of Lindberghs. The music for this dramatic cantata was written jointly by Weill and Paul Hindemith. Brecht's other 'Lehrstueck', presented at Baden-Baden, with music by Hindemith, had a similar theme and was in some ways an extension and elaboration of *The Flight of the Lindberghs*. It has the cryptic title *Das Badener Lehrstueck vom Einverstaendnis (The Didactic Play of Baden on Consent)* and deals with the fate of a group of transatlantic flyers whose aircraft has crashed. While the pilot rebels against his fate, the mechanics consent to die in the cause of human progress. In the course of an interlude, designed to demonstrate man's inhumanity to man, a huge figure on stilts has his arms and legs sawn off by two clowns. During the first performance of the *Badener Lehrstueck* members of the audience fainted during the course of this gruesome scene with its reminiscence of Brecht's experiences in the Augsburg military hospital. The then grand old man of the German theatre, Gerhart Hauptmann, left in disgust.

Brecht's preoccupation with the theme of consent, which in this context means the individual's willingness to sink his private feelings in the common cause of human progress, and to agree to become part of an anonymous and disciplined mass, reflects his own difficulties in the face of his decision to throw in his lot with the Communist party. The immoralist, the anarchist and nihilist Brecht felt that he *must* find a positive creed. And in those years when the new barbarism of the Nazi movement already loomed on the horizon, the Communists seemed to many German intellectuals the only effective counter-force. That is why the need for the individual to divest himself of his freedom in the interests of a higher cause forms the recurring theme of the 'Lehrstuecke'. For Brecht this decision always had the emotional colour of a religious act. His next 'Lehrstueck', the school opera *Der Jasager* (*He Who Says Yes*), openly derives the individual's consent from a Japanese religious ritual. This short opera, for which Weill also wrote the music, is based on Arthur Waley's translation of a Japanese Nō play, *Taniko*. During a journey through the mountains a boy falls ill, and thereby endangers his travelling companions. In accordance with an ancient tradition, he consents to be killed rather than slow down their progress.

Ironically enough, when this school opera was presented in Berlin, in 1930, it was enthusiastically received by circles which saw it as a tract in favour of the Prussian virtues of obedience, discipline, and self-sacrifice. Brecht and Weill visited a number of schools that were rehearsing the play and changed the text according to the wishes and suggestions of the children. The pupils of the Karl Marx Schule pointed out that there was no need for the boy in the play to be killed. Characteristically, Brecht let himself be convinced. He re-wrote the play and now called it *Der Neinsager* (*He Who Says No*), and turned it into a passionate plea for the rethinking of ossified beliefs:

> The answer that I gave was false, but your question was even more false. He who says *A* does not have to say *B*. He can also recognize that *A* was wrong. . . . And as to the great ancient custom, I see no reason in it. Instead I require a great new custom, which we must introduce forthwith, namely the custom to think anew in any new situation. . . .[1]

Brecht's decision to alter the 'Jasager' into the 'Neinsager' at the request of a group of schoolboys shows that he genuinely tried to ke~ an open mind and that he wanted to resist the temptation of bec~ dogmatic. It is significant, however, that, when he took u~ theme for the third time, transferring the action from

[1] Brecht, *Der Neinsager, Versuche 4*, p. 32

to Communist agitators in modern China, the hero again consented to be killed. The ancient custom of discipline and obedience to orders prevailed, whether the discipline was Prussian, Samurai, or Stalinist, the orders those of an ancient religious rite or Communist policy. On this play *Die Massnahme* (*The Measure*) – one of Brecht's greatest achievements – he worked with a different composer: Hanns Eisler.

The culmination of Brecht's collaboration with Kurt Weill was undoubtedly the opera *Rise and Fall of the City of Mahagonny*, which had its first performance at Leipzig in March 1930. This opera had the aim of putting an end to the era of mere enjoyment in the opera house. It was an attack against the whole conception of opera as a pleasure of the senses. Bourgeois society that made these pleasures its sole pre-occupation was depicted as a lawless frontier town, where everything is permitted according to the principle of *laissez-faire* and the only crime is lack of money. At the climax of the action, when the hero is sentenced to death for having failed to pay his debts, the bourgeois public was directly addressed by an inscription flashed on a screen:

MANY AMONG YOU MAY WATCH THE NOW FOLLOWING EXECUTION OF PAUL ACKERMANN WITH DISTASTE. BUT YOU TOO IN OUR OPINION WOULD NOT WANT TO PAY FOR HIM. SO HIGHLY IS MONEY ESTEEMED IN OUR TIME.[1]

The first night in the Leipzig opera house again produced a first-class scandal, one of the most memorable in the history of the German theatre. The critic Alfred Polgar has immortalized it in the following description:

Here, there, above, below in the electrically charged theatre contra-dictions flashed like lightning and aroused further contradictions which in turn gave rise to more contradictions in geometrical progression. And soon the epic form of the theatre spread from the stage to the auditorium. . . . The woman on my left had a heart attack and wanted to leave. But when it was pointed out to her that this was an historic moment she stayed. . . . A man behind me on the right was heard to observe: 'I'll only wait till that fellow Brecht turns up!' He smacked his lips. Readiness is all. War cries echoed through the auditorium. In places hand-to-hand fighting broke out.

[1] Brecht, *Aufstieg und Fall der Stadt Mahagonny, Versuche 2*, p. 98.

Hissing, applause, which sounded grimly like faces being slapped.
. . . And in the end: the *levée en masse* of the malcontents, smashed
by thunderous applause. There were impressive episodes: a worthy
gentleman with the face of a boiled lobster had taken out his bunch
of keys and waged a heroic struggle against the epic theatre . . . he
had pressed one of the keys against his lower lip and caused streams
of air of an extremely high rate of vibration to pass over the hole at
its end. The noise which this instrument produced had an implacable quality. It cut right through one's stomach. Nor did his spouse
desert him in this hour of trial: a large, round woman, she was the
ride of the Valkyries all over, with a bun and a blue dress with yellow
flounces. This lady had put two fat fingers into her mouth; she
closed her eyes, blew up her cheeks, and produced a whistle louder
than the key. . . .[1]

This pattern was repeated in a number of other provincial cities where
Mahagonny was performed. The political atmosphere of the times was
already tense, and here the bourgeois public felt themselves personally
attacked. They did not expect to be insulted, in an opera house of all
places. Instead of uplift they were given a picture of immorality, and
then told that this was an image of their own society. In the provincial
parliament of Oldenburg the caucus of the National Socialist Party
demanded the cancellation of the scheduled performance in the local
theatre, because *Mahagonny* was a 'concoction of vile and immoral
content'.[2] But the left was equally dissatisfied with *Mahagonny*. *Die
Weltbuehne* attacked it for its negative attitude and its lack of relevance
to the problems of the moment: 'Life is not like that, not even in the
Klondike of yesteryear, certainly not in the America of today; and the
relevance of it all to the Germany of 1930 is very thin. This is stylized
Bavaria. . . .'[3]

And so *Mahagonny*, however successful it might have been as a
satirical spectacle and as a musical experiment, had failed as an
expression of Marxism on the stage.

Brecht, who had become so fascinated with the Marxist philosophy

[1] Alfred Polgar, 'Theaterskandal' in *Handbuch des Kritikers*, Zurich, 1938,
p. 32.
[2] Schumacher, p. 275.
[3] Peter Panter (i.e. Kurt Tucholsky), 'Proteste gegen die Dreigroschenoper',
Die Weltbuehne, 8.4.1930.

that he had conscientiously attended lectures at the Marxist Workers' College (Marxistische Arbeiter Schule) in Berlin throughout 1928 and 1929, decided to tackle a more directly Marxist subject: what fascinated him most about the Communist party was the problem of the subordination of the individual to the collective will. And so he fused the theme of the Japanese schoolboy from *Der Jasager* with reports of the Communist party's attempt to organize the workers of China and produced *Die Massnahme*. Hanns Eisler wrote the music for this austere didactic oratorio. Brecht got the idea for it from Hanns Eisler's brother Gerhard, who had been sent to China by the Comintern a few years earlier.

Die Massnahme, which is discussed at greater length elsewhere in this book, was originally intended for the 'New Music' Festival in Berlin in the summer of 1930. But the committee of the 'New Music', to which Paul Hindemith belonged, had qualms about putting on so openly political a work and demanded to see the text. Brecht and Eisler indignantly refused. This led to a breach between Hindemith and Brecht, and so *Die Massnahme* was first performed by the Greater Berlin Workers' Choir (Arbeiterchor Grossberlin) on 10 December 1930. The oratorio, which depicted the liquidation of a deviationist by a group of Communist party workers, aroused a storm of indignation – not only among the non-Communists but in Communist party circles as well (see Chapter VII: 'Brecht and the Communists').

Brecht's conversion to an austere didactic creed also expressed itself in the form in which he now began to publish his works. His earlier poems and plays had appeared in gay little volumes. From 1930 Brecht issued his current work in continuously numbered grey brochures, made to look like the drabber kind of school primer, and entitled *Versuche* (which can mean 'drafts' or 'essays' or 'experiments' and was intended to allude to all three of these meanings). Most issues of *Versuche* contained more than one work by Brecht; the series was something like a periodical appearing at irregular intervals and devoted to the continuous publication of Brecht's work in progress. Each separate play, essay, or cycle of poems in the series was numbered, on the pattern of opus numbers of the works of composers. To show the collective nature of the work, each item was signed in characters of equal size with the names of the collaborators: 'Brecht. Hauptmann. Caspar Neher. Weill' (in the case of *Mahagonny*); 'Brecht. Suhrkamp'

(Note on *Mahagonny*), etc. That this fiction of collective authorship, however, was largely affectation is shown by the title-page of each issue which laconically proclaims the author and contents as BRECHT: VERSUCHE.

Seven numbers of the *Versuche* appeared between 1930 and 1933. In 1949 Brecht resumed publication of these grey brochures. Number 15, the last, came out shortly after he died.

In spite of the rather pained reception of *Die Massnahme* by the Communists, Brecht resolutely continued to work for the party. With a loyalty and readiness to accept criticism, most remarkable in a professed cynic and immoralist, he resolved to learn from the 'mistakes' of his first attempt and to do better next time. The result was his adaptation of Gorky's *The Mother*, which had its first performance early in 1932. This play was too openly designed as propaganda to be judged as a work of art by the non-Communist press. Nor was it intended for a more general public. Neher had designed sets which could easily be transported and re-erected in public houses or local halls, and *The Mother* began to move from one district party centre to the next through the Berlin working-class quarters. The government of the day tried to stop these performances, even if only on the ground that the halls in question had not been passed for theatrical performances and did not comply with fire regulations. This led to the actors giving mere readings of the play, closely watched by the police, lest they began to impersonate the characters. Brecht was delighted: the effect of mere reading was as great if not greater than that of a fully acted performance – conclusive proof of his pet theory that the actors should not even try to pretend to be the characters they impersonate. Despite its propagandist purpose *The Mother* is a moving and impressive play. Hanns Eisler again wrote very effective music for it.

His attempts to make the film version of *The Threepenny Opera* a vehicle of left-wing propaganda having failed, Brecht was eager to make a real Communist propaganda film. With the help of various Communist organizations he succeeded in producing *Kuhle Wampe* in 1932. *Kuhle Wampe* is the name of an allotment area on the working-class outskirts of Berlin where the unemployed lived in shacks. The film was written by Brecht and Ernst Ottwalt. The music was again

47

by Hanns Eisler and Brecht's friend, the young Bulgarian film director, Slatan Dudow, directed it.

Kuhle Wampe describes the plight of the unemployed during the great economic crisis and, among other things, bitterly attacks the Social Democrats for their old-fashioned, petty bourgeois outlook. After showing the demoralization of some young workers by idleness and hopeless waiting for jobs, it ends in a surge of optimism and activity symbolized by a workers' sports rally.

Kuhle Wampe immediately ran into trouble. The government banned the film on the ground that it offended the President of the Republic by linking a young worker's suicide with the appearance of a presidential emergency decree; that it maligned the administration of justice in depicting the eviction of a family by the police; and exposed religion to ridicule by showing naked youths plunging into the river to the sound of church bells.

In a posthumously published account Brecht has described the interview between the producers of the film, himself, Eisler and Dudow, and the censor. The censor criticized the film because it neglected the individual features of the characters and showed them as generalized types. The young worker who committed suicide thus appeared not as an individual instance but as the representative of all young workers who were denied the right to live, etc. 'No, gentlemen,' he exclaimed, 'you have not acted as artists. You were not concerned in showing a tragic individual case. We would never have denied you the right to do that!'[1]

The makers of *Kuhle Wampe* were pained. The censor had very precisely summed up their original intention. They had done their work too well and had been found out. Brecht, with his usual cynicism, came to the rescue:

> I rose and, in spite of my revulsion against speeches, I made a speech. I stuck strictly to the untruth. I quoted the individual features we had given our unemployed: for example, that he had put away his wristwatch before jumping out of the window. . . . I protested against the horrible accusation that we had not acted strictly as artists . . . and I shamelessly asserted that my honour as an artist had been called into question. . . .[1]

[1] Brecht, 'Kleiner Beitrag zum Thema Realismus', *Der Sonntag*, East Berlin, no. 6, 1958, p. 9.

In the end this cynical manœuvre succeeded. The film was
with a few minor cuts. Brecht notes:

Leaving the building we did not conceal our high opinion
censor. He had penetrated the essence of our artistic intentions with
far greater sagacity than our most benevolent critics.[1]

Kuhle Wampe, which was shown in America under the title *Whither
Germany?*, was the only Communist film ever produced in the Weimar
Republic.

In the winter of 1930–1, when unemployment was at its peak in
Berlin, Brecht and Elisabeth Hauptmann had roamed the soup kitchens
of the Salvation Army. Ever since 1926 Brecht had wanted to write
a play on the workings of capitalist society: the writings of Lincoln
Steffens and other muck-raking American authors, Upton Sinclair's
Jungle and accounts of the destruction of coffee and wheat to raise
prices contributed to the somewhat crude idea he had formed of the
great buccaneers of capitalism like Dan Drew or Commodore Vander-
bilt. His original idea of a play on the wheat speculators of the Chicago
Stock Exchange had come to nothing. Another play, *Der Brotladen*
(*The Bread Shop*) which uses a chorus of unemployed (who rhapsodize
on the mysterious actions of the rich with their unfathomable consequences for the poor in the same vein as the chorus in a Greek tragedy
would bewail the equally unfathomable workings of fate), also
remained unfinished. In this play Brecht had introduced a Salvation
Army girl to show the absurdity of wanting to solve economic problems by mere charity. This character, Miss Hippler, coalesced with
the Salvation Army girl in the abortive musical *Happy End* into that
of Joan Dark (i.e. d'Arc), the heroine of *St Joan of the Stockyards*.

St Joan of the Stockyards is one of Brecht's greatest and most
characteristic works. Like all his best plays, it moves on several levels.
On one of these levels it is a devastating parody of German classical
drama; above all, of one of the silliest plays in the German classical
canon, Schiller's *Maid of Orleans*, and of Goethe's *Faust*. The meat-
packers of the Chicago stockyards talk in the bombastic blank verse of
Schiller's romantic heroes:

> *Remember Cridle how some days ago*
> *We crossed the stockyard as the evening fell*
> *And standing by the newest canning plant*
> *Remember, Cridle, how we saw that ox*

Great, blond and sullen looking at the sky
As it received the deathblow: oh, I felt
It had been meant for me; oh Cridle, Cridle
Ours is a bloody business. . . .[1]

It is also an attempt, and a rather naïve one, to look behind the scenes of big business and stock-exchange operations. And thirdly, *St Joan of the Stockyards* returns to the question of ends and means. The capitalist Pierpoint Mauler is shown with the hardly concealed admiration that Brecht, like Shaw, had for the ruthless millionaire operator. In fact, *St Joan of the Stockyards* combines features of Shaw's *St Joan* and *Major Barbara*.

It was a portent of the times that by 1932 Brecht, although an acknowledged and famous playwright, could not get a theatre to put on *St Joan of the Stockyards*. Apart from a shortened radio version, broadcast from Berlin in the spring of 1932, *St Joan of the Stockyards* remained unperformed until 30 April 1959, when it had its first stage performance in Hamburg.

Throughout the eight years of this first Berlin period Brecht retained the public *persona* of the literary *enfant terrible*. At the height of his fame and prosperity he continued to sport his highly personal get-up: he wore waistcoats with cloth sleeves, a leather tie, a mechanic's or lorry driver's leather jacket and a dirty visored cap. He was still unshaven. But some of the more malicious observers of the time alleged that he wore exquisite silk shirts under this proletarian costume. His hair was combed forward in a fringe and the steel-rimmed glasses of a minor civil servant or village schoolmaster were the most prominent features of his face. He drove round Berlin at great speed and considerable risk to himself and his passengers in an open Steyr car, earned by writing an advertising jingle for the makers, a mercenary act for which the defenders of the romantic view of the German poet's ethereal and spiritual mission held him in contempt.

With his strange appearance and studied arrogance Brecht aroused feelings of physical disgust and violent loathing in the breasts of many respectable people – which was precisely what he intended. He loved being taken for a very 'dangerous fellow', and enjoyed paining worthy literary critics by remarking in a condescending tone: 'I have nothing

[1] Brecht, *Die Heilige Johanna der Schlachthoefe*, *Versuche 5*, p. 362.

against Ibsen or Schnitzler. They are very good – for their own time and their own class.'[1] But what disconcerted his detractors most was his exasperating habit of switching his standpoint in the middle of a discussion and suddenly agreeing with everything his opponents had said, pointing out that precisely this had always been his opinion, so that in the end one did not know whether he really agreed or was merely exercising a subtle form of derisive irony.

Much of this was part of a systematic attempt to destroy the idea of the poet which Stefan George and Rilke had tried to embody: romantic beings singled out by Providence, too delicate to soil themselves by contact with the real world, the secret kings and priestly law-givers of the nation. Hence Brecht's ostentatiously unromantic and businesslike air. As his friend George Grosz has said:

> In spite of the fact that he was anything but a colourless person, he loved the colour grey, not the opaque grey of obscurity, but the sober grey of the theoretician, commentator, and schoolmaster. He clearly would have liked to have had a sensitive electric computer in the place of his heart and in place of his legs the spokes of a motor-car's wheel. . . .[2]

In his desire to destroy the legend of the poet's mysterious and lonely act of creation Brecht liked to work surrounded by crowds of friends.

> On a long table by the window his typewriter stood always open and ready for work surrounded by numerous folders containing cuttings from European and American papers. If a visitor came Brecht regarded this as excellent for his work – he read out a difficult passage to test the quality of the writing against the visitor's reaction, or discussed it with him at length. Immediately he rushed to the typewriter to write down a new version. He believed that it was good for his work if many people participated in it. And so he collected young people around him as collaborators. They did research, discussed his plans with him, made suggestions for alterations and amendments. In the printed versions of his works they appear as his co-authors.[3]

[1] Willy Haas, *Die literarische Welt*, Hamburg, 1955, p. 134.

[2] George Grosz, *Ein kleines Ja und ein grosses Nein*, Hamburg, 1955, p. 181.

[3] Bernhard Reich, 'Erinnerungen an den jungen Brecht', *Sinn und Form*, Second Special Brecht Issue, 1957, pp. 434–5.

His influence on these young people was so strong that they all began to look like Brecht:

Brecht, Klabund, Dudow, Caspar Neher, and Paul Samson Koerner (the boxer), all sported exactly identical haircuts . . . the hair was sliced off abruptly all around the head after two or three inches growth, and hung down vaguely like the coiffure you see on busts of Roman emperors.[1]

It was a closely knit circle. Carola Neher, one of Brecht's favourite leading ladies (in spite of her name no relative of Caspar Neher, the designer), was the wife of Brecht's friend, the consumptive poet Klabund. Polly and *St Joan of the Stockyards* had been written for her. Kurt Weill was married to Lotte Lenya, another of the leading ladies of *The Threepenny Opera* and *Mahagonny*.

Brecht himself, whose first brief marriage to Marianne Zoff, the sister of the writer Otto Zoff, had ended in divorce, was by this time married to the actress Helene Weigel, who had played the female lead in the 1927 Berlin production of *Mann ist Mann*. Two years younger than Brecht, Helene Weigel, who came from Vienna, was the product of a famous girls' school run by a militant suffragette, resolved to prove that she could produce girls more intelligent and intellectual than the best boys' school. A whole generation of brilliant girls, Helene Weigel among them, was evidence that this had not been an empty boast: Helene Weigel combines the emotional intensity of a great, though always an intellectual actress, with an acute and culti- vated mind and prodigious organizing ability. At the same time she was always a very competent housewife and mother. Her loyalty and devotion to Brecht never faltered. In spite of his inveterate and irrepressible polygamous tendencies Brecht and Weigel remained devoted to each other for thirty years.

Inside the circle of his own admirers Brecht lost the sinister air with which he liked to appear in public. He became kind, gentle and genial, bubbling over with ideas. The Russian writer Sergei Tretyakov, who met Brecht repeatedly in 1931 and 1932, has left a vivid picture of his conversation at the time. Puffing the poisonous cheap cigars he smoked incessantly and resembling 'a note blown through a slender clarinet, his hooked-nosed face recalling that of Voltaire or Rameses'[2] he

[1] Ernest Borneman, 'The Real Brecht', *Encore*, London, July/August 1958, p. 26.

[2] S. Tretyakov, 'Bert Brecht', *International Literature*, Moscow, May 1937.

would hold forth on the German character, tell stories of his early life, throw out ideas for dozens of new plays, or develop his project for a new kind of theatre, that would

> function like a court room. Two trials an evening each lasting an hour and a quarter. For example, the trial of Socrates, a witches' trial, the trial of Karl Marx's *Neue Rheinische Zeitung*, the trial of George Grosz on the charge of blasphemy for his cartoon of Christ in a gas-mask. Brecht was carried away by his enthusiasm. He began to elaborate: 'Let us suppose that the trial of Socrates is over. We organize a short witches' trial, where the judges are armoured knights who condemn the witch to the stake. Then the trial of George Grosz begins, but we forget to remove the knights from the stage. When the indignant prosecutor storms at the artist for having insulted our mild and compassionate God . . . the knights . . . are moved to applause. . . .'[1]

In January 1933 Anatoly Lunacharsky – until 1929 Soviet Commissar for Education – came to Berlin for an eye operation. He had met Brecht on earlier occasions and went to visit him. Lunacharsky's widow has described how the conversation circled round the impending catastrophe: Hitler's rise to power. The members of Brecht's circle who were present spoke of the probable need to emigrate, and Lunacharsky tried to comfort Brecht by pointing out that, after all, he could continue to write his plays even in exile. 'One of the actresses laughed: "Brecht can't live without a theatre . . , he would rather work as a prompter than be without one!" – "He would even be ready to become the backstage fireman!" said someone else.'[2]

A few weeks later Hitler had come to power. On 27 February fire broke out in the Reichstag building, and storm-troopers started rounding up Communists and left-wing intellectuals. On the following day Brecht went into exile.

[1] S. Tretyakov, 'Bert Brecht', *International Literature*, Moscow, May 1937.
[2] Natalya Rosenel, 'Brecht und Lunatscharsky', *Neues Deutschland*, East Berlin, 8.2.1958.

Chapter III

EXILE
(1933-1948)

... changing countries more often than shoes. ...
BRECHT, An die Nachgeborenen

To teach without pupils ·
To write without fame
Is difficult. . . .
BRECHT, *Ueber das Lehren ohne Schueler* (1935)

In our age of political and racial persecution, passport chicanery, and labour permits, the fate of the refugee is hard enough in itself. But that of the refugee writer, suddenly cut off from the medium of his skill, his language, is harder still.

Brecht's case was particularly cruel: he was not merely a poet, dependent on his mastery of his language, but also an experimenter and innovator in the theatre; to do his work and to widen his range he needed a stage, scenery, actors – and a public. At the age of thirty-five, just when he had achieved fame – or at least notoriety – and financial success, his career had suddenly come to a virtual end.

He might have derived certain hopes from the success of *The Threepenny Opera* outside the German-speaking world, brought about to a large extent, and ironically, by Pabst's film which had been produced simultaneously in French and German versions. *The Threepenny Opera* was also produced on the stage in the main capitals of Europe and even in New York (in 1933 – with little success), and the royalties from the musical numbers also brought Brecht a certain income, right up to outbreak of war. But his chances of writing and producing new works were greatly reduced: to rely on translations for launching new plays is to ensure failure. And the possibilities of getting new plays produced in German were cruelly diminished.

There were still a few countries, not yet controlled by Hitler, that had a German-speaking population and some outlets for German artists: Austria, Switzerland, and certain areas of Czechoslovakia, some places in the Balkans and even in Soviet Russia, where the Volga Germans had their own autonomous region, much publicized at the time. But with the exception of Vienna, Prague, or Zurich these places were largely provincial in their tastes and standards. And even in Vienna, Prague and Zurich the possibilities were strictly limited and far too small for the sudden influx of writers, producers, composers, actors and journalists from Hitler's Reich.

Some German refugee writers had the courage and the ability to jettison their own language and to master another; but these (Arthur Koestler, Robert Neumann, and a few others) were exceptions. The remainder had to rely on the few publishers outside the Nazi orbit who were prepared to risk losing the German market by publishing writers persecuted by Hitler, and on the numerous but ephemeral anti-Nazi literary magazines that sprang up in Vienna, Prague, Amsterdam, or Paris. They spent their days planning and launching such ventures in the cafés of Europe. In the beginning they still hoped for the sudden collapse of Hitler's régime. Later they tried to convince themselves, with steadily diminishing success, that the great powers would not stand idly by while Hitler openly planned the war against them. But the years went by and nothing effective was done. It was a truly terrible situation in which these intellectuals found themselves: they knew Hitler and they knew what was going to happen, but were condemned to pour out their warnings in unread refugee periodicals, to have their rousing plays, designed to open the world's eyes, performed in the back rooms of cafés, where only other refugees who did not need to be converted came to see them, to move among people unaware of their former importance or fame, and to beg for grants from charitable organizations. It is not surprising that many of these German refugee writers committed suicide or drank themselves to death.

On the day after the Reichstag fire Brecht had fled to Vienna, accompanied by his wife and his little son, Stefan. His name had always been high up in the Nazis' liquidation lists; as early as 1923, at the time of the first Hitler *putsch*, Brecht figured as number five on the list of people to be arrested – mainly for having besmirched the honour of the German front-line soldier in his *The Legend of the Dead*

Soldier. When the Nazis burned the books of their chief opponents soon after they had come to power, Brecht's books were among the first to be thrown into the flames. And later he was deprived of his German citizenship – again as the author of *The Legend of the Dead Soldier*.

All the more serious was it that the younger of his and Helene Weigel's two children, the two-year-old girl Barbara, had been left behind in Germany, in the care of Brecht's father. In the course of March 1933 rumours reached Vienna that the Nazis intended to use this child as a means to blackmail Brecht into returning to Germany. An Englishwoman, who was doing welfare work in Vienna, heard about this dangerous situation and offered to smuggle the little girl out of Germany. On 1 April 1933 this rescue operation was successfully, if precariously, carried out: little Barbara was picked up in the country outside Augsburg and put on the train that took her to Switzerland, where her parents had in the meantime gone.

In the months that followed, Brecht, like so many of his fellow-writers, was travelling through Europe in search of a place to live and a chance to work: Prague, Vienna, Paris were the conventional stopping places on these depressing prospecting tours. In the spring of 1933 a group of prominent anti-Nazi writers held a kind of council of war at Sanary-sur-Mer to discuss their plight: Thomas and Heinrich Mann, Feuchtwanger, Arnold Zweig, Thomas Mann's son, Klaus Mann, Ernst Toller, and Brecht. It was the first of innumerable similar gatherings that followed, all devoted to the earnest and searching examination of the problem of what writers could do to help to bring about the downfall of Hitler. To keep their self-respect and their sanity they had to believe that their efforts mattered a great deal. In fact, they mattered little enough.

A few weeks after Whitsun, Brecht went to Denmark on the invitation of the Danish novelist, Karin Michaelis. He decided to make Denmark his base, and Karin Michaelis helped him to find a temporary home there. Denmark was remote from the centres of the emigration with their depressing cliques and distracting and futile intrigues and bogus projects. And Denmark was relatively near to Germany: Brecht liked to think of himself as taking part in the underground struggle of the German workers, a myth to which he and so many of his colleagues stubbornly clung, although very little corresponded to it in reality:

Escaped beneath the Danish thatched roof, friends,
I follow your struggle. . . .[1]

This Danish thatched roof was that of a farm-house on the island of Langeland in the province of Svendborg. The former stables had been whitewashed and turned into a workroom for Brecht: an immensely long table ran along one of the walls, beneath the window, where he would sit by his typewriter, tapping out satirical poems, plays, essays, and articles on to his favourite grey tissue paper; meticulously pasting corrections over the discarded passages; and cutting out piles of pictures and news photographs from illustrated magazines and newspapers – material for future work. Brecht believed in documentation and collected voluminous scrapbooks filled with images of human folly. After the war he published one of these: *Kriegsfibel* (*Primer of War*); it consists of photographs from a number of papers – *Life* magazine occurs most frequently – each of them accompanied by a bitter, biting quatrain.

On one of the oak beams supporting the roof of this former stable he had fixed an inscription, which proclaimed in large letters the first article of his artistic and philosophical creed: THE TRUTH IS CONCRETE. And

> *. . . in front of the whitewashed wall*
> *There stands the black soldier's suitcase with the manuscripts.*
> *On it the smoking utensils with the copper ashtrays.*
> *The Chinese scroll that shows the doubter*
> *Hangs above it. . . .*[2]

These were his favourite possessions which he carried round the world with him: his manuscripts, his smoking things, and the scroll with the painting of a Chinese philosopher, probably Confucius.

From the courtyard he could hear the voices of his children playing on their swing. But however idyllic it might appear, he never saw himself as settled, but as ever prepared and ready to be on the move again –

> *. . . the house has four doors from which to escape. . . .*[3]

From this base in Denmark Brecht carried out his varied, almost feverish, but never very profitable activities.

[1] Motto to *Svendborger Gedichte*, London, 1939.
[2] Brecht, 'Auf der Flucht', *Lieder und Gedichte*, West Berlin und Frankfurt, p. 102.   [3] Brecht, 'Zufluchtsstaette', ibid., p. 103.

In Paris in the spring of 1933 he and Kurt Weill had written a ballet: *Die sieben Todsuenden* (*The Seven Deadly Sins*), designed as a vehicle for Weill's wife, Lotte Lenya. Georges Balanchine's company, 'Les Ballets 1933', presented it at the Théâtre des Champs-Elysées in June of that year. The ballet tells the story of an American girl who goes out into the world to make money and has to avoid the seven deadly sins, the indulgence of her own natural instincts, which might prevent her from achieving her objective. Anna is shown as a split personality: her emotional side is danced (Tilly Losch created this part) while her rational side (Lotte Lenya) admonishes her in song. Caspar Neher came to Paris to design the décor. But the performance achieved hardly more than a *succès d'estime*. From 1 to 15 July this ballet was presented at the Savoy Theatre in London under the title *Anna Anna*. Here too it was found impressive, but *The Dancing Times* criticized it for abandoning 'the Latinity of style from which ballet has culled so much beauty' and complained that there was 'nothing to clarify or elucidate the heavy darkness of the Germano-American text. . . .'[1] This was only the first in a long series of painful reminders that success outside Germany was not merely a matter of translating Brecht's words from German into English or French. It was the spirit of his work, his whole approach, which appeared alien and incomprehensible to a non-German public.

In spite of this Brecht repeatedly returned to Paris and London to discuss the possibility of having one of his plays performed. Towards the end of 1935 the left-wing Theatre Union in New York decided to put on Brecht's *The Mother*, and he went to New York, mainly to try to stop the enthusiastic company from laboriously changing his 'epic' style into a conventional one by putting in all the things he had purposely left out: the kitchen smells and the naturalistic detail. He did not quite succeed, the performance fell between two stools, and the critics confessed that they were puzzled by it all.

In 1936 Brecht became co-editor of a newly founded anti-fascist literary review, *Das Wort*, published in Moscow. The other two editors were Lion Feuchtwanger and Willi Bredel. The appearance of Brecht's name on the title-page of *Das Wort* had led many people, and some compilers of reference books, to assume that he lived in Moscow at that time. In fact, in the years of his exile he visited Moscow only on a few occasions and never for longer than a few days.

[1] *The Dancing Times*, London, August 1933.

Considering that Feuchtwanger did not stay in Moscow much longer and that Willi Bredel was fighting in the Spanish Civil War, *Das Wort* must have been edited by a peculiar postal method. Brecht published a certain amount of his current output in the paper, but otherwise there is little trace of his editorial influence to be noticed in its policy or contents – some of the writers he most detested were among the regular contributors. On the other hand, this editorship gave him a certain financial security.

At the time of the Nazi-Soviet pact in the summer of 1939 *Das Wort* came to an inglorious end.

To make ends meet he had to work hard: he is even said to have written the shooting script of a film version of *I Pagliacci* with Richard Tauber. 'The film was almost catastrophically bad, but it still showed the touch of the master in such unlikely scenes as the epilogue in which Tauber suddenly turned to address the audience like a commissar in a "Lehrstueck".'[1] But this was not the only way in which the situation militated against his real talent: even in his more serious work the feeling that he must in some way play his part in the day-to-day struggle against Hitler led him not only to make speeches at congresses of anti-fascist writers but to produce a whole series of political *pièces d'occasion*, both poetry and plays, many of them skilful and witty, yet always marked by the ephemeral quality and inevitable mediocrity of this kind of writing. The *German Satires*, a group of poems written for broadcasting by the anti-Nazi 'German Freedom Station', for example, are interesting as experiments in an extremely free kind of free verse, but they have worn badly. Today they appear not only dated but politically naïve. Brecht's Communist views hindered rather than helped him to penetrate to the true nature of National Socialism: he regarded it as a kind of conspiracy of the rich against the poor and completely overlooked the genuinely revolutionary and really frightening side of the Nazis, who were by no means merely the stooges of the generals or the industrialists whom they used, but also ruthlessly betrayed. And Brecht not only missed this point but also misunderstood many of the more sinister aspects of totalitarianism, such as the efficacy of its propaganda which made the people actually love their oppressors. In accordance with the Communist party line he continued to depict the German working

[1] Ernest Borneman, 'The Real Brecht', *Encore*, London, July/August 1958.

class as filled with sullen hate against the 'rulers', and concentrated a
good deal of his fire on such relatively unimportant symptoms as the
shortage of butter or oranges. There, as in so many other instances,
Marxism proved an extremely fallible tool of social analysis. The
Ribbentrop-Molotov pact finally shattered Brecht's, and many of his
fellow-refugee writers', naïve views on the phenomenon of totalitarian
dictatorship.

This political *naïveté* also mars the plays Brecht wrote between 1933
and 1938: *The Roundheads and the Peakheads* (a tract against racialism)
and a series of one-act plays and short sketches collected under the
title *Furcht und Elend des Dritten Reiches* (*Fear and Misery of the Third
Reich*). A version of this was produced in the United States in 1945 as
The Private Life of the Master Race. Some of these scenes are brilliant
proof that Brecht could write in the conventional, naturalistic style.
But most of them fail to convince. To do his duty in the Spanish
Civil War, Brecht wrote another play in the conventional dramatic
form he so despised: *Die Gewehre aer Frau Carrar* (*Señora Carrar's
Rifles*) which was performed in German by refugee actors in Paris in
1937. Helene Weigel played the name part. This play (vaguely based
on Synge's *Riders to the Sea*) is very effective theatre, but also rather
oversimplified politically and clearly a pot-boiler. Brecht himself
acknowledged this fact by a note in the collected edition of his plays
which insists that this

> is Aristotelian (empathy) playwriting. The drawbacks of this tech-
> nique can be compensated, up to a point, by presenting the play
> together with a documentary film on the events in Spain, or by
> linking it with some propagandistic occasion'.[1]

Brecht's only large-scale novel, the *Threepenny Novel*, published in
Amsterdam in 1934 and published in an English translation in 1937,
also suffers from political oversimplification. This long elaboration of
the unused screen story for *The Threepenny Opera* film gallantly
attempts to unmask the workings of capitalist society: it contains many
brilliantly written passages and much bitter satire in the vein of
Swift's *Modest Proposal*, but it fails to convince – its competing chains
of multiple shops that sell only stolen goods and syndicates of
respectable businessmen who get rid of rotten hulls to the Admiralty
as troop transports, knowing that they cannot keep afloat, simply

[1] Brecht, *Stuecke VII*, p. 60.

cannot be accepted as valid images of the real workings of the capitalist system.

But as if to make up for the dry, ephemeral and oversimplified nature of all this political pamphleteering in these years of exile, Brecht also wrote some of his most moving poetry. He had planned to publish most of this in the fourth volume of a collected edition of which two volumes only appeared, printed in Prague in 1938 but with the publisher's imprint 'Malik Verlag London'. The third volume was in the press when Czechoslovakia fell, and only a small number of copies of the *Svendborger Gedichte* (*Svendborg poems*) appeared as an advance extract from the abortive volume four of this collected edition. It contains what is perhaps Brecht's most personal poem – *An die Nachgeborenen* (*To Posterity*) in which he begs the generations of a happier age to forgive him for the harshness of his writing –

> *For we know:*
> *Even the hatred of evil*
> *Distorts the features,*
> *And anger over injustice*
> *Also hoarsens the voice. Alas, we*
> *Who wanted to prepare the ground for friendliness*
> *Could not ourselves be friendly. . . .*[1]

As the illusion that he could influence the course of events by his writing receded, Brecht returned to his deeper and more poetical vein of playwriting. Those who had followed his development only in what he published in the refugee magazines had almost written him off as a real poet and believed that he had not fulfilled the promise of his earlier works. They could not know that from 1937 onwards Brecht had thrown off the shackles of political propaganda and had begun to write a series of plays which showed his talent not only undiminished, but considerably matured and purged of the more puerile antics of his *enfant terrible* period: *The Life of Galileo* (1937-8); *The Trial of Lucullus* (1938); *The Good Soul of Setzuan* (1938-40); *Mother Courage* (1938-9). It is significant that all these plays were produced at a time when the situation had grown so bad that political pamphleteering had become quite clearly futile, when war was imminent, and when the alliance between the Nazis and Stalin had damped the spirit of even the most ardent German Communists.

[1] Brecht, 'An die Nachgeborenen', *Svendborger Gedichte*, p. 60.

Even in exile Brecht gathered a circle around him. He could not live without working in the theatre, and so he took an active part in the amateur dramatics of the Danish left wing. *The Roundheads and the Peakheads* had its first performance in Copenhagen in 1936 by actors of the Danish working-class theatre movement, and among Brecht's theoretical writings on the art of acting, there is a long didactic poem, entitled: *Speech to Danish Working-class Actors on the Art of Observation.*

In Denmark, Brecht added two more names to the list of his loyal women friends: one of them, Margarete Steffin, appears as co-author of *Fear and Misery of the Third Reich, The Good Soul of Setzuan, The Trial of Lucullus,* and *Arturo Ui.* Together with her, Brecht translated Martin Andersen-Nexoe's story of his childhood into German. Margarete Steffin also translated Nordahl Grieg's play on the Paris Commune, *The Defeat,* which Brecht published in *Das Wort* and which later gave rise to his counter-play *The Days of the Commune.*

The Danish actress Ruth Berlau not only appears as collaborator on *The Days of the Commune, The Caucasian Chalk Circle,* and *The Good Soul of Setzuan,* etc., but also became the photographer who created the complete pictorial records of Brecht's productions, which formed the basis of his 'model books'.

In the summer of 1939, when war had become inevitable and Denmark appeared more and more unsafe, Brecht moved to Sweden. After the German invasion of Denmark and Norway, however, Europe could not offer any real safety to a man as hated by the Nazis as Brecht. So in the course of 1940 he again moved his family – and some of his helpers and collaborators – to Finland, where for some reason it seemed easier to get an American visa. In Finland he was the guest of the writer Hella Wuolijoki, whose folk-tales he used as the basis for his play *Herr Puntila und sein Knecht Matti (Mr Puntila and his Hired Man Matti)*, later the cause of another accusation of plagiarism. In preparation for America he was also working hard to complete a play with which he wanted to conquer the U.S. stage: *Der Aufhaltsame Aufstieg des Arturo Ui (The Resistible Rise of Arturo Ui)*, a transposition of the rise of Hitler into a Chicago gangster milieu. On 10 March Brecht noted the first idea in his diary; by 28 March the whole play, except for one scene, had been completed.

On 3 May 1941 the U.S. Vice-Consul in Helsinki issued Brecht

a quota immigration visa. At the beginning of June he and his family
and some of the members of his circle set out on the long journey to
America – from Finland across the entire Soviet Union to Vladivostok
by the Siberian express. They interrupted their journey briefly in
Moscow. Bernhard Reich, who had been one of the artistic directors
of the Munich Kammerspiele in the early twenties and now lived in
the Soviet Union, visited the travellers in the Hotel Metropole:
'Everywhere there lay suitcases and parcels. In the rocking chair the
boy Steff (Stefan Brecht). In a corner crouched Barbara; Helli
(Helene Weigel) put some order into the luggage. Somewhere, quite
forlorn, sat Margarete Steffin. Brecht occupied a table. A family of
migrants! When, years earlier, we had lightheartedly laughed about
the Chaplin film we had no inkling of the prophetic relevance of this
movie parable.' Margarete Steffin, who had difficulty in obtaining an
American entry visa and was suffering from consumption, had to remain behind in Moscow and died there soon afterwards. Ten days
after the party left Vladivostok aboard a Swedish ship, Hitler's troops
invaded Russia, and Finland entered the war as an ally of Germany.
While Brecht was preparing to leave, the country had already been
swarming with German troops. It had been a last-minute escape.

After a long sea voyage of which he later liked to remember the
porpoises playing in the sea of Japan and the little horse-carts in the
streets of Manila – soon to be overrun by the Japanese – Brecht
arrived at San Pedro, California, on 21 July 1941.

He settled on the fringe of Hollywood, where so many other Central
European writers were sitting out the times of war and exile. Many of
his old friends had preceded him: Lion Feuchtwanger, after an adventurous and dangerous journey through German-occupied France; the
composer Hanns Eisler; the Austrian poet and producer Berthold
Viertel, whom Christopher Isherwood has immortalized in *Prater
Violet*, a fiery and kind-hearted genius; and many others. But in spite
of the help and support of these friends, the times were hard and the
atmosphere was anything but congenial:

> *Every morning to earn my bread*
> *I go to the market, where they buy lies. . . .*[1]

The high-flown hopes that some of his plays might be performed
on the American stage had come to nothing. The gangsters of *Arturo*

[1] Brecht, 'Hollywood', *Hundert Gedichte*, East Berlin, 1951, p. 308.

Ui were far too unlike the originals to give that ambitious play a chance. Apart from a performance of some of the scenes of *Furcht und Elend des Dritten Reiches*, by a group of refugee actors under Berthold Viertel's direction in New York in May 1942, there seemed as yet no chance of gaining a foothold in the American theatre. And so Brecht's time was spent in trying to think up plots that might be sold to a film studio: this was the period of films on the underground struggle in occupied Europe, and Brecht was working on a number of projects of this type. On the struggle of occupied France he and Feuchtwanger were planning a modern version of the story of Joan of Arc, which later crystallized into a novel by Feuchtwanger and Brecht's *Die Gesichte der Simone Machard* (*The Visions of Simone Machard*), one of his most tender plays whose little resistance heroine has clumsily naïve visions of herself as an anachronistic Joan of Arc.

In the end Brecht did succeed in selling a story: it dealt with the assassination of Heydrich by Czech patriots and was filmed by Fritz Lang under the title *Hangmen Also Die*. Hanns Eisler wrote the music. But the final product bore little resemblance to Brecht's outline and he dissociated himself from it.

Far away in Zurich, the gallant band of anti-Nazi actors who made the Schauspielhaus the chief exponent of the free German theatre gave Brecht the only reason to feel himself not completely forgotten: they scored great success with three of the plays he had written in Denmark: *Mother Courage*, *The Good Soul of Setzuan*, and *The Life of Galileo*. In his American exile, however, he could not find anyone to print his poems, so that he had to issue some of his *Gedichte im Exil* (*Poems in Exile*) in typewritten and photostated form for distribution to a few of his friends. But he continued to write: his new version of Schweik – *Schweik in the Second World War* and *The Caucasian Chalk Circle*.

At this time Brecht lived at Santa Monica. He was now in his middle forties and had mellowed considerably, but he had adapted his favourite costume to Californian conditions only in so far as he now wore trousers and jackets of blue denim and tieless, open shirts. Instead of German 'Virginias' he now smoked American five-cent cigars and stubbornly refused to have anything to do with more expensive varieties, even when he received whole boxes of them as gifts.

He astonished his Hollywood friends by managing always to appear with a two-days' growth of beard: never clean-shaven, but never a three-days' growth either. Nobody could explain how he did it.

He moved largely in the narrow world of German and Austrian refugee intellectuals and was frequently at loggerheads with those American circles one would have thought most likely to appeal to him: the many left-wing, fellow-travelling and Communist Americans of Hollywood. But these actors, writers, and producers were largely under the spell of the Russian theatre and enthusiastic followers of the Stanislavsky method, which was a red rag to Brecht. Artistic contradictions cut across possible political affinities.

And so he remained the centre of a mainly German-speaking circle. Ironically enough, Brecht, whose writing in his youth had centred round a mythical conception of an Anglo-Saxon, and largely American, world, found very little contact with the real America. After he had set foot on American soil, the American scene, which had dominated his early works, disappeared from his writing. And while he admired the productive achievements of the United States, he had no contact with its cultural climate; distrusted its politics, wrongly believing that after the war the U.S.A. would inevitably relapse into isolationism; and disliked its cooking. When served some fanciful American dish he would push it away, saying: 'We don't eat that kind of thing in Augsburg.' As to the beauties of the Californian landscape. . . . A friend once took him on a drive along the coast road through the most breath-taking scenery. Brecht remained silent and morose. But when the car turned into the disreputable quarters of the Los Angeles waterfront his face lit up: 'What beautiful scenery!' he said. And he meant it. Brecht, whose early poetry was full of ecstatic praise of the beauties of nature, had come to fear them as a temptation, which might lure him away from his duties as a social critic.

He continued to consult his friends while writing his plays or poems and spent hours discussing the course of the war with them. To make himself clear he would act out any situation: what he imagined Roosevelt might have said to Stalin or Hitler to Himmler. Thus he turned abstract, political argument into his own kind of dramatic reality. For to him truth was always concrete. The slogan which had adorned the oak beams of Svendborg also greeted the visitor from the wall of his apartment at Santa Monica. Always striving for Confucian politeness, Brecht would occasionally lose his temper, particularly if he was reminded of painful facts that did not fit into his political scheme of things, such as the Moscow trials and the Stalinist terror. When his composer friends, Hanns Eisler and Paul Dessau, whom he had met during a visit to New York in 1942, came to see him, there would be a great deal of rumbustious music-making and sometimes Brecht himself would sing his ballads in his high, thin voice, just as he had sung them in his youth in the taverns of Bavaria.

Slowly, gradually, nevertheless, Brecht gained a foothold in the United States. His name had been known to a few enthusiasts for a new kind of theatre since the early thirties, and in spite of the failures of the first New York productions of *The Threepenny Opera* (1933) and *The Mother* (1935) he had retained some followers. Mordecai Gorelik, who had been present at the Copenhagen production of *The Round-heads and the Peakheads*, had written about the 'epic theatre' in *Theatre Workshop* as early as 1937. Clement Greenberg had drawn attention to Brecht's poetry in *Partisan Review* a few months before Brecht's arrival in America.

Shortly after he had settled in California he met Eric Bentley, who was to become his chief advocate among the academic and theatrical *avant-garde*. As Bentley himself has described it: 'I met Brecht late 1941 or early 1942. I was just out of graduate school. . . . I asked Brecht to help me with my translation of . . . Stefan George. He read me his own poems and I started translating.'[1] Other translators were equally keen on presenting his works to a new audience; in 1943 H. R. Hays published his impressive translation of *The Trial of Lucullus*, which was later set to music by Roger Sessions. (Brecht and Dessau based another opera on the original German text in 1951.)

The conquest of the American stage was more difficult. As early as 1942 Max Reinhardt, Brecht's former employer and now a fellow exile in Hollywood, had planned a performance of *Furcht und Elend des Dritten Reiches*, which Bentley translated as *The Private Life of the Master Race*. Brecht had written a very effective framework for the short, unconnected scenes and sketches – an armoured troop carrier rolling through wartime Europe with its load of Nazi soldiers was to link groups of scenes illustrating the environment from which the German troops had emerged to ravage Europe. Nothing came of Reinhardt's project. But Bentley's translation was performed at Black

[1] Eric Bentley, in a letter to the author.

Mountain College during the war – the first of a long line of performances of Brecht's plays in American colleges and universities. It
is significant that Brecht, who remained consistently unsuccessful on
the commercial and professional stage, should have established himself in America through such amateur performances by student
players, even at a time when his political views were widely frowned
upon throughout the country.

The Private Life of the Master Race reached the professional New
York stage in June 1945. Originally Piscator was to have directed it,
but shortly before opening night he dropped out and Berthold Viertel
took over. A number of the leading roles were played by German
refugee actors whose command of English left much to be desired.
Brecht tried to improve things by making longer and longer cuts, until
some of the scenes became unintelligible. And he added some weird
touches that further confused the audience. A Negro actor who appeared in the part of an S.S. man, for example, was given dead-white
make-up. No wonder that the first-night reception was a pained one.
The New York *Times* gave the production a lukewarm but fairly
favourable notice. Burton Rascoe in the New York *World-Telegram*
summed up the other camp's point of view in the succinct phrase,
'It was perfectly awful.'

Nevertheless, by the time the war in Europe ended, there seemed
to be a good chance that Brecht might yet make his mark in America.
Like most German refugees he was none too eager to hasten back to a
devasted Germany with its ruined cities, its hate-ridden population,
its misery, and its black markets. Brecht felt that it was worth his
while to bide his time and see whether he might not, after all, succeed
in creating a place for himself in the United States. He had taken out
first citizenship papers immediately after his arrival in 1941, and he
now considered applying for a Guggenheim Fellowship.

To bring out their own works in German for the reviving German
market, a group of German refugee writers founded a publishing
house in New York, the Aurora Verlag. Brecht, Doeblin, Feuchtwanger, Heinrich Mann, Viertel and F. C. Weiskopf were among the
partners in this venture.

And for Brecht the pace quickened. Reynal and Hitchcock was
interested in publishing a translation of his collected works. Eric and
Maja Bentley completed their translation of *The Caucasian Chalk
Circle*, which was produced at Carleton College, Minnesota, in 1948,

and *The Good Soul of Setzuan.* H. R. Hays was bringing out a volume of translations of Brecht's *Selected Poems* and, most important of all, Brecht himself was working on an English version of his *Galileo* with Charles Laughton, who wanted to play the name part.

As far back as 1943 Orson Welles and Mike Todd had planned a joint production of *Galileo* with Laughton. This plan had come to grief when the clash of these two strong temperaments led to the inevitable quarrel. But Laughton's interest had been aroused. In 1945 he asked Brainerd Duffield and Emerson Crocker to prepare an acting version from an existing literal translation. The two young men retired to the country and emerged with a text that pleased Laughton. But in the meantime Brecht had begun to reshape the play, and eventually he and Laughton embarked on a joint revision so radical and enjoyable that they completely lost sight of the existence of other translators or translations. Brecht himself later suggested an almost miraculous process of collaboration through mutual inspiration: 'The unfortunate circumstance that one of the translators knew no German and the other only little English forced us from the start into play-acting as a method of translation.'[1]

Brecht admired Laughton as a very great actor and was amazed at his intuition of the underlying reality of the historical situation and the deeper layers of the character. 'So great was his desire to show things as they really are that, in spite of his indifference, even timidity, in all political matters, he would demand considerably sharper formulations, or even suggest them himself, in more than a few places; merely because he regarded these passages as "somehow weak", by which he meant that they did not do justice to things as they really are.'[1] The two collaborators met at Laughton's house, 'overlooking the Pacific Ocean, because the catalogues of synonyms were too heavy to carry about. . . . [Laughton] used these heavy tomes much and with untiring patience'.[1] To illustrate a point of translation Laughton would read from the Bible, Aesop, Molière, or Shakespeare. 'We used to work in L.'s small library, in the mornings. But L. rushed to meet me in the garden, running out in his shirt and trousers, barefoot, across the wet lawn. . . .'[1] While the translation was still in progress the externals of the production were increasingly discussed in ever more meticulous detail. 'When L. heard about the delicate sketches of scenes that Caspar Neher used to make so that the actors could

[1] Brecht, *Aufbau einer Rolle: Laughtons Galileo*, East Berlin, 1958.

group themselves according to the designs of a great artist, he immediately asked an excellent artist of the Walt Disney Studios [John Hubley] to make such sketches. They turned out somewhat malicious; L. used them, but with caution.'

The production of *Galileo* was Brecht's greatest chance to break into the American theatre. All his former efforts had failed. He had tried to persuade Thornton Wilder to adapt *The Good Soul of Setzuan*, but had met with a rebuff. He had adapted *The Duchess of Malfi* for Elisabeth Bergner, together with H. R. Hays and W. H. Auden, but when Bergner finally did the play on Broadway Brecht's version was not used. Now a great star of the stage and screen had recognized Brecht's importance and was ready to launch him. Moreover, *Galileo* was a great play, and highly topical as well. The dropping of the first atom bomb had made the problem of the scientist's responsibility to society one of the most burning issues of the day.

On 30 July 1947 *Galileo*, directed by Joseph Losey, opened at the Coronet Theatre in Beverly Hills. 'L.'s main worry was the heat. . . . He demanded that trucks full of ice blocks should be placed around the theatre and that the ventilators should be turned on so that "the audience should be able to think".'[1] But whether the ice was placed around the theatre or not, the public remained cool towards the whole enterprise. Laughton was robustly magnificent. But the unusual, cerebral play was lost on an audience unprepared for a new kind of dramatic convention. Not knowing Brecht's views about a theatre without mounting climaxes and 'well-constructed' scenes, they had come expecting the usual effects of suspense and emotional intensity and were not prepared for a loosely strung together sequence of dialogues on a stage of Spartan simplicity. As *Variety* remarked, the 'script' did not seem to make the grade and left an overall impression of dullness. There was still another chance: *Galileo* was to go to New York as well. But Brecht's thoughts had already turned to Europe.

This was not simply because he had failed to gain success and appreciation; existence on the fringes of American society and intellectual life was becoming less and less comfortable for foreigners with pronounced left-wing views. The cold war was on. Subversion was being suspected in all kinds of places. Hollywood was one of them.

---

[1] Brecht, *Aufbau einer Rolle: Laughtons Galileo*, p. 13.

Communist infiltration of the motion-picture industry was on the agenda.

In the course of September 1947 Brecht received a subpoena to appear before the Committee on Un-American Activities to testify on this subject.

While some of the members of his circle were terrified by the prospect and suggested ways and means to avoid his having to face this ordeal, Brecht himself was only too eager to pit his impertinence and Schweikian servility against what he considered the darkest and most evil forces in the country. He had always enjoyed such encounters and delighted in misleading pompous representatives of authority by 'sticking strictly to the untruth', as he had done when summoned before the censor of his film *Kuhle Wampe*.

On Thursday, 30 October 1947, he faced the Committee on Un-American Activities under the chairmanship of Representative Parnell Thomas.

The record of the proceedings on that morning is a curious document. Anyone who approached it with the expectation of finding the full horrors of the witch-hunt in it would be greatly disappointed. What is most striking is the utter innocence of the investigators, their inability to understand an intellectual, and, even more puzzling, the sketchiness of the preparation of their case. One might have expected that if one wanted to prove the Communist sympathies of a world-famous writer, someone might have been found to read his works in the original, so that he could confront him with his own words and opinions. But nothing of the sort had been done. The few scattered poems or plays of Brecht's that had been translated or had found their way into American Communist literature seem to have been the main basis of the Committee's knowledge of Brecht, together with one or two articles about him that were available in English. This gave Brecht the opportunity of roundly denying any Communist tendency in the poems quoted at him by insisting that the translation had changed his meaning. And when he noticed that none of the members of the Committee had any real knowledge of his writings, Brecht subtly misled them even on those points where they most clearly had a case.

Mr Robert E. Stripling, the Chief Investigator of the Committee, for example, read him a passage from *Die Massnahme* and asked:

Now, Mr Brecht, will you tell the Committee whether or not one of the characters in this play was murdered by his comrades because it was in the best interests of the party, of the Communist Party; is that true?[1]

This, though it may be somewhat crudely put, is indeed the plot of *Die Massnahme*. But Brecht calmly confused the issue. He replied:

No, it is not quite according to the story. . . . You will find when you read it carefully like in the old Japanese play where other ideas were at stake, this young man who died was convinced that he had done damage to the mission he believed in and he agreed to that, and he was about ready to die in order not to make greater such damage. So he asks his comrades to help him, and all of them together help him to die. He jumps into an abyss and they lead him tenderly to that abyss and that is the story.[1]

In fact, the three Communists in *Die Massnahme* say quite categorically:

> *Then we shot him and*
> *Threw him into a lime pit. . . .*[2]

But Brecht intentionally confused *Die Massnahme* with the earlier play *Der Jasager*, which *was* based on a Japanese legend and had been a kind of preliminary study for *Die Massnahme*. In that play the young man concerned *did* jump into an abyss. If challenged, Brecht could always have excused himself with having simply confused two of his plays that have much in common. But the Committee, of course, did not know the facts. The chairman merely remarked:

I gather from your remarks . . . that he was just killed, he was not murdered.

Brecht: He wanted to die.

Chairman: So they kill him?

Brecht: No; they did not kill him – not in this story. He killed himself. . . .[3]

[1] *Hearings Regarding the Communist Infiltration of the Motion Picture Industry*, Washington, 1947, pp. 491–504.

[2] Brecht, *Versuche 4*, p. 358.

[3] *Hearings Regarding the Communist Infiltration of the Motion Picture Industry*, Washington, 1947, pp. 491–504.

And there the matter rested. The Chief Investigator gallantly returned to the charge. He read out at length the article about Brecht by Sergei Tretyakov in the Moscow periodical *International Literature,* in which Brecht was quoted as openly sympathizing with the Communists (as indeed he had since 1928). Triumphantly the Chief Investigator turned to Brecht:

Do you recall that interview, Mr Brecht?

Brecht: No. [Laughter.] It must have been written twenty years ago or so. . . . I do not recall the interview in exact. I think it is a more or less journalistic summary of talks or discussions about many things.

The Chief Investigator shifted his ground again:

Have many of your writings been based upon the philosophy of Lenin and Marx?

Ever since 1930 Brecht had openly based all his writing on a Marxist standpoint. But he replied with complete confidence in the ignorance of the Committee:

No. I don't think that is quite correct. But of course I studied; I had to study as a playwright who wrote historical plays; I, of course, had to study Marx's ideas about history. I do not think intelligent plays today can be written without such study. Also history now, written now, is vitally influenced by the studies of Marx about history.[1]

Again the Committee was left speechless; and this point too went by default. When asked point-blank whether he had ever applied to join the Communist Party, Brecht denied it. The Committee produced some more of Brecht's openly Communist marching songs from an American Communist song-book.

Did you write that, Mr Brecht?

No, I wrote a German poem, but that is very different from this. [Laughter.]

Whereupon there remained nothing for the chairman to do but to close the proceedings:

[1] *Hearings Regarding the Communist Infiltration of the Motion Picture Industry,* Washington, 1947, pp. 491–504. ·

Chairman: Thank you very much, Mr Brecht. You are a good example to the witnesses of Mr Kenny and Mr Crum.[1]

And so Brecht left Washington with the thanks of the Committee on Un-American Activities for his exemplary behaviour as a co-operative witness. No wonder that his friends were in raptures. As one of them put it, it had been as though a zoologist had been cross-examined by apes.

To his chagrin Brecht had not been allowed to read the prepared statement he had brought with him to Washington. This, later published in Mr Gordon Kahn's book *Hollywood on Trial*, is a very typical exercise in Brechtian irony and Schweikian subservience. It begins by describing his career in the twenties:

> . . . in Germany voices could already be heard that free artistic expression and free speech should be silenced. Humanist, socialist, even Christian ideas were called 'un-deutsch' (un-German), a word which I can hardly think of without Hitler's wolfish intonation. . . .[2]

After thus openly equating Hitler's attacks on 'un-German' activities with the Chauvinism of the 'un-American' witch-hunt, Brecht proceeded to list the places he had passed through during his exile: Denmark, Finland, Manila, all of which were afterwards submerged in the tides of authoritarian invasion. The implication was clear that the same thing was now happening in the United States. And he went on:

> My activities, even those against Hitler, have always been purely literary activities of a strictly independent nature. As a guest of the United States I refrained from political activities concerning this country even in a literary form. . . . Being called before the Un-American Activities Committee, however, I feel free for the first time to say a few words about American matters: looking back at my experiences as a playwright and a poet in the Europe of the last two decades, I wish to say that the great American people would lose much and risk much if they allowed anybody to restrict free competition of ideas in cultural fields, or to interfere with art, which must be free in order to be art. . . .[3]

[1] *Hearings Regarding the Communist Infiltration of the Motion Picture Industry*, Washington, 1947, pp. 491-504.
[2] Gordon Kahn, *Hollywood on Trial*, New York, 1948, pp. 121-9.
[3] ibid.

When Brecht had asked to read this statement into the record of the Committee, the chairman had demanded to see it, had read it, and had replied:

Mr Brecht, the Committee has carefully gone over this statement. It is a very interesting story of German life, but it is not at all pertinent to this inquiry. Therefore we do not care to have you read the statement.[1]

Brecht had gone to Washington with the reservation for his flight to Europe in his pocket. Shortly after he got back to New York from his excursion to Washington he left America.

A friend who ran into him in Paris a few days later expressed surprise at seeing him back in Europe. Brecht replied: 'When they accused me of wanting to steal the Empire State Building, I thought it was high time for me to leave.'

And so, having travelled right round the world in the course of his exile, Brecht was back in Europe, with his suitcase containing his manuscripts on microfilm, a recording of his testimony before the Un-American Activities Committee, and the scroll with the picture of the cheerful, sceptical Chinese sage.

But he was in no hurry to return to Germany. In his sly, cautious way he took his time over getting the feel of things, surveying the ground and weighing up the pros and cons before finally making up his mind.

At first he went to Switzerland: Zurich was undoubtedly the most favourable vantage-point for such a reconnaissance – on the very borders of Germany with easy access not only to Western Germany but also to the Soviet zone and within easy reach of Austria. Moreover, it had sufficient German-speaking theatres to give Brecht a chance to work, at least for a while.

He took an apartment at Herrliberg outside Zurich, on the top floor of a gardener's cottage. In the main room he set up his workshop as he had done at so many transitory stopping-places in the years of exile: the typewriter stood by the window from which he could look out over the lake. The scroll depicting the Chinese sage was unrolled on the wall and folders with newsphotographs cut out from magazines littered the room.

[1] *Hearings Regarding the Communist Infiltration of the Motion Picture Industry*, Washington, 1947, pp. 491–504.

From Herrliberg one can take the train right to the centre of Zurich. Not far from the station, at the Café Odeon, one was at that time at the very centre of the intellectual life of Central Europe.

The Zurich Schauspielhaus, which had held high the honour of the German-speaking theatre throughout the years of Hitlerism and war, was reviving *Mother Courage* and preparing the world première of *Puntila*. The Municipal Theatre at Chur (Coire), the capital of the Grisons, invited Brecht to put on his adaptation of the *Antigone* of Sophocles, which he had freely based on Hoelderlin's great translation.

His old schoolmate and friend Caspar Neher came to design the set. Helene Weigel played Antigone, and the performance was a memorable demonstration of the Brechtian style of production. Ruth Berlau has made a detailed photographic record of it.[1]

This healthy and pleasurable plunge back into Brecht's favourite element, practical work in the theatre, also stimulated his theoretical activity: he composed a summary of his beliefs on the 'non-Aristotelian' drama in seventy-seven tersely formulated paragraphs, the *Little Organon for the Theatre*. And he began to write a play, *The Days of the Commune*. It was the last play he completed.

The Swiss novelist, dramatist, and architect, Max Frisch, who spent a good deal of time with Brecht in those months in Zurich, has given us a memorable and sensitive picture of Brecht at that time: reading poems to his guests in the quiet, matter-of-fact tone of a man showing you words as one would show interesting stones, pieces of cloth,

> or other things that have to speak for themselves; in the attitude of a man who, smoking his cigar, feels impelled to read out a text, merely because it is not generally available, as one would read a letter: in the tone of *communication*. He is not disturbed when the door-bell rings, or a further visitor enters the room. . . . 'I am', he says to the new arrival, 'reading a poem; it is called *To Posterity*.' He says this to make the new arrival wait for a moment before starting on his conversation, and in the voice of sober communication continues to read what he wants to tell posterity. . . .[2]

Frisch was fascinated by his discussions with Brecht: by his seriousness and dedicated loyalty to his Marxist creed, which made him reject

[1] Brecht and Neher, *Antigonemodell 1948*, East Berlin, 1949.
[2] Max Frisch, *Tagebuch 1946–1949*, Frankfurt, 1950, p. 226.

any social order existing at present and wholly align himself to the future.

Christians are aligned to a beyond; Brecht is aligned to this world. That is one of the differences between him and those priests to whom he bears no little resemblance, however much he may . . . mock them; the doctrine of the ends that sanctify the means produces similar features even when the ends are diametrically opposed. Materialist Jesuits also exist. . . .[1]

When it was time to go Brecht would sometimes take Frisch to the station:

He waits till I have got on the train, makes a spare, somewhat shy gesture with his hand, without taking off his grey cloth-cap; that would be out of style; avoiding the crowd, he leaves the platform with rapid, short, rather light steps, his arms hardly swinging, his head held slightly sideways, his cap drawn into the forehead as if to conceal his face, half conspiratorially, half bashfully. If you look at him like that, he gives the impression of a workman, a metal worker; yet he is too slight, too graceful for a workman, too much awake for a peasant, altogether far more volatile than the local breed of people; reserved, yet observant, a refugee, who has left innumerable stations, too shy for a man of the world, too knowing not to be anxious, a stateless person . . . a passer-by of our time, a man called Brecht, a scientist, a poet without incense. . . .[2]

[1] Max Frisch, *Tagebuch 1946–1949*, Frankfurt, 1950, p. 288.
[2] ibid., pp. 292–3.

Chapter IV

EAST BERLIN
(1948–1956)

> . . . Before me come the bombers. Deadly swarms
> Announce my return. Raging fires
> Precede the son.
>
> BRECHT, *Rueckkehr* [1]

> . . . I do not like the place I have come from
> I do not like the place I am going to. . . .
>
> BRECHT, *Der Radwechsel* (1953). [2]

On 22 October 1948 Brecht arrived back in Berlin. To reach the Soviet Zone, and the Eastern Sector of Berlin, he had been compelled to travel from Zurich via Prague. But he was not, by any means, certain that he wanted to stay.

On the morning after his arrival he went out by himself and wandered through the ruins. 'I went to the Reich Chancellery to smoke a cigar there,' he wrote in his diary. [3] A reporter wanted to know what his impressions were: 'Before I say anything, I want to see what it is like . . .,' he replied. [4]

The Communist Kulturbund gave a reception in his honour. There were long speeches. Brecht, who was sitting between the East German Communist leader Wilhelm Pieck (who later became President of the 'German Democratic Republic') and the Soviet Political Officer, Colonel Tulpanov, patiently listened to the long and fulsome orations. When his turn came to reply, Brecht rose, and

with his bird's head slightly stretched forward he blinkingly eyed the expectant circle of faces, then with a wide, sweeping gesture

[1] *Hundert Gedichte*, East Berlin, 1957, p. 313.
[2] *Sinn und Form*, Second Special Brecht Issue, 1957, p. 340
[3] Arnolt Bronnen, 'Bertolt Brecht und Berlin', *Berliner Zeitung*, East Berlin, 9.2.1958.
[4] H. C. Meier, 'Gespraech mit Brecht', *Hamburger Freie Presse*, 6.11.1948.

solemnly shook hands first with Pieck, then with Tulpanov, sat down again, and started to eat his soup. . . .[1]

Brecht had been invited to East Berlin to produce *Mother Courage* at the Deutsches Theater, where Reinhardt had once watched the rehearsals of *Drums in the Night*. Erich Engel, who had produced *Im Dickicht* in Berlin back in 1924, was to be his co-producer. Helene Weigel was to play Mother Courage. After long rehearsals the play opened on 11 January 1949. It was a brilliant performance and one of Brecht's greatest triumphs as producer and author. This, if not formally, was in fact the birth of the Berliner Ensemble.

Brecht returned to Zurich. Now he had to make up his mind: here was the possibility of obtaining what he had wanted all his life, a theatre of his own and lavish means to experiment to his heart's content. But he still hesitated. He, who had refused the invitation to settle in Moscow at the beginning of his exile, still had some doubts as to the advisability of moving too far into the Soviet orbit. Only after the Soviet blockade of West Berlin had been defeated by the Allied airlift and the prospect of a more normal life in East Berlin, with relatively free access to the West, seemed assured for at least a while, did he finally make up his mind.

For a man in Brecht's situation, and of Brecht's convictions, the decision to throw in his lot with the Communist part of Germany seems natural enough: in the West he had failed to make his mark, and he felt that America had not only rejected him as an artist but also proscribed him as politically undesirable. And America seemed the dominant force in the Western half of Germany. Moreover, Brecht had always followed the Communist party line in believing that Nazism had merely been a front for the magnates of German industry. To the adherents of this dogmatic view the Western Powers' efforts to put German industry – private industry – back on its feet were bound to appear as an attempt to restore the forces of German nationalism. Brecht's long poem *Freiheit und Democracy*, written in 1947, a ballad modelled on Shelley's *Mask of Anarchy*, expressed this conviction: under the banner of Anglo-Saxon freedom and democracy militarism and Chauvinism return to Germany followed by all the motley crew of their erstwhile adherents.

On the other hand, Brecht had no illusions as to the danger and

[1] Gody Suter, 'Brecht', *Tagesanzeiger*, Zurich, 1.9.1956.

hardship of life in the Soviet Zone. In his characteristically sly and circumspect manner he took his precautions to make himself independent of some of the main drawbacks of life in the East.

Brecht never allowed his political convictions and socialist ideals to interfere with his healthy peasant sense of thrift: there are many instances of his preferring to put a play of his into the hands of a rich entrepreneur rather than some poor struggling left-wing collective that would have needed his support to establish itself. When his financial advantage was at stake, these considerations simply ceased to exist.

And so at the very moment he moved to Eastern Germany, he put the copyright of his works into the hands of a West German publisher, Peter Suhrkamp, his old friend and collaborator on *Mahagonny* who had become one of Western Germany's leading publishers. This not only put Brecht outside the effective range of East German censorship, but gave him a source of Western currency, a financial bridgehead in the non-Communist world, which made him, up to a point, independent of his new Eastern patrons. To this day East German editions of Brecht's plays have to carry the imprint: 'By permission of Suhrkamp Verlag, Frankfurt on Main'.

Another proof of Brecht's circumspect approach to the question of his final domicile in Europe emerges from the efforts he made to secure a foothold in a German-speaking area that would have saved him from the necessity of deciding between West and East Germany. It was clear that Switzerland could not provide such a permanent residence. But shortly after his arrival in Zurich, Brecht had been approached by the Austrian composer Gottfried von Einem, at that time one of the most active promoters of the Salzburg Festival, to inquire whether he would be interested in lending his name to that famous but then tarnished institution. Von Einem, whom Caspar Neher, designer of many productions at Salzburg, had introduced to Brecht, felt that he might become for postwar Salzburg what Max Reinhardt, the great director, and Hugo von Hofmannsthal, the author of the *Everyman* play annually performed in front of the cathedral, had been in the twenties. Brecht was to come and live in Salzburg and be one of the artistic directors of the festival. He was greatly interested by the project and began to sketch out a *Salzburg Dance of Death* as a successor to the *Everyman*. 1949 was also the bicentenary of Goethe's birth: there was discussion of a *Faust* adaptation by Brecht.

In a letter dated 23 May 1948 – six months before Brecht's first visit to East Berlin – Brecht wrote to von Einem: '. . . I persist in my firm intention to come, if the matter can be arranged at Salzburg.' In the autumn of 1948 Brecht went to East Berlin. But after his return to Zurich in April 1949, he again wrote to von Einem: '. . . I am sitting here with Cas [Caspar Neher] and we have been talking about the festival play; it looks as though that would work. And I now also know of a reward, worth more to me than any advance of whatever kind: that would be a place of sanctuary, in other words a passport. If this were at all possible, it should be done, of course, without any publicity. And perhaps one way to do it, like the following, would be best: Helli [Helene Weigel] is after all a born Austrian – Viennese – and like myself stateless since 1933, and now there exists no German government. Could she get an Austrian passport back ? And could I then get one, simply as her husband ? You understand: I don't know the legal way. But, indeed, a passport would be of immense importance. I cannot, after all, settle in one part of Germany and then be dead for the other part. . . .'

Von Einem advised Brecht that he would have to apply formally for Austrian citizenship. The Austrian authorities were at that time prepared to grant naturalization fairly easily to distinguished artists, writers and scientists who wanted to settle in that small, newly independent country. Austrians have always been conscious of the value of their cultural prestige and saw this as an opportunity to re-establish their country as a cultural centre. But applications of this kind *had* to come from people who already lived in Austria. Brecht had no address in Austria, so his application is dated as from von Einem's residence in Salzburg. In his official application Brecht explained his desire to become an Austrian citizen in these terms: 'My longing for Austria is by no means due to external circumstances but can be explained by the fact that I, who have now reached the age of fifty, want to do my intellectual work in a country which can offer me a suitable atmosphere. Austria is such a country. . . . I should like to stress that I feel myself only a poet and do not want to serve any particular political ideology, nor do I especially want to be represented as the exponent of such an ideology. For certain specific reasons I refuse to be repatriated to Germany.'

This application was written before Brecht's return to East Berlin in the autumn of 1949. It is not clear whether he had already decided to settle in East Germany and merely wanted to obtain an Austrian passport as a safeguard and a means to travel in the West, or whether he had not yet made up his mind. What is certain, however, is that *after* the foundation of the Berliner Ensemble and after his final settlement in East Berlin Brecht continued to press for his naturalization in Austria. On 2 March 1950 – at a time when the German Democratic Republic already officially existed and he could easily have become its citizen – Brecht wrote to von Einem: '. . . Believe me I am as much interested as before, even more so. You *must* help me. So much depends on it for my artistic work (and collaboration with others), as many countries, including West Germany, could not be visited without a travel paper. . . .'

In April 1950 Brecht's application for Austrian citizenship was finally granted. The formalities to obtain the passport itself took some time. He obtained his Austrian passport in the autumn of 1950. By that time the whole episode of his application for naturalization had become known in Austria and had caused a public scandal, as anti-Communist circles reproached the government for having been taken in by a well-known Communist. There was even, for a time, a boycott of Brecht's plays in Austria, outside of the Soviet sector of Vienna. But he retained his Austrian nationality to the end. With his Austrian passport he could freely travel in the many countries that did not recognize the East German régime. If any Western visitor inquired whether Brecht might be able to come to a performance of his plays or a congress in Western Europe, Brecht would break into a broad grin and say with his most Schweikian expression: 'But of course; I have an Austrian passport. . . .'

Moreover, the Berliner Ensemble, which emerged from the company that had appeared in Brecht's and Engel's production of *Mother Courage* at the Deutsches Theater, was at first planned as a mobile, a touring company. In the first years of its existence the Berliner Ensemble, while it was given excellent rehearsal accommodation and ample financial means, had no permanent home of its own: it appeared as a fleeting tenant of the stage of the Deutsches Theater and spent a good deal of time on the road. In the autumn of 1949, before the Berliner Ensemble was formally constituted, *Mother Courage* had toured Western Germany. The East German authorities clearly regarded the *avant-gardist* style of Brecht's theatre as even more useful for propaganda purposes in the West than within their own sphere, where Brecht's theories and practice were regarded with some suspicion as formalism. But the East German authorities' aim suited Brecht admirably; it gave him, at least in theory, the best of both worlds: East German money to put on his plays and ample opportunity of travel and acclaim in the West.

And what is more, in East Germany he felt that he could exercise a real influence on the course of events. His prestige as an internationally famous figure who had thrown in his lot with the régime, the very fact that his presence was being used for purposes of propaganda, seemed to give him an opportunity to make his views count. He knew many of the leading figures of the régime from his years of exile, so that he was sure he would always have access to the authorities. In the West he would have been only an artist and intellectual on the fringe of affairs. In the East he would be in the very centre of things. In the words of Brecht's *alter ego* Herr Keuner, the city of B was preferable to the city of A, because 'in the city of A they asked me to dine; but in the city of B they asked me into the kitchen'.[1]

And so, in the autumn of 1949, Brecht finally moved to Berlin, to become 'artistic adviser' to the Berliner Ensemble, which was placed under the direction of his wife, Helene Weigel. After thirteen preliminary and forty-eight stage rehearsals the new company's first production, *Mr Puntila and His Hired Man Matti*, opened on 8 November 1949.

Brecht, who had left Berlin as the *enfant terrible* of his time now returned to it as the grand old man of German literature. He found it difficult to fill that role adequately. Considerable efforts were made to give him a more tidy and better groomed appearance: but without much success. On one occasion, when he turned up for a reception at the House of Soviet Culture, shabbily dressed and unshaven, he was turned away at the door as unworthy to grace so respectable a gathering of dignitaries. Hastily, and much relieved, he hurried away before his identity might be discovered.

With his austere grey suit, which was cut on the lines of a workman's overall, and his cloth cap, he did not look like a person of weight. One day when he had to get some papers stamped at some ministry, the minor official at the door made him feel the power of

[1] Brecht, 'Zwei Staedte', *Versuche 12*, p. 154.

authority by making him fill in a long document with all the details of where he wanted to go and whom he wanted to see. Scrutinizing this document, he spelled out the applicant's name – '"Bertolt Brecht". Are you a relative of Bert Brecht?' he asked. 'Yes, I am my own son,' said Brecht, and disappeared, muttering: 'In every hole you still find a Kaiser William II.'[1]

He refused to make use of a sumptuous official car and drove around in an old Steyr cabriolet, exactly like the one he had earned in the twenties by writing a publicity poem. And this car he had *bought* and paid for himself. If, as he drove up in his car, the porter hastened to hold the car door open for him, he ostentatiously got out on the other side.

Yet he did not refuse some of the other, and more solid, benefits and privileges enjoyed by members of the ruling circle of a Communist country: a flat in town and a country house at Buckow on the lakeshore of the Scharmuetzelsee with a large park surrounding the villa that had once belonged to a rich Berlin business man. Brecht himself preferred to stay in the gardener's cottage.

The flat in town was at the back of an old building in the Chausseestrasse. It overlooked the Huguenot cemetery, where Hegel is buried. Helene Weigel had a separate flat on the floor below where she lived with her young daughter Barbara, an actress in the Berliner Ensemble. Brecht's son had stayed behind in the United States.

Now that Brecht could indulge his tastes, he surrounded himself with objects he liked.

. . . Curiously shaped chairs that did not match, very small tables, a minute harmonium, a portable typewriter. Half-smoked cigars were lying on pewter plates; on the walls an engraving, oriental masks and two little old photographs, one of Marx when his beard was still black, the other of Engels in his early youth; all horizontal areas were covered by mountains of paper: music, manuscripts, letters, posters, books. . . .[2]

The clock on the wall of one of the rooms had a case made of an old copper saucepan. For Brecht loved old, well-worn things:

---

[1] Ruth Berlau, 'Wie war Bert Brecht?' *Das Magazin*, East Berlin, February 1958.
[2] V. Pozner, 'bb', *Sinn und Form*, Second Special Brecht Issue, p. 453.

Of all the works of man I love most
Those that are much used.
Copper vessels, dented, buckled, with flattened rims;
Knives and forks with wooden handles
Worn smooth by many hands: such forms
I thought most noble. . . .[1]

And in his own surroundings as much as in the theatre he disliked any attempt to cover up the workings of machinery by hiding it behind genteel disguises. When he asked one of the decorators of the Berliner Ensemble to fix him some curtain wire in his study at Buckow, this workman hid the wire behind a beautiful oak pelmet. Brecht was horrified: 'Fischer,' he said to the man, 'you are covering up the technical apparatus. One must be able to see how things work. . . .'[2]

So Brecht created an island for himself to which he could withdraw from the strains and stresses of the outside world: he was appalled by what he found on his return to Germany: the bureaucracy of the authorities, the vulgar, petty bourgeois tastes of the population, the horrible tastelessness of the goods offered for sale – and eagerly bought by the people. Where was the upsurge of good taste the left-wing intellectuals of the twenties had always associated with the coming of the revolution? Now Brecht had to explain it all away by the argument that people of a class which has come to power first desire an abundance of the things they had seen in the homes of the class they have displaced. The trouble was, however, that the working class of Eastern Germany did *not* feel that it had come to power. They merely wanted any consumer goods they could get hold of, whether they were ugly or not.

But from these realities the members of the ruling clique in Eastern Germany were mercifully isolated: they had no contact with the people or with popular feeling. The immense difference in their way of living completely cut off the few, with their town flats and country houses, their cars and their privilege of free travel – and shopping – in the West, from the down-trodden, fear-ridden masses of the people. The intellectuals within this narrow ruling class had little in common with the hard-boiled party functionaries. They had to fall back on the even narrower circle of their fellow-intellectuals: for Brecht in many ways this became a replica of the equally isolated world of the German

[1] Brecht, 'Von allen Werken', *Gedichte und Lieder*, p. 46.
[2] 'Dreizehn Buehnentechniker erzaehlen', *Sinn und Form*, Second Special Brecht Issue, 1957, p. 476.

émigrés in the United States; Hanns Eisler and Paul Dessau, who had been among Brecht's closest friends in America, belonged to this circle. Arnold Zweig had also returned from exile; Herbert Ihering, Brecht's discoverer and critical champion, had kept his position under Hitler and had now landed on his legs in the Soviet Zone as well.

For Brecht the main escape from this parochial world of super-annuated intellectuals was his work with the young members of his theatre and with the young writers who were his pupils in the German Academy of Arts. In these young people Brecht inspired a fanatical devotion, and among them he found a considerable number of brilliant talents: Manfred Wekwerth, Hans Joachim Bunge, Peter Palitzsch, Kaethe Ruelicke, Egon Monk, and a number of other members of the literary and production staff of the Berliner Ensemble formed the nucleus of a band of disciples who more than once provoked the wrath of the party stalwarts by their unorthodox views and even their un-orthodox and somewhat uniform appearance. Among the young writers with whom Brecht worked or who followed his teaching from the distance were some of the outstanding talents of the younger genera-tion: the poets Heinz Kahlau and Guenter Kunert, and the young dramatist Peter Hacks, now the main exponent of the Brechtian drama in Germany. It is significant that these young writers are all considered to belong to the opposition against the hide-bound party orthodoxy of the old guard intellectuals. They have often been the target of attacks from the inner circles of the party and have sometimes bravely hit back. Monk and Palitzsch left East Germany and for many years have been working in West Germany where they have been responsible for the transplanting and continuation of the Brechtian style of production and revolutionary political approach to the theatre.

In 1954 the Berliner Ensemble was given its own theatre: the Theater am Schiffbauerdamm, which had seen some of Brecht's greatest triumphs in the twenties, became its permanent home. A startling poster designed by Picasso invited the people of East Berlin to the opening performance and immediately aroused a storm of protest from people who considered it a typical example of formalistic, bourgeois art.

The Schiffbauerdamm theatre had been modernized and brought up to date. Brecht was so grateful to the technicians that he wrote them a letter in which he asked them to remind him of the debt he owed them, if and when he should become too rude during rehearsals. The technicians, remembering many terrible rows that Brecht had made, painted the relevant sentence from Brecht's letter on to an enormous streamer which always hung in the flies to be lowered into view at the appropriate moment should Brecht ever become too angry. But it was never used.

Now that Brecht was master of his own theatre he had achieved one of the greatest ambitions of his life: a company of about 60 actors and actresses, a total personnel of more than 250 – actors, designers, producers, Dramaturgen, mechanics, musicians, scene-painters – was at his disposal. New productions could be rehearsed for periods from three to five months, and Brecht could indulge his habit of trying out everything in practice before rejecting or adopting it. Half jokingly, but half seriously, he had often maintained that he considered himself the greatest producer in the world – with the single exception of Charlie Chaplin. And now he could put this boast to the test. In the few years that were left to him, he proved his claim: when the Berliner Ensemble visited Paris – in 1954 with *Mother Courage* and in 1955 with *The Caucasian Chalk Circle* – its European fame was assured. Visitors from all over Europe came to East Berlin to watch Brecht at work as he sat in his special producer's chair in the front row of the auditorium, quietly watching the rehearsal and weighing up the many different ways in which a single gesture could be performed until the only one that was really right was found. In his last years every word he said during rehearsals was reverently tape-recorded by his disciples. He had indeed become a grand old man.

But in spite of this outward success, membership of the Academy of Arts, the award of the National Prize First Class for Art and Literature and later the Stalin Peace Prize, relations between Brecht and the East German Communist authorities were by no means smooth: however isolated the privileged class of artists and intellectuals might have been from the down-trodden and long-suffering population, who showed their true feelings by crossing the border into Western Germany in their thousands,[1] reality broke in upon them in the rising of 17 June 1953. Nor could Brecht, who did not suffer fools gladly, remain unaffected by the stupidity and low intellectual calibre of many of the bureaucrats with whom he came into contact: the party

[1] 199,000 in 1950; 165,000 in 1951; 182,000 in 1952; 331,000 in 1953; 184,000 in 1954; 242,000 in 1955; 279,000 in 1956.

and State functionaries responsible for allocating paper, passing the plans for the theatre's future repertoire, etc. Having become a Communist in protest against the empty nationalism of the German bourgeoisie, he was now supporting a régime which was indulging in propaganda even more violently Chauvinistic and hollow. This clash between the reality of the Communist State and the ideal picture he had believed in presented Brecht with a continuous conflict of conscience, which is described in greater detail elsewhere in this book.[1] The difficulties he had with his and Paul Dessau's opera *The Trial of Lucullus* were followed by a ban on his play about the Paris Commune, *The Days of the Commune*, which the authorities considered too defeatist; his *Kriegsfibel* (*Primer of War*), the fruit of his collection of news photographs, was at first refused the imprimatur of the authorities as being too pacifist. Only when Brecht threatened to bring the whole matter before the World Peace Council was permission finally granted.[2]

Even more grotesque, in the light of Brecht's previous struggle with capitalist film makers to protect *The Threepenny Opera* from being distorted in its film version, was the conflict in which he was involved in connexion with a projected film of *Mother Courage*. The East German State film concern DEFA planned *Mother Courage* as a monster Cinemascope epic in colour. Work on the film, which was to be directed by Wolfgang Staudte, then East Germany's leading director (he has since fled to the West), was started in the autumn of 1954. Brecht insisted that the actors of the Berliner Ensemble should appear in the film in the parts they had played on the stage. Staudte refused and work was suspended. But in the summer of 1955 the project was taken up again. To increase the film's appeal in the West, Staudte had invited two leading French stars (Simone Signoret and Bernard Blier) to appear in *Mother Courage*. A three-cornered fight ensued between Brecht who still wanted Helene Weigel to play the name part, Staudte who preferred another actress, and the party authorities who insisted on various changes in the text, designed to make the film conform with the current political line. Both Brecht and Staudte tried to resist this interference. On the other hand, Brecht made such a nuisance of himself by demanding a say in all kinds of details of the filming, right down to the historical authenticity of the

[1] See Chapter VII, 'Brecht and the Communists'.
[2] 'Brecht – beinahe verboten', *Frankfurter Allgemeine Zeitung*, 19.11.1955.

shoes the characters should wear, that the director obtained an order banning Brecht from the precincts of the studios.

After much wrangling and deadlock the film was abandoned for the time being. Having sat idly in Berlin for weeks, Simone Signoret and Bernard Blier returned to Paris. Some years later – after Brecht's death – a less ambitious film version of *Mother Courage* was completed; this was, essentially, a transfer of the Berliner Ensemble's production, with the Berliner Ensemble's actors, to the screen.

In spite of all these difficulties and annoyances Brecht loyally continued to lend the East German Communists his support. Cynic that he was, he still felt under an obligation to repay the financial support he received from the authorities. Talking to a Swiss newspaper man about his troubles with *Lucullus* he once said: 'Let Adenauer put the means for so far-reaching an experiment at my disposal! After all, the patrons have a right to make their wishes felt. . . .'[2] In this spirit Brecht played his part in the various campaigns of the East German authorities. He sent telegrams to Einstein and other American personalities when the campaign to obtain a reprieve for the Rosenbergs was at its height, and repeatedly addressed appeals to West German intellectuals during the agitation against the rearmament of the Federal Republic. From time to time he appeared on the platform at press conferences arranged by the East German propaganda authorities for the benefit of Western journalists: looking much older than his age and having grown somewhat fat and flabby, he would intervene with particular venom against the 'war-mongers' of the West. There can be no doubt that on this point he was sincere: he had succeeded in making himself believe that the old militarists were being helped back into the saddle in West Germany by the Americans; and with his memories of the horrors he had seen in the military hospital of the First World War this conviction enabled him to overlook the most blatant sins of the East German régime – including their rearmament started on the best Prussian lines long before a West German defence contribution had even been discussed.

But even in his valiant efforts to make propaganda for them, the East German régime often let him down. During a discussion with

[1] This account of the affair of the *Mutter Courage* film is based on 'Streit um Mutter Courage', *Frankfurter Allgemeine Zeitung*, 29.10.1955, 'Brecht und der Film', *Neue Zuercher Zeitung*, 1.9.1956, and private information.

[2] Gody Suter, 'Brecht', *Tagesanzeiger*, Zurich, 1.9.1956.

Western intellectuals attended by Brecht and the East German Minister for Culture, Johannes R. Becher, Melvin J. Lasky, the editor of the liberal West Berlin monthly *Der Monat*, offered Brecht space in his magazine to put his views before a Western audience – provided the same privilege was granted Lasky in an East German publication. Brecht laughed off any suggestion that the East German authorities would not dare to have any article of Lasky's published, and eventually, if somewhat reluctantly, accepted the challenge. But no article from Brecht arrived. Clearly he had overestimated the liberalism of his political friends. And so he had to undergo the humiliation of seeing *Der Monat* appear with a blank page – reserved for Brecht's article on artistic freedom.[1]

No wonder Brecht looked tired and worn in these years of his greatest outward success: the poems he wrote in this period show a deep feeling of guilt, malaise, and a nostalgic, tender yearning for the Augsburg of his youth. Was it this tiredness that kept him from writing anything of major significance after his return to East Berlin? Was it the oppressive lack of freedom? Or was it, as has been argued by some defenders of the East German regime, merely that Brecht was too eager to see his old plays staged to write any new ones? All these factors undoubtedly contributed to Brecht's sterility. That he was just too busy seems difficult to believe: not only did he work extremely fast, when he came to grips with an idea, he also in fact spent a great deal of time on adapting existing plays: Lenz's *Hofmeister* (*The Private Tutor*), a combined version of two comedies by Gerhart Hauptmann (*Biberpelz* and *Roter Hahn*), an adaptation of Farquhar's *Recruiting Officer* (*Pauken und Trompeten*), and a version of *Coriolanus*. For Brecht working on an adaptation of this kind was hardly less arduous than writing a new play of his own. On the other hand, it was safer to work on existing material. The East German authorities were constantly urging him to write a propaganda play on one of the great contemporary issues of the Communist transformation of their republic. And it is known that Brecht was in fact working on one such play, which was to have dealt with the life of the shock worker Hans Garbe. But it is also known that he abandoned work on it when it became clear that his way of treating the subject would not meet with the approval of the party authorities. So Brecht confined his literary support of the régime to a number of political marching

[1] *Der Monat*, West Berlin, January 1955.

songs, an anti-Adenauer cantata (*Herrnburger Bericht*), and a long poem on the improvement of the growing of millet in the Soviet Union (*Erziehung der Hirse*).

When he died Brecht left an almost completed but unrevised play, *Turandot oder der Kongress der Weisswaescher* (*Turandot or the Congress of Whitewashers*), a satire in a Chinese setting directed against intellectuals who defend the capitalist system. He is also reported to have been planning a counterplay to Beckett's *Waiting for Godot*.

Helped by his Austrian passport, Brecht took every opportunity to travel in the West, whether it was to a PEN Congress in Amsterdam or a guest appearance of the Berliner Ensemble in Paris, a première of one of his plays in Western Germany, a production of *The Three-penny Opera* in Milan, or some East-West discussion in West Berlin.

He particularly enjoyed his visits to Paris; France and French culture had always been his particular love. Vladimir Pozner has described one of these visits to Paris: Brecht buying mountains of paper-back crime stories in English (his favourite reading) or inhaling the delicious odours of a large plate of cheeses in a restaurant. 'I should like to exhibit this plate of cheese in the foyer of my theatre in Berlin', he said, 'to teach the Germans the meaning of culture!'[1]

In the spring of 1955 Brecht fell seriously ill. Henceforth he was haunted by forebodings of death. When his Swiss friend Max Frisch came to visit him in the summer of that year, Brecht asked him about the chances of buying a small house by the Lake of Geneva to which he could retire.

He did not look ill, but exhausted . . . and his politeness, a very individual kind of graceful courtesy which he maintained even after the most heated discussions, this time only accompanied me to the door of his apartment, so that I had to look for the way out of the house by myself. Real discussion, the open cut and thrust of conflicting views – that had been buried long ago. . . .[2]

On his fifty-eighth birthday, on 10 February 1956, Brecht was in Milan to attend the first night of Giorgio Strehler's production of *The Threepenny Opera* at the Piccolo Teatro. Talking to an old

[1] Vladimir Pozner, 'bb', *Europe*, January/February 1957, p. 30.
[2] Max Frisch, 'Brecht ist tot', *Die Weltwoche*, Zurich, 24.8.1956.

acquaintance about his heart trouble, he said with a smile: 'At least one knows that death will be easy. A slight knock at the window-pane, and then. . . .'

Shortly afterwards his old school friend and favourite stage designer, Caspar Neher, came to see him. They talked about the adaptation of *Coriolanus* on which they were working, and Neher quoted the Roman custom of appearing in sackcloth and ashes – 'in luctu et squalore' – when applying for public office. Brecht pointed to the cemetery under his window and said: 'Soon you will stand down there in luctu et squalore. . . .'[1]

The Berliner Ensemble were rehearsing for their London season which was to start on 27 August 1956. On 5 August one of the young producers of the Ensemble, Manfred Wekwerth, had gone to visit Brecht at his country place and found him in the best of spirits. He typed out a brief note to the actors on how to succeed with the British: '. . . in England there is an old fear that German art (literature, painting, music) is terribly weighty, long-winded, complicated, and pedestrian. Therefore we must play in a fast, light, and vigorous manner. . . .'[2] Wekwerth also discussed at length the problem of the production of *The Days of the Commune* which had at last been passed by the authorities and which Wekwerth was to produce at Karl-Marx-Stadt (Chemnitz). Brecht talked about the importance of *naïveté* in his conception of aesthetics. 'The naïve', he said, 'is an aesthetic category, the most concrete of all.'[3] And he mentioned the paintings of Breughel, which had always influenced his ideas of décor and grouping, as good examples of what he meant by the truly naïve in art. 'The opposite of a naïve approach is naturalism.'[3]

On 10 August Brecht attended a rehearsal at the theatre. He felt very tired afterwards, and his condition gradually deteriorated. During the night from the 13 to the 14 August it became critical. He died of coronary thrombosis at a quarter to midnight on 14 August 1956. Among the four doctors who signed the medical bulletin on his death was Dr Muellereisert, his schoolmate at Augsburg.

[1] Caspar Neher, 'Dem Gedaechtnis meines Freundes', *Sinn und Form*, Second Special Brecht Issue, 1957, p. 437.

[2] 'Brecht, 'Zum Londoner Gastspiel'. Leaflet in programme of London Season of Berliner Ensemble.

[3] M. Wekwerth, 'Auffinden einer Aesthetischen Kategorie', *Sinn und Form*, Second Special Brecht Issue, 1957, p. 267.

Brecht was buried, as he had requested, in the old Huguenot cemetery beneath the window of his last apartment. He had specifically forbidden any speech-making at the funeral. So the speeches had to be made at a ceremony in the Schiffbauerdamm theatre.

Today the apartment in the Chausseestrasse has become the Brecht archive. Brecht's enormous mass of manuscripts, draft plays, diaries, and jottings of all sorts is being microfilmed and sorted by devoted disciples. A complete critical edition of all his works is in preparation. There can be no doubt whatever that the loyal band of Brechtians in charge of this work is determined to carry it through with the utmost faithfulness to the text and to publish every scrap Brecht ever wrote. But whether such a publication will in fact ever be possible in the present circumstances in Eastern Germany is another, and an open, question.

Part Two: The Artist

Chapter V

THE POET:
BRECHT'S LANGUAGE
AND ITS SOURCES

Brecht was a poet, first and foremost a poet. However much interest his writings may have aroused as expressions of the problems and anxieties of the age, as political pamphlets, manifestoes of stage reform, or social documents, their chief distinction lies in being 'memorable speech'. This is their primary significance. It underlies, from it derives, any other significance they may possess.

Brecht's plays may be discussed and imitated as examples of a new kind of dramatic construction or stage technique. Nevertheless their main importance lies in their poetic quality. The new dramatic convention they represent lives above all through the grace of their language and the poetic vision of the world it conveys. Without the stamp of greatness impressed upon them by their poetry, these plays could never have exercised such an influence. They would not even have been noticed. And so it is with Brecht's ideas in other fields. They become important only as the ideas of a major poet.

But this also makes any discussion of Brecht particularly difficult outside his own linguistic sphere. While writers like Sartre or Thomas Mann lose relatively little by translation and their ideas come across in any language, Brecht's ideas, in their own way as significant as theirs, are so intimately bound up with the manner in which they are expressed that any account of Brecht's work which has to ignore this quality becomes unreal. Hence the champions of Brecht in the English-speaking world so often appear to be overstating their case. Brecht's poetry does not translate well. Its power, to a large extent, lies in its directness and simplicity, in the bold use of hackneyed words in unhackneyed contexts. Inevitably in translation simplicity often turns into mere simple-mindedness or banality and the common word subtly used into the merely commonplace.

It is clearly futile to try and *describe* the beauties of a poet's style at second-hand. Yet an attempt must be made here to convey, without deeper analysis of Brecht's use of words, syntax, and imagery, some of the features which account for its impact, and to trace the varied sources and influences that lie behind it.

Literary German, and above all stage German, is essentially an artificial, a dead language. While standard English, standard French, or standard American are spoken, if not by the whole population so at least by important sections of it, standard German only exists on paper and on the stage. In ordinary life even the most educated Germans have their clearly defined regional accent and vocabulary. It is thus far more difficult in German to write dramatic dialogue which sounds like real speech that is free from the local overtones and limitations of mere dialect. Some of the greatest achievements of German dramatic literature are in fact dialect plays and confined to a limited area: the Viennese folk theatre of Raimund and Nestroy, or the Darmstadt comedies of Niebergall. When naturalism reached the German stage, its first successful exponent, Gerhart Hauptmann, wrote his early plays in Silesian and later in Berlin dialect. He turned to standard 'poetic' German only when he took up a vague and bloodless romanticism.

In poetry, even more so than in the drama, the language used tends to diverge from real speech and to assume a highly formalized hieratic tone, which some poets like Stefan George and Rilke have used with consummate skill and great effect, but which tends to degenerate into empty and abstract phrase-making in the hand of lesser men.

Brecht, however, achieved the rare feat of creating in his poetry and plays a language all his own, which suggested the rhythms and gave the feeling of real speech without being tied to any particular regional dialect. It is still not a language spoken by anyone in reality – with the exception perhaps of Brecht himself. But while it is a synthesis, this language is such a vital and original synthesis, so deeply rooted in a number of different traditions, that it creates the illusion of real speech.

This was the quality which overwhelmed the audience even in Brecht's first chaotic plays. As one critic said at that time:

If it weren't for Brecht's diction! Again and again it simply forces you to listen. His characters may talk the silliest stuff for quarters of an hour on end. In parts what they say is completely devoid of sense. But the point is: *how* they say it! No other writer has caught the speech of the masses of the people as Brecht has. In comparison Tollers' leading-article German is ridiculous; even Hauptmann sounds like reams of paper beside him. . . . For Brecht language is no longer a secondary, indirect matter, no longer merely a question of intellectual expression, but something elementary, a function of the body. . . . This language rises up from depths in which the conscious self only flickers as a far off, little taper. It is no coincidence that in Brecht's plays there are so many drunkards, and that almost all his characters are good drinkers: *in vino veritas*. This language never lies, there is not the least bit of padding in it. All rational inhibitions are here dissolved. . . . The choice of words itself is *banal*, but the way they are put together almost amounts to genius. . . . [1]

This intensely personal idiom, chaotic and uncontrolled in his early years, disciplined into severe and monumental simplicity later on, is the product of the fusion of many diverse and disparate elements.

Ernest Borneman has most perceptively isolated the four main sources of Brecht's language:

1 – the daily speech of Southern Germany; 2 – an anti-metaphorical poetry of colours, textures, and other concrete images; 3 – bureaucratic jargon; 4 – Anglicisms and exotic expressions. [2]

These elements, which are already clearly present in Brecht's earliest published writings, are the basis of his personal idiom: the regional Bavarian accent is always to be detected, but never lapses into mere local colour. It is stylized and fused with archaic elements from an earlier, *baroque* layer of the German language. The use of phrases and constructions from the jargon of the civil service is in itself a somewhat baroque device. The stilted locutions of the bureaucrats are to a large extent historical relics, and Brecht used their dusty flavour and demented pedantry not only as parody but somehow turned it into poetic imagery through which the desiccated, fossilized clichés suddenly sprang into new and unexpected life.

On the other hand, Brecht's language has a firm basis in the chief

[1] Harry Kahn, 'Bert Brecht', *Die Weltbuehne*, Berlin, 17.1.1928.
[2] E. Borneman, 'Ein Epitaph fuer Bertolt Brecht', *Sinn und Form*, Second Special Brecht Issue, 1957, p. 142.

source of modern standard German. Once, when asked by a magazine to name the strongest literary influence in his life, Brecht replied in a single sentence: 'You will laugh: the Bible!'[1] And in fact the vigorous, outspoken language of Luther's Bible pervades the writings of the atheist and blasphemer Brecht. He made masterly use of Biblical constructions: the juxtaposition of contrasted half-sentences, parallelism, repetition, and inversion.

Equally marked throughout Brecht's life was the influence of the street ballad, the 'Moritat' (morality), as it was sung by ballad-mongers at country fairs, lurid accounts of murders and executions couched in the strident language of larmoyant sentiment and naïve horror. Brecht turned to this 'vulgar' style in protest against the gentility and respectability of the bourgeois society he abhorred. Disgusted by the insipid classical poetry taught at school, he revelled in the powerful emotions and garish colours of the entertainments of the common people, the songs of kitchen maids and the pleasures offered by the sideshows of fair-grounds and beer-gardens.

In protesting against the canons and conventions of German poetry, the stately idealism of Goethe or Schiller which he had been taught at school, Brecht in fact returned to the last relics of an older tradition which these reformers of the German language and purgers of its 'coarseness' and 'irregularity' had tried to eradicate. Goethe and Schiller had been the crowning glory of the literary movement of the eighteenth century, whose aim it had been to base the greatness of the united German nation they sought to create upon the sure foundation of a German national literature as respectable and regular, as elegant and polite as those of France and England. To achieve this aim the exuberance of the baroque, the earthiness of the folk tradition had to be banished from polite society. The victory of the reformers seemed complete. And yet among the comics of the beer-gardens, in the peep-shows, and fair-ground 'panoramas' the old German baroque drama, the earlier traditions of Hans Sachs, the Austrian and Bavarian forms of the Italian Commedia dell' Arte, and even some relics of the mystery plays of the Middle Ages were still alive when Brecht was young.

The Austrian and Bavarian folk theatre, which reached its peak in the Viennese popular drama of the late eighteenth and early nineteenth century, is a branch of the same tradition which also survives

[1] *Die Dame*, Berlin, 1.10.1928.

in English pantomime. The only example of the genre which has achieved international fame is Schikaneder's *Magic Flute*, carried to immortality by Mozart's music. If one imagines the *Magic Flute* with the music much reduced in weight, it can serve as a good example of its type: the main plot is a fantastic fairy-tale with a strong moral lesson, but parallel to it there always runs a coarsely comic plot which parodies and debunks the high-faluting antics of the noble lovers and matches their ethereal sentiments with earthy common sense. While the 'high' plot is intended as historical drama, the 'low' plot lapses into constant anachronisms. The spoken dialogue is interrupted by musical numbers – 'couplets' with recurring refrains that resemble the comic character songs of Victorian music-hall.

This is a genuinely common, 'plebeian' kind of theatre: as the romantic plot is no longer taken seriously, the higher world of upper-class sentiments is presented from the ruthless viewpoint of the common people. The heroes are seen through the eyes of their valets and chambermaids. And this produces a characteristic duality of language: the high-flown bombast of the 'noble' characters stands against the homely, vigorous common sense of the people.

The sketches that Brecht's greatly admired friend Karl Valentin performed in the beer-gardens of Munich were direct descendants of this tradition. He was the last in a long line of great clowns and Hans-Wursts stretching back to the eighteenth century.

Brecht's theatre with its use of fairy-tale elements, musical numbers, and broadly comical characters is a continuation of this old and once despised tradition, and has re-established it as a vehicle for the expression of ideas. His language drew much of its vigour and force from the earthy speech of clowns who never failed to call a spade a spade.

The affinities between this comico-heroic drama and Shakespeare are clear enough, and the early Brecht was deeply indebted to the Elizabethans, both directly, and indirectly through their greatest follower in German literature, Georg Buechner, the author of *Woyzeck* and *Danton's Death*. Brecht regarded Buechner as the greatest German dramatist and modelled his early plays on Buechner. In *Baal* and *Drums in the Night* we find the same feverish, rhythmic prose, tender and coarse in turn, direct and daring in its images:

And love is like letting one's naked arm swim in the water of a pond, with weeds between one's fingers; like the torment of which the drunken tree begins to sing as it creaks when the wild wind rides it; like drowning in the wine you gulp down on a hot day, and her body pours into you like very cool wine and penetrates every fold of your skin; soft like plants in the winds are the joints; and the force of the impact to which you yield is like flying against a storm and her body tumbles over you like cool gravel. . . .[1]

This ecstatic prose of Brecht's first play also shows the influence of another great rebel among German dramatists, Frank Wedekind (1864–1918), another follower of Buechner, who spent his life struggling for the sexual liberation of mankind, like D. H. Lawrence after him, acted in his own plays and sang his ballads in the Munich cabarets.

Brecht saw himself as one of this band of outsiders. He was fascinated by all the *poètes maudits* of world literature: François Villon, whose ballads he used in *The Threepenny Opera*, Baudelaire, Verlaine, and Rimbaud. The plot of *Baal* contains echoes of the relationship between Rimbaud and Verlaine, and so does another early play, *Im Dickicht der Staedte*, in which Brecht quotes extensively from *Une saison en enfer* in K. L. Ammer's translation. Many of the poems in Brecht's first published collection *Hauspostille* are modelled on Rimbaud's language.

All the more surprising it may seem at first sight that Brecht was at least as strongly influenced by a poet of an entirely different stamp: Rudyard Kipling. Yet it was the same impulse which drove him from the drab respectability of provincial society to the vagabonds among the poets, street entertainers, and fair-ground comics that also made Brecht dream of the wide, wide world he found in the Barrack Room Ballads. And there too he met a vigorous plebeian language – spiced with deliciously exotic names of places and things that breathed an air of boundless freedom and adventure.

Kipling was the main source of the exotic, mythical Anglo-Saxon world which forms the background to a great deal of Brecht's earlier writing. Other elements in it come from Swift and Gay, Upton Sinclair, Jack London, the Chicago stories of the Danish novelist J. V. Jensen (*The Wheel*), Dickens, innumerable crime stories, and gangster films. This world, in which English and American elements are inextricably mixed up, is as unlike real England or America as it could possibly be: it is a world inhabited by huge, hard-drinking

[1] *Baal. Erste Stuecke I*, p. 18.

lumber-jacks from the Yukon *en route* for Benares, laden with gold and
ready to spend it; a world where Chicago merges into Soho, and John
Gay's rogues and highwaymen are blood-brothers to bootleggers and
gangsters. This is the world of *The Threepenny Opera*: eighteenth-
century London inhabited by highwaymen, whores, and Victorian
bankers, ruled by the police chief Brown, who is addressed as 'Sheriff'
and has served with Macheath in the Indian Army, where they freely
made mincemeat out of any brown or yellow race they met between
'the Cape and Cooch Behar'. Chicago, on the other hand, is the home
of the daemonic merchant Shlink in *Im Dickicht der Staedte*, who
happens to be a Malay from Yokohama and is lynched for having
lived with a white girl; in Chicago too we find, in *St Joan of the
Stockyards*, the mighty canned meat king Pierpont Mauler in whose
factories careless workers disappear into the mincing machines to
reappear in the form of meatloaf; Pierpont Mauler, who ruins whole
industries by his ruthlessness on the Stock Exchange and has his
starving locked-out workers beaten up by the police. Everything in
this mythical Anglo-Saxon empire which extends from Alaska to the
South Seas is bigger than life-size, savage, adventurous, and free.
Brecht was so fascinated by it that he even wrote a number of 'songs'
in his own peculiar English, which he thought could alone express its
flavour:

> *There is no whisky in this town*
> *There is no bar to sit us down*
> *Oh!*
> *Where is the telephone?*
> *Is here no telephone?*
> *Oh Sir, God damn me:*
> *No!*
> *Let's go to Benares*
> *Where the sun is shining*
> *Let's go to Benares!*
> *Johnny, let us go.*[1]

Brecht's ostensible loathing of the capitalist ruthlessness of this dream-
land can never quite conceal the magnetic attraction its size, its
freedom, and adventurousness had for him. The drunken pirates of
the *Ballade von den Seeraeubern* who murder and rape their way across

[1] 'Benares Song', *Hauspostille*, Berlin, 1927, p. 42.

a boundless azure sea, the Kiplingesque soldiers of *Mann ist Mann*, who ransack the treasures of ancient pagodas if they want to pay for a pint of beer and storm the mountain fastnesses of Tibet, are the symbols of Brecht's passionate protest against the respectability of small-town bourgeois life in a landlocked country. His love for these images thus springs from precisely the same roots as his anti-bourgeois, anti-capitalist politics. Even at a later stage of his development, in so openly political a poem as the one in which at the time of the great depression he somewhat prematurely mourned the *Forgotten Glories of the Giant City of New York*, we can detect an undertone of awe and nostalgia:

> *. . . Harmonious sounds at evening time of the waters of Miami!*
> *Irresistible gaiety of generations driving fast along unending highways!*
> *Powerful sorrows of singing women, hopefully bewailing*
> *Broad-chested men, but still surrounded by*
> *Broad-chested men!*[1]

Such was the curious mixture of influences that shaped Brecht's early poetry and the tense, extravagant prose of his first plays. While the Expressionist fashion of the period also left some superficial traces on his style, his basic attitude remained fundamentally different from that of the Expressionists. They were entirely preoccupied with their own ego and projected their own personal emotions on to a cosmic plane, while Brecht's poetry, even in its wildest effusions of riotous imagery, remains strangely impersonal. Like the ballads of the street singers, whose strident tones he tried to reproduce, most of his poems are reports on the accidents and crimes of other people, or dramatic monologues whose first person singular or plural is clearly that of historical or imagined characters. The only really personal poems in Brecht's first published volume of poetry, *Hauspostille* (*Domestic Breviary*), are relegated to an appendix, headed 'Of poor B.B.' (an echo of 'pauvre François Villon'), and even here the lyrical self-portrait of the author is put forward in the exhibitionist tone of a music-hall performer presenting a character sketch, masking the private emotion by the posturing of a public performance.

The publication of *Hauspostille* marks the transition to an even more impersonal approach than that represented by many of the early poems

[1] 'Verschollener Ruhm der Riesenstadt New York', *Hundert Gedichte*, East Berlin, 1951, p. 130.

collected in that book. By the time Brecht published these poems (1926) his attitude had become austere and didactic. He had made himself one of the main exponents of 'Gebrauchslyrik', the view that poetry should not be an outlet of private emotions, but that it should be judged solely by its social usefulness. Hence the arrangement of *Hauspostille* on the model of a religious breviary as a kind of blasphemous prayer-book, in which each poem is designed for use in a certain situation. The collection is prefaced by a detailed 'Direction for Use of the Lessons contained in this Book', which starts with the injunction:

This domestic breviary is designed for the use of readers. It must not be gobbled up in a senseless manner.[1]

Detailed indications follow as to the situations in which the poems should be used:

Chapter 2 ('Ballad on Many Ships') is to be read in hours of danger. . . . Chapter 6 ('Ballad of the Pirates') is mainly designed for the light nights of June; but the second part of this ballad, as far as it deals with the sinking of the ship, can still be sung in October, etc.[2]

This is parody, but behind the jest there was a serious and growing conviction. As the frenzy of the Expressionist era died down and the fooleries of Dadaism lost their novelty, many of the younger poets and artists in Germany tried to get back from the fruitless preoccupation with their own selves to the real problems of the age. The plush curtains and ornamental bric-à-brac of the previous now discredited generation had been torn down and cast aside. The new beauty of the machine, its economy of outline resulting from perfect adaptation to the function for which it had been created now became the ideal before the artist. This was the creed of a movement labelled 'Neue Sachlichkeit'. If social usefulness, however, was to be the new criterion of beauty, literature and the stage would also have to be didactic and to serve the community by teaching it how to live.

And so Brecht's language cast off all ornament and became functional and austere. The 'Lehrstuecke' and 'school operas' are meant to be 'teaching aids' rather than art, and their language is severely

---

[1] *Hauspostille*, Berlin, 1927, p. ix.   [2] ibid., p. xi.

factual. In *The Flight of the Lindberghs*, for example, the chorus which embodies the collective personality of the hero introduces itself:

> My name is Charles Lindbergh
> I am twenty-five years old
> My grandfather was Swedish
> I am American.
> I have picked my aircraft myself
> Its name is 'Spirit of St. Louis'
> The Ryan Aircraft works in San Diego
> Have built it in sixty days. . . .[1]

The poetry of facts and figures is extracted from the most unpromising material:

> I carry with me:
> 2 electric torches
> 1 coil of rope
> 1 roll of string
> 1 hunting knife
> 4 red flares, sealed in rubber tubes
> 1 waterproof box of matches, etc., etc.[1]

It is a measure of Brecht's stature as a poet that he did succeed in achieving the effect of functional elegance he aimed at and that some of the later 'Lehrstuecke' have a monolithic, stark beauty of their own. The sudden rejection of the anarchic exuberance of his early style reflects Brecht's yearning for discipline and order which led him to Marxism, and it is significant that one of the models for his new didactic style was provided by a civilization which followed a pattern of equally strict military discipline: the Japan of the samurai. The school operas *Der Jasager* and *Der Neinsager* are based on a Japanese Nō play, *Taniko*, in Arthur Waley's translation, and Brecht's most important didactic play *Die Massnahme* also derives from this Japanese model.

Arthur Waley's translations of *Chinese* poetry made a deep impression on Brecht in his next, more mellowed and relaxed stage of development. The Confucian urbanity and courtesy, the quietly ironical tone and free rhythm of these translations became a decisive influence in his progress towards mature simplicity. The gentle politeness of the Chinese, the undogmatic authority of their classical

[1] *Der Flug der Lindberghs*, *Versuche 1*, p. 3.

teachers represented for him the ultimate Socialist ideal of friendliness as the basis of human relations. Brecht made German versions of a number of Waley's Chinese poems, and some of his most successful later verse is clearly modelled on them. In one of these poems, which relates a dream vision of a visit to the once exiled poets in the land of the dead, Brecht sees himself in the company of the shades of Po Chü-i and Tu-fu, together with those of Villon, Dante, Heine, Voltaire, Shakespeare (exiled to Stratford by James I!), Euripides, and Ovid.

Brecht, who knew his own facility in writing verse, deliberately attempted to get away from smooth, easy rhythms. When he was working on the adaptation of Marlowe's *Edward II* with Lion Feuchtwanger, Brecht would bring his blank verse to have it roughened up by his collaborator. 'I needed a heightened language, but I was repelled by the oily smoothness of the usual iambic pentameter,'[1] he writes in his essay *On Unrhymed Verse with Irregular Rhythms* in which he describes his efforts to find a style that could dispense with rhymes and regular rhythms and yet remain poetry, a poetry expressing the disharmonies of society.

As a consequence, apart from ballads and rhymed (political) songs for the masses, I wrote more and more poems without rhyme in irregular rhythms. It must be remembered that my main work was done for the stage; I always thought of the spoken word. And I had worked out a special technique for the speaking of prose or verse. I called it *gestisch*. . . .[1]

i.e. a language in which the words already contain the gesture that must accompany them. Characteristically Brecht illustrates what he means by quoting the Bible. To say 'pluck out the eye that offends thee' is far less effective than 'If thy eye offend thee, pluck it out'. Here the language itself implies and compels the corresponding action. Brecht argues that it is this element of implied gesture which can make unrhymed, irregular verse still keep the quality of poetry. He describes how he discovered the power of such irregular rhythms in the slogans shouted in unison by demonstrating masses of unemployed workers and in the headlines called out by newsvendors at the street corners of Berlin.

[1] 'Ueber reimlose Lyrik mit unregelmaessigen Rhythmen', *Versuche 12*, p. 143.

Apart from political marching songs, for which he used a rhymed stereotype of German 'folk song' and some of the songs in his plays, most of Brecht's later poetry is in this unrhymed, irregular verse, the rhythmic subtleties of which he compared to those of the syncopations of jazz or tap-dancing. This highly personal style is equally effective in the robust anti-Nazi *German Satires* he wrote for broadcasting from the 'German Freedom Station' before the war and the elegiac poetry of exile, as well as in the very short, epigrammatic poems resembling Japanese 'Haiku' he composed with masterly economy of words in the last years of his life.

But it is in the great plays he wrote between 1937 and 1947 that the overflowing richness of his early language and the didactic severity of the phase that followed are blended in a masterly idiom unequalled by any other German dramatist of this century. The Biblical allusions, the Bavarian local accent, the exotic names, the archaisms, and the garish rhythms of the street ballad are still there but controlled and put into their place by the conciseness and economy acquired in the austere atmosphere of the didactic plays, and mellowed and relaxed by the influence of the Chinese example. Each play has its own individual tone: *Mother Courage* the earthy flavour of seventeenth-century German and the picaresque novels of Grimmelshausen; *Puntila* a racy folk language; *Galileo* the richness of baroque scientific and religious disputation; *The Good Soul of Setzuan* a Confucian urbanity; *The Caucasian Chalk Circle* a different blend of oriental colours; and *Schweik in the Second World War* a brilliant pastiche of the language of Hašek's novel.

The various and openly acknowledged influences which have shaped Brecht's work throughout his life have inevitably led to his being accused of plagiarism and lack of originality. In fact, his originality consisted in his uncanny ability to absorb and assimilate the most diverse and seemingly incompatible elements. Under the influence of the Romantics an even greater value is attached in Germany than elsewhere to the quality of uniqueness, the originality which is said to be the essence of genius. Brecht thought little of this cult of originality. In one of his Keuner stories he makes his *alter ego* quote the example of the Chinese philosopher Chuang Tzu, who wrote a book of a hundred thousand words, nine-tenths of which consisted of extracts from other books.

Such books can no longer be written in our country, because we have not enough intelligence. That is why we manufacture ideas only in our own workshops. Anyone who is unable to put enough of them together feels that he is lazy. That is why there are no ideas worth taking up, and no phrases worth quoting. . . . They build their huts without help and with nothing but the miserable amount of material a single person can carry. They know no larger buildings than those one man can build by himself![1]

Brecht loved to adapt and to modify the work of others. He needed the challenge of another mind to get the best from his own talent. He based many of his plays on existing originals – Marlowe's *Edward II*, Gay's *Beggar's Opera*, Hašek's *Schweik*, old Japanese or Chinese legends. Again and again he drew on motives from Shakespeare. The satire against racialism, *The Roundheads and the Peakheads*, contains elements from the plot of *Measure for Measure*; in *Arturo Ui*, in which the rise of Hitler is parodied by that of a Chicago gangster, the character of the villainous hero is modelled on Richard III so that the murder of Roehm echoes the downfall of Buckingham and the Hitler-character woos the widow of one of his victims. But while the Shakespearian models are used with reverence and admiration, the German classics are always ruthlessly parodied. Brecht even went so far as to parody the Bible: Macheath, for example, is betrayed by a kiss on a Thursday evening.

Besides reverent adaptation or cruel parody, Brecht had a third way of assimilating the work of others: the counter-play, written as a reply to, or refutation of, an existing work. His first play *Baal* was written to show how Johst's *Der Einsame* could be bettered. *The Days of the Commune* was a reply to Nordahl Grieg, and at the time of his death Brecht planned a counter-play to Beckett's *Waiting for Godot*.

It would be tedious to pursue the countless literary parallels, concealed quotations, and examples of pastiche and parody in Brecht's work. This will provide employment for generations of students to come. Brecht shares his predilection for literary allusion with writers like T. S. Eliot, Ezra Pound, or James Joyce. It marks him out as an intellectual, in spite of his sincere attempts and avowed intention of writing for the common people. The use of parody, moreover, particularly the iconoclastic mockery of the German classics, the Bible, and

[1] 'Herr Keuner und die Originalitaet', *Versuche* 5, p. 456.

religious hymns and anthems, reveals Brecht's ambivalent attitude towards these models. Parody gave Brecht an opportunity of fulfilling an unconscious desire to emulate and follow these examples. Under the cover of ridicule he could indulge the 'high-minded', even religious impulses, which his rational, cynical self would not allow him to acknowledge. It is significant that in his later phase, when he had found a positive framework of belief and had attained recognition as a classic of his own time, this tendency to parody great literary examples disappeared, while his love for open adaptation and imitation continued unabated.

Brecht's readiness to sink his own personality in the work of his predecessors and contemporaries, to use the whole storehouse of past literature as so much material for his own handiwork, was in accordance with his views about the nature of poetry itself and the poet's function in society. Here too he rejected the mystical, romantic view of the poet as the vessel of divinely inspired intuitions, called upon to fulfil and to express his unique personality. To him the poet was a craftsman serving the community and relying on his reason and acquired skill, a man among men, not a being set apart by virtue of some special quality or power. That is why Brecht was ready to accept the advice of numerous collaborators, whom he conscientiously named when his works were published. As he did not consider the work of art as divinely inspired he never hesitated to alter, and often debase, his own work, according to the circumstances of the moment.

After the banning of the operatic version of *The Trial of Lucullus* Brecht told a Swiss journalist that he regarded the indignation of his Western admirers about the interference of the authorities with an artist's work as sheer hypocrisy. After all, the authorities had paid for his opera, so they could demand alterations from the craftsman they employed. 'When princes commissioned works of art, they too interfered a great deal with the artists.'[1]

Within his own sphere of craftsmanship, however, Brecht never suffered from undue humility. Lion Feuchtwanger tells how he used to counter criticisms of his often very unorthodox use of grammar by saying: 'Ego, poeta Germanus, supra Grammaticos sto.'[2] And when

[1] Gody Suter, 'Brecht', *Tagesanzeiger*, Zurich, 1.9.1956.
[2] Lion Feuchtwanger, 'Bertolt Brecht', *Sinn und Form*, Second Special Brecht Issue, 1957, p. 106.

during his stay in the United States someone drew his attention to a literal translation of an English idiom, pointing out that such a phrase did not exist in German, Brecht replied: 'All right. So it exists from now on!'[1]

But this arrogance remained confined to the sphere in which he regarded himself as a craftsman, an expert. It never led him to regard the poet as a higher being. For, as he said in a poem dedicated to the Danish writer Andersen-Nexoe, the time will come when the works of the most exquisite poets will be looked at with different eyes:

> *. . . not for their elevated thoughts*
> *Will their books be searched through; but*
> *Some casual sentence, which allows conclusions*
> *As to some feature of those who were weavers of coats*
> *Will be read with interest. . . .*[2]

[1] H. Winge, 'Brecht en privé', *Europe*, January/February, 1957, p. 46.
[2] 'Die Literatur wird durchforscht werden', *Hundert Gedichte*, East Berlin, 1951, p. 173.

Chapter VI

THE BRECHTIAN THEATRE–
ITS THEORY AND PRACTICE

Terms like 'epic theatre', 'non-aristotelian drama', 'alienation effect' ('*Verfremdungseffekt*'), and other catchphrases from Brecht's theoretical writings have become more widely known than any of his creative work (with the exception perhaps of the song of 'Mac the Knife'); having been taken up by enthusiasts of theatre reform on both sides of the Atlantic, they have found their way into the currency of daily and weekly theatrical criticism and must have puzzled countless readers who had never heard of Brecht, let alone seen any of his plays.

Such Teutonic neologisms seem to exercise a powerful spell even on Anglo-Saxon minds, not excluding those who appreciate their usefulness in the sphere of lifemanship; from Kant to Marx down to our own times the difficulty and obscurity of a specialized and impenetrable jargon has contributed much to the success and influence of German ideologies. Brecht, unwittingly, achieved a similar result in his own, more modest theorizing: for even he, the clearest and most concrete of writers in his poetry and plays, often succumbed to the ponderous tradition of German aesthetic philosophy, when he tried to expound the underlying principles of his work.

Yet basically these principles are neither very complicated nor very new, however stimulating and revivifying their influence may yet prove in the present-day theatre. Towards the end of his life Brecht made repeated efforts to dissipate the fog of the Brechtian theories he himself had created in his youth.

The accounts (of my theatre) and many of the assessments based on them [he wrote] are applicable not to the theatre that I myself produce, but to the theatre that my critics imagine from reading my treatises. . . . My theories are altogether far more naïve than one might think – more naïve than my way of expressing them might allow one to suspect.[1]

[1] Brecht, 'Gespraech auf der Probe' (1953), *Schriften zum Theater*, pp. 285–6.

Brecht has always acknowledged his debt to a wide range of old theatrical conventions and traditions: the Elizabethan, the Chinese, Japanese, and Indian theatre, the use of the chorus in Greek tragedy, the techniques of clowns and fair-ground entertainers, the Austrian and Bavarian folk-play, and many others. Yet he somehow created the impression that he was advocating something radically new and entirely revolutionary – perhaps by the dogmatic and didactic tone of his earlier pronouncements, perhaps by his often excessive insistence that *his* was the only stage theory to meet the needs of a new, revolutionary, scientific age.

Nor must the Brechtian theory of the drama be regarded as a single, homogeneous body of doctrine: throughout his life it changed, developed, and finally mellowed in accordance with the changes in his styles of writing and stage production. The primary factor was always his creative work: the theories he put forward were postscripts to plays or poems rather than *a priori* principles on which these had been based. The rationalist Brecht deeply distrusted inspirations and intuitions. So he constructed his theories as rationalizations of changes in his style, taste, or stage practice. That is why so much of the discussion of these theories as general principles has proved barren and unreal: it remains yet to be proved that they have any validity apart from Brecht's own works – and productions – which they were intended to explain and justify.

Brecht was a rebel. The Brechtian theatre can only be understood in the light of what he rebelled against: the theatre as he found it in Germany around 1920 and as it still remains in many parts of the world to this day – a theatre in which bombastic productions of the classics alternate with empty photographic replicas of everyday life, whether in melodrama or drawing-room comedy, a theatre which oscillates between emotional uplift and after-dinner entertainment.

We are so used to the concept of the stage as a faithful representation of the world that we tend to forget how recent a growth the naturalistic theatre really is: before the second half of the nineteenth century, before the introduction of modern lighting techniques and stage machinery, historically accurate costumes, and three-dimensional properties, the theatre could not even pretend to create a complete illusion of actual life, observed through a missing fourth wall. On such a stage the styles of acting also had to be kept openly theatrical to match the surrounding scenery and lighting. Declamation, asides, and monologues formed part of a convention never intended to convey the illusion of real happenings on which the audience was merely eavesdropping.

So great was the effect of the new stage techniques that emerged from the efforts of producers like the Duke of Saxe-Meiningen, Stanislavsky, Antoine, Brahm, Granville Barker, and Reinhardt, that the naturalistic theatre in the widest sense had become accepted as the only possible stage convention by the time Brecht was born. The previous convention only survived in the form of parody (as it does to this day in the skits on Shakespeare and Victorian melodrama one still sees in English music-halls).

The reaction against this theatrical convention, which had to come, is entirely analogous to the reaction against representational painting which came at the same time: for centuries painters had tried to get nearer and nearer to reality; the Impressionists had finally captured the very flicker of daylight, just as the naturalistic stage could simulate the changing light from the blazing sun of noon to the bluish tints of the moon at night. Such perfection having been attained, the next step *had* to be a new beginning, the initiation of an entirely different line of development: in painting away from nature into the realms of the primitive and the abstract; in the theatre away from the illusion of eavesdropping on real events.

Brecht belonged to the generation which had to make this new beginning; and his solution is one of many that were put forward by his contemporaries: German Expressionism, the poetic drama of T. S. Eliot, the satires of Mayakovsky, the Russian theatre of Meyerhold and Tairov, the monster pantomines of Max Reinhardt, Piscator's political theatre with its use of film and posters are all part of the same striving to overcome the limitations of the 'theatre of illusion'.

When Brecht began to formulate his ideas in the late nineteen-twenties he had already experimented in a variety of techniques: he had written plays which showed the influence of the Expressionist trend in their loose construction, their treatment of the characters as types rather than individuals and their highly concentrated, poetic language; and he had worked in close collaboration with Erwin Piscator, the exponent of the 'political theatre' whose stage made use of every new technique in order to turn the theatre into a forum for the discussion of current affairs.

Brecht's theories show the influence of all these experiments. He too was convinced that the theatre must become a tool of social engineering, a laboratory of social change.

> Today [he wrote in 1931] when human character must be understood as the 'totality of all social conditions' the epic form is the only one that can comprehend all the processes, which could serve the drama as materials for a fully representative picture of the world.[1]

Why did Brecht consider the existing stage convention incapable of providing such a picture of the world? His objections against the theatre of illusion concern both the means employed and the uses to which these means are put.

In formulating his theory of 'epic' theatre Brecht was reacting against the German classics' theory of drama: in 1797 Goethe and Schiller, the two giants of the German tradition, had jointly presented their point of view in an essay, 'On Epic and Dramatic Poetry'. It is against this specific theory that Brecht offered his counter-theory.

Goethe and Schiller had described the distinction between the epic and dramatic genres of poetry as follows: 'Their great essential difference lies in the fact that the epic poet presents the event as totally past, while the dramatic poet presents it as totally present.' Goethe and Schiller had urged their readers 'always to keep before (their) mental eyes a rhapsodic singer and an actor, both being poets: the one surrounded by a circle of quiet listeners, the other by impatiently watching and listening spectators'. Thus the epic poet, the rhapsodic singer, relates what has happened in calm contemplation '. . . he will freely range forward and backward in time. . . . The actor, on the other hand, is in exactly the opposite position: he represents himself as a definite individual; he wants the spectators to participate . . . in his action, to feel the sufferings of his soul and of his body with him, share his embarrassments and forget their own personalities for the sake of his. . . . The spectator must not be allowed to rise to thoughtful contemplation; he must passionately follow the action; his imagination is completely silenced. . . .'

It was this conception that Brecht abhorred, and that he called, knowing that Goethe and Schiller had based their theory on Aristotle's

---

[1] Brecht, 'Anmerkungen zur Dreigroschenoper' (1931), *Schriften zum Theater*, p. 35.

Poetics, the Aristotelian concept of drama, the drama of catharsis by terror and pity, the drama of spectator-identification with the actors, the drama of illusion, which tries to create magical effects by conjuring up events which are represented as 'totally present', while palpably they are not. Such a theatre therefore was a fraud. Brecht, the rationalist, demanded a theatre of calm contemplation and detachment, a theatre of critical thoughtfulness; in other words, a theatre to correspond to the mood described by Goethe and Schiller as an attribute of the rhapsodic singer of epic poetry: an *epic* theatre.

Brecht regarded a theatre of illusion and identification as downright obscene:

> looking around one discovers more or less motionless bodies in a curious state – they seem to be contracting their muscles in a strong physical effort, or else to have relaxed them after violent strain . . . they have their eyes open, but they don't look, they stare . . . they stare at the stage as if *spellbound*, which is an expression from the Middle Ages, an age of witches and obscurantists. . . .[1]

Identification with the characters on the stage appeared equally indecent to Brecht:

> How long are our souls going to have to leave our 'gross' bodies under cover of darkness to penetrate into those dream figures up there on the rostrum, in order to share their transports that would otherwise be denied to us ?[2]

Such an audience, Brecht argues, may indeed leave the theatre purged by its vicarious emotions, but it will have remained uninstructed and unimproved. For them the theatre will be a means of mental refreshment in the same sense as a good meal, which is consumed with enjoyment, provides physical refreshment, but leaves no lasting trace behind. Brecht regarded the art of the theatre as more than a mere article of consumption and despised what he called the 'culinary theatre', the theatre which merely provides mental foodstuffs, to be gobbled up and then forgotten. The audience, in his view, should not be made to feel emotions, it should be made to *think*. But identification with the characters of the play makes thinking almost

[1] Brecht, 'Kleines Organon fuer das Theater' (1948), para. 26, *Versuche 12*, p. 119.
[2] op. cit., para. 34, ibid., p. 122.

impossible: the audience whose souls have crept into that of the hero will see the action entirely from *his* point of view, and as they are breathlessly following a course of events which, in suspension of disbelief, they accept as really happening before their very eyes, they have neither the time nor the detachment to sit back and reflect in a truly critical spirit on the social and moral implications of the play. And all this because the author, the producer, and the actors have conspired to create so powerful an illusion of reality!

Brecht's answer is clear: the theatre must not only not attempt to create such an illusion, it must do its best to destroy in the bud any illusion of reality as it will continuously, and mischievously, tend to arise.

It must therefore at all times be made apparent to the spectators that they are not witnessing real events happening before their very eyes at *this very moment*, but that they are sitting in a theatre, listening to an account (however vividly presented) of things which have happened in *the past* at a certain time in a certain place. They are to sit back, relax, and reflect on the lessons to be learnt from those events of long ago, like the audience of the bards who sang of the deeds of heroes in the houses of Greek kings or Saxon earls, while the guests ate and drank. Hence the term *epic* theatre. While the theatre of illusion is trying to re-create a spurious present, by pretending that the events of the play are actually taking place at the time of each performance, the 'epic' theatre is strictly *historical*; it constantly reminds the audience that it is merely getting a *report* of past events.

Moreover, the audience must be *discouraged* from losing its critical detachment by *identification* with one or more of the characters: the opposite of identification is the maintenance of a separate existence by being kept apart, alien, strange – therefore the producer must strive to produce by all the means at his disposal effects which will keep the audience separate, estranged, alienated from the action. That is the meaning of the famous 'Verfremdungseffekt', a term which has never been successfully rendered in English, because terms like alienation or estrangement have entirely different, and unfortunate, emotional overtones. In French *distantiation* is a happier term.

The abolition of the old theatre of illusion which Brecht once described as having sunk to the level of a 'branch of the bourgeois drug traffic' not only frees the critical faculty of the audience, it also absolves the playwright from being cramped by the narrow and rigid conventions which the pretence of presenting real happenings imposes on the dramatist: in the realistic convention one can show only the action of the characters themselves, it is quite impossible to supply the sociological background to their actions or to comment on them from a higher viewpoint than their own. In the 'epic' theatre the author is able to dispense with the tedious ritual of the naturalist exposition through which the characters laboriously have to establish their names and relationships in the framework of seemingly casual, 'natural' conversation; he can now make them introduce themselves directly to the audience, or flash their names on to a screen. He can go further: he can tell the audience in advance how the play will end, thus freeing their minds from the distraction of suspense; he can supply background material of all kinds by letting a narrator describe the thoughts and motives of the characters or, as in Brecht's adaptation of Gorky's *The Mother*, by flashing the prices of basic foodstuffs on to the backdrop during a scene in which the cost of living is mentioned in the dialogue. Brecht claimed that the 'epic' theatre alone could present the complexity of the human condition in an age in which the life of individuals could no longer be understood in isolation from the powerful trend of social, economical, or historical forces affecting the lives of millions.

By abandoning the pretence that the audience is eavesdropping on actual events, by openly admitting that the theatre is a theatre and not the world itself, the Brechtian stage approximates to the lecture hall to which audiences come in the expectation that they will be informed; but also to the circus arena, where an audience, without identification or illusion, watches performers exhibit their special skills. What distinguishes the theatre from the lecture room or the circus, however, is the fact that it 'produces living illustrations of historical or imaginary happenings among human beings'.[1]

To what purpose are these happenings re-created? It is in this point that Brecht's thought changed most radically between his earlier and later periods. In the beginning Brecht proclaimed his conviction that the theatre had to be strictly didactic: he saw it as his task 'to develop the article of consumption into a teaching aid and to refashion certain institutions from places of entertainment into organs of information'.[2]

---

[1] Brecht, 'Kleines Organon fuer das Theater' (1948), para. 1, ibid., p. 110.
[2] Brecht, 'Anmerkungen zur Oper Aufstieg und Fall der Stadt Mahagonny' (1930), *Schriften zum Theater*, p. 28.

In this period of the 'didactic plays' and 'school operas' the a of Brecht's conception was such that he wrote plays which serve for the instruction of the *participants alone*. 'They n audience.'[1]

By 1948 he had mellowed to the extent of openly repudiating much of this severity of approach:

Let us therefore recant . . . our intention of emigrating from the realm of the pleasing and let us . . . proclaim our intention of settling in this realm. Let us treat the theatre as a place of entertainment. . . . But let us inquire what kind of entertainment we regard as acceptable.'[2]

Brecht answered this question by rejecting the old idea of entertainment through emotional catharsis. The pleasure which his theatre was now permitted to give was the pleasure we feel when we discover new truths, the exhilaration we experience when we enlarge our understanding. In this scientific age Brecht wanted his audience to experience some of the exaltation felt by the scientist who has uncovered one of the mysteries of the universe. For Brecht, whose own curiosity and thirst for knowledge were boundless, regarded the 'instinct of inquiry as a social phenomenon not less pleasurable, nor less imperious, than the instinct of procreation'.[3]

To keep the audience relaxed and yet receptive, to stimulate their critical faculties and to make them think, the 'epic' theatre employs a variety of means. In Brecht's view, the abolition of the dramatic illusion alone removes a good many of the less desirable implications of the 'Aristotelian' theatre: the very fact that the action was each time assumed to be happening anew before the eyes of the audience implied that the passions and attitudes of the characters were unchangeable expressions of a fixed 'human nature'; the dynamic, tautly logical construction of such plays indicated the relentless course of fate and made it appear unfathomable and incapable of being influenced by human initiative. In the 'epic' theatre therefore there is no attempt to create fixed, highly individualized characters. Character emerges from

---

[1] 'Anmerkung zu den Lehrstuecken'; Brecht, *Stuecke V*, p. 276.

[2] Brecht, 'Kleines Organon fuer das Theater (1948) Vorrede', *Versuche 12*, p. 109.

[3] Brecht, 'Anmerkungen zu *Leben des Galilei*', *Stuecke VIII*, p. 205.

the social function of the individual and changes with that function. As Brecht once put it, character

> should not be regarded like a stain of grease on a pair of trousers, which, however much you try to rub and wipe it away, will always come up again. In actual fact the question is always how a given person is going to act in a specified set of circumstances and conditions'.[1]

The construction of the plays of the 'epic' theatre, which rejects the logically built, well-made play, is free from the need of creating suspense, loosely knit, and episodic; instead of mounting to a dynamic climax, the story unfolds in a number of separate situations, each rounded and complete in itself. The total effect of the play will be built up through the juxtaposition and 'montage' of contrasting episodes. While the 'Aristotelian' drama can only be understood as a whole, the 'epic' drama can be cut into slices which will continue to make sense and give pleasure, like the favourite chapters of a novel that can be read by themselves, or the extracts from plays of great length that are performed as self-contained units in the Chinese classical theatre.

Just as isolated episodes of the play retain their individual significance, even if taken out of the context of the play as a whole, the non-literary elements of the production – décor, music, and choreography – also retain their independence; instead of serving as mere auxiliaries of the text, reinforcing it by stressing some of its features and painting in atmosphere, mood, or descriptive details, they are raised to the level of autonomous elements; instead of pulling in the same direction as the words, they enter into a dialectical, contrapuntal relationship with them. The musical numbers are no longer smuggled in at the point when the emotional charge of a scene rises to a climax and speech merges into song – but are introduced as entirely distinct ingredients of the play, which interrupt its flow, break the illusion, and thereby render the action 'strange'. And within the musical numbers themselves the music does not merely express the mood of the words: it often stands in contradiction to them, comments on them, or reveals the falsity of the sentiments they express.

The stage designer, who is no longer bound by the necessity of

[1] H. J. Bunge, 'Brecht probiert', *Sinn und Form*, Second Special Brecht Issue, 1957, p. 324.

trying to create the illusion of a real locality in which the action takes place, is now free to supply his own, independent contribution to the play by providing background material of all kinds (in *Galileo* Caspar Neher backed the action by projections of maps, documents, and works of art of the Renaissance) or even by duplicating the action by showing it from a different angle (in the first production of *Mahagonny* the scene in which greedy Jakob eats himself to death was played in front of a backdrop showing a large portrait of Jakob eating, so that the audience saw the episode split into two).

Thus the 'epic' theatre does not use décor and music to produce a Wagnerian 'Gesamtkunstwerk' with its, in Brecht's view, diabolically strong narcotic and hypnotic effect and concerted onslaught on the senses, but to destroy the illusion of reality. As Brecht put it, 'sie verfremden sich gegenseitig' ('they mutually make each other appear strange').

The destruction of stage illusion, however, is not an end in itself. The 'Verfremdungseffekt' has its positive side. By inhibiting the process of identification between the spectator and the characters, by creating a distance between them and enabling the audience to look at the action in a detached and critical spirit, familiar things, attitudes, and situations appear in a new and strange light, and create, through astonishment and wonder, a new understanding of the human situation. The great discoveries of mankind, Brecht points out, were made by men who looked at familiar things as if they had never seen them before – Newton at the falling apple, Galileo at the swinging chandelier – and in the same way the theatre public should be taught to look at the relationships between men with the critical 'estranged' eye of the discoverer. 'The natural must be made to look surprising.'[1]

This is how Brecht has summed up the distinction between the old convention and his own conception of the theatre:

The spectator of the *dramatic* theatre says: 'Yes, I have felt the same. – I am just like this. – This is only natural. – It will always be like this. – This human being's suffering moves me, because there is no way out for him. – This is great art: it bears the mark of the inevitable. – I am weeping with those who weep on the stage, laughing with those who laugh.'

The spectator of the *epic* theatre says: 'I should never have thought

---

[1] Brecht, 'Vergnuegungstheater oder Lehrtheater' (1936), *Schriften zum Theater*, p. 63.

so. – That is not the way to do it. – This is most surprising, hardly credible. – This will have to stop. – This human being's suffering moves me, because there would have been a way out for him. This is great art: nothing here seems inevitable – I am laughing about those who weep on the stage, weeping about those who laugh.'[1]

Brecht has written a great deal about the methods of production and the technique of acting he required to translate these theories into practice. And he has left detailed records of some of his most successful productions in the form of 'model books' – scene-by-scene descriptions of the performances illustrated by photographs of every movement on the stage.

The basis of the Brechtian technique of acting is the conception that the actor should not regard himself as impersonating the character so much as *narrating* the actions of another person at a definite time in the past. To illustrate these actions and to make them fully understood by the audience he goes through the motions the character made, imitates the tone of his voice, repeats his facial expression, but only to the extent of *quoting* them. The Brechtian style of acting is acting in quotation marks.

Brecht liked to illustrate his basic concept of acting by the example of an everyday occurrence one might observe in any large town: a street accident has happened. A crowd has collected on the scene, and an eyewitness is telling the bystanders what has taken place: he wants to indicate that the old man who has been run over walked very slowly, and so he will imitate his gait to show exactly what he means. He is in fact *quoting* the old man's walk. And he is only quoting *those elements of the old man's movements which are relevant* to the situation that he wants to describe. The eyewitness concerned is far from wanting to *impersonate* the victim: 'he never forgets, nor does he allow anyone to forget, that he is not the one whose action is being demonstrated, but the one who demonstrates it'.[2] The character who is being shown and the actor who demonstrates him remain clearly differentiated. And the actor retains his freedom to *comment* on the actions of the person whose behaviour he is displaying.

A theatre which aims at preventing the identification of the audience

[1] Brecht, 'Vergnuegungstheater oder Lehrtheater' (1936), *Schriften zum Theater*, pp. 63–4.
[2] Brecht, 'Die Strassenszene' (1940), *Schriften zum Theater*, p. 99.

with the characters cannot allow the identification of the actor with the character either. Brecht was fully aware of the contagious nature of anything that takes place on the stage, which is the essence of the mystery and magic of the theatre. He did not deny the teaching of Stanislavsky in this respect: if the actor believes that he is Lear, the audience will also believe it and will share his emotions. But Brecht did not want the audience to be taken in. For the 'epic' actor, he says, the assertion: 'he did not merely act Lear, he *was* Lear', would be a devastating criticism.[1]

As the 'epic' actor does not intend to put his audience into a trance, he must also keep *himself* free from any state of trance.

> His muscles must remain relaxed, for even a turn of the head with tensed muscles 'magically' carries away with it the eyes, and even the heads of the spectators – and this would reduce their ability to reflect or feel emotion about this gesture. . . . Even if playing one possessed, the actor must not appear possessed himself: how else could the spectators find out what it is that possesses the possessed ?[2]

These views express Brecht's revulsion against the cramped and convulsive style of acting which is still widely prevalent in the German theatre, where actors still tend to be rated according to the violence, the frenetic intensity of the emotions they portray. The frantic 'Ausbruch' (outburst) represents the highest peak of acting to the adherents of this style. The Brechtian actor is always loose-limbed and relaxed, always clearly in control of himself and his emotions. In Brecht's view the actor's task is far wider, and far more complex, than the mere identification with the character, the merging of actor and character, postulated by Stanislavsky. At one stage in his preparatory work the Brechtian actor also has to feel himself into the character; but the results of this process of empathy are only one among a number of elements which fuse in the final performance on the stage. They must be supplemented by acute and fully rational observations; by implied comment on the character's actions so that the audience can see the actor's approval or disapproval, his pity, or contempt for the character. Moreover, the actor must also show that he is never taken by surprise by the character's experiences, that, in fact, he knows exactly where the character's conduct will eventually lead him.

[1] 'Kleines Organon', para. 48, *Versuche 12*, p. 127.
[2] ibid., para. 47, *Versuche 12*, p. 126.

And he must also be able to suggest to the audience that the character's behaviour is by no means the only possible course of action, that there are always alternatives. The actor must be able to suggest at suitable moments

> apart from what he does, something else . . . he does *not* do: i.e. he acts in such a manner that one can see the alternative course of action, so that the acting allows the audience to detect the other possibilities, so that any given action can be seen as only one among a number of variants.[1]

In other words, the actor's attitude must always be so conscious, so fully rational, and demonstrative, that he is in fact telling the public: 'I have decided to go left rather than right. I could have gone to the right, but I am going to the left and *not* to the right.' This implies a deliberateness of action, a consciousness of the presence of the audience, which is diametrically opposed to Stanislavsky's ideal of an actor who is completely alone, completely wrapped up in himself and unaware of being observed. In fact, Brecht compares the style of acting he advocates to the manner in which the producer would demonstrate an intonation to his cast. He too, by the deliberateness of his demonstration, says in effect: 'I want it done this way and not *that* way.' Nor can there be any question of the actor's thought or action arising spontaneously from the situation: there must be nothing improvised in the delivery of the lines. As Brecht puts it: 'the actor's performance must present an attitude which denotes the delivery of a finished product'.[2]

Like all attempts to describe a style of acting in theory, these maxims appear more complicated than they are in fact: the villain as he was acted in Victorian melodrama is the perfect example of a style of acting without identification between the actor and the character he portrays; there too the audience is never left in doubt as to what the actor thinks of the character, nor that he knows that he will come to a bad end, nor that he enjoys the virtuosity with which he portrays wickedness, nor that he behaves in a manner to which there would be a clear and obvious alternative. And this applies to some extent to all the villains in drama. As Brecht pointed out: 'Why is the principal

[1] Brecht, 'Neue Technik der Schauspielkunst' (1940), *Schriften zum Theater*, pp. 108–9.
[2] 'Kleines Organon', para. 76, *Versuche 12*, p. 140.

negative character so much more interesting than the positive hero? Because he is performed in a spirit of criticism.'[1]

In the theatre of illusion and identification the actor works through introspection. He delves into the character he is to portray and tries to merge with him. Only after this work is accomplished are the characters brought into relation with each other. The nature of the characters determines their relationships. The basic unit of such a theatre is the single character.

Brecht's theatre, on the other hand, is extrovert. The inner life of the characters is irrelevant to him except in so far as it is expressed in their outward attitudes and actions. 'For the smallest social unit is not one human being, but two human beings.'[2] The eyewitness in the example of the street accident

> derives his characters wholly from their actions. He imitates what they have done and thus permits inferences as to their nature. A theatre which follows him will to a large extent break with the habit of the conventional theatre, which derives its action from the nature of the characters. . . .[3]

The study of human *nature* is thus replaced by that of human *relations*. Not the characters, but the story in which they are involved becomes the main concern of the epic, narrative, historical, theatre. 'Everything depends on the *story*; it is the centre-piece of the performance.'[4] For the *story* (Brecht uses the German word *Fabel*, with its didactic overtones) is the sequence of events which constitutes the social experiment of the play; it provides the dialectical field for the interplay of social forces, from which the lesson of the play will be seen to emerge.

Characters acting and reacting upon each other thus become the basic unit of the Brechtian theatre. The basic attitudes of human beings are expressed by what Brecht called *Gestus*, a term which does not merely mean 'gesture' but covers the whole range of the outward signs of social relationships, including 'deportment, intonation, facial expression'.[5] Each scene of a play has its *basic Gestus* (Grundgestus).

[1] Brecht, 'Einige Irrtuemer ueber die Spielweise des Berliner Ensembles', *Sinn und Form*, Second Special Brecht Issue, 1957, p. 258.
[2] 'Kleines Organon', para. 58, *Versuche 12*, p. 131.
[3] Brecht, 'Die Strassenszene' (1940), *Schriften zum Theater*, p. 96.
[4] 'Kleines Organon', para. 65, *Versuche 12*, p. 135.
[5] op. cit., para. 61, ibid., p. 132.

By his emphasis on 'Gestus' – the clear and stylized expression of the social behaviour of human beings towards each other – Brecht shifts the emphasis from the inner life of characters towards the way in which they *behave* towards each other: the way in which the down-trodden tutor in *Der Hofmeister* bows to his master, the way in which the kindly prostitute of Setzuan moves differently when she turns into her ruthless cousin, assumes a greater importance than the supposed inner life or emotions of these characters. Brecht wanted to arrive at a 'Gestus' so simple and expressive that it could be quoted with the same ease as a well-turned line of dialogue is quoted. And he placed great emphasis on writing dialogue which would contain the appropriate 'Gestus' and almost force the actor to assume the correct stance, movement, and tone of voice. He himself was a master of this 'gestische Sprache' (*gestic* language). His sentences, with their contrapuntal construction, subtle rhythms, and cunningly placed pauses, their Biblical parallelism and sudden changes of cadence compel the speaker to follow the author's intentions and to act as he utters them.

Brecht's 'songs' also have this *gestic* character. They are even more pronounced, even more clearly magnified, *exhibits of basic attitudes*, for the music makes the fusion of words and gesture even more compelling. Brecht used to point to the way street singers render the more vulgar kind of popular song with large and simple gestures. His own 'songs' were designed to achieve a similar effect on actor and audience alike by crystallizing an essential, fundamental attitude and exhibiting it with the utmost clarity: despair or resignation, defiance or submission.

The fundamental importance of the 'Gestus' determines the method by which actors and producer tackle the play. By analysing the action they determine the basic story line (*Fabel*), which is then broken down into smaller and smaller elements until each scene appears as the expression of one simple, basic action, which can be translated into a single sentence (e.g. 'Richard Gloucester woos the widow of his victim' or 'God wagers against the devil for the soul of Dr Faustus' or 'Woyzeck buys a cheap knife to kill his wife'). This sentence or title contains the basic 'Gestus' of the scene which the producer and the actors will now have to put on to the stage. The arrangement and grouping of the actors, their manner of speaking and moving must be made to convey all the implications of this 'basic Gestus' with the greatest possible expressiveness, elegance, and economy of means. It is entirely irrelevant what the scene concerned might have looked like in real life, the producer is only concerned with bringing out its social content and significance.

The new theatre uses the simplest kind of grouping which will express the meaning of the action in the clearest possible manner. Any 'accidental' grouping which might try to simulate 'real life' . . . is to be avoided. The stage does not reflect the 'natural disorder' of things. The opposite of 'natural disorder' which it aims at is 'natural order'. The point of view adopted to achieve this order is historical and sociological.[1]

Once the basic elements of the story have been isolated, they must be linked together again, but not in such a way that they imperceptibly merge into each other. The links between the separate sections must be clearly marked, so that the audience has time to use its judgment instead of drifting helplessly through the story. The component parts have to be carefully juxtaposed to set each other off, preferably by the use of written chapter headings which will not only indicate what will happen next (and thereby inhibit suspense) but also set the tone of the ensuing scene by the way in which they are phrased – 'In the style of a chronicle or a ballad or a newspaper or a description of manners and customs.'[2]

As Brecht sought to banish trance, illusion, magical effects, and orgies of emotion from the theatre, he tried to replace them by lucidity, rationality, and elegance. The numerous and varied devices by which the illusion of reality was to be dispelled must bear the hallmark of honest craftsmanship, the perfection which comes from the unpretentious use of undisguised materials.

Above all, the stage must be bathed in light:

> *Give us light on the stage, lighting engineer! How can we,*
> *Playwrights and actors, present our images of the world*
> *In semi-darkness? Nebulous twilight*
> *Lulls to sleep. But we need the spectators'*
> *Wakefulness, even watchfulness. Let them dream*
> *In blazing clarity!*[3]

[1] Brecht quoted in Wekwerth, 'Sechs Punkte zum erzaehlenden Arrangement Bertolt Brechts', *Theater der Zeit*, East Berlin, supplement to no. 11, 1956.

[2] 'Kleines Organon', para. 67, *Versuche 12*, p. 136.

[3] Brecht, 'Die Beleuchtung', from 'Der Messingkauf', *Schriften zum Theater*, pp. 260–1.

Brecht was against the use of lighting effects to create atmosphere and mood. The coming of night was indicated, in his theatre as in that of the Elizabethans, by properties such as lamps or the appearance of a moon disk, not by a dimming of the uniformly bright light in which his stage was bathed. To dispel any illusion of reality he insisted that the sources of light should remain visible to the public. 'Nobody would expect the spotlights over a boxing ring to be hidden,'[1] why should they therefore be concealed in the theatre?

Nor was the curtain to be used to allow illusions to be prepared in secret:

> . . . and make
> My curtain half high, don't seal off the stage!
> Leaning back in his chair, let the spectator
> Be aware of busy preparations, made for him
> Cunningly; he sees a tinfoil moon
> Float down, or a tiled roof
> Being carried in; do not show him too much,
> But show him something! And let him notice
> That you are not wizards,
> Friends, but workers. . . .[2]

The curtain often also serves to show the projected titles of the scenes. When it parts, it reveals sets which suggest the locale of the action rather than depicting it. Brecht's favourite designers – his childhood friend Caspar Neher, Teo Otto, and Karl von Appen – each in his individual way leave much to the imagination of the spectator. The backdrops are often intentionally two-dimensional and derived from known pictorial models (old prints in *Der Hofmeister*, or Persian miniatures in *Der Kaukasische Kreidekreis*, etc.). The use of décor to supply independent comment on the action has already been mentioned.

Just as the sources of light remain unconcealed, the source of any music must also remain visible. Often the musicians are placed on the stage itself.

The musical numbers and 'songs' are used to interrupt the action and to give the audience an opportunity to reflect. The coming of such an interruption is usually announced beforehand by some visible

[1] Brecht, 'Die Sichtbarkeit der Lichtquellen' (1940), *Schriften zum Theater*, p. 262.
[2] Brecht, 'Die Vorhaenge', *Schriften zum Theater*, p. 260.

change on the stage: the title of the song may flash on to a screen, special lights may be put on, or a symbolic emblem (e.g. flags and trumpets) may come down from the flies.

These mechanical devices may help the actors in creating the 'Verfremdungseffekt', but they nevertheless leave the brunt of the work of 'making things strange to the audience' to them. The temptation to identify himself with the character must always remain strong for the actor. Brecht used a variety of techniques to enable him to overcome this temptation.

During rehearsals the actors were invited to translate their text into the third person, so that they were made to relate the story of the actions and speeches of the characters they were later to act. Brecht has published a number of examples of this technique. In scene three of his adaptation of Lenz's play *Der Hofmeister* (*The Private Tutor*) there occurs the following passage:

> (Enter Count Wermuth. After a few silent compliments he sits down on the sofa.)
> COUNT: Has Your Excellency seen the new dancing master who has arrived from Dresden? He is a Marchese from Florence. His name is. . . . On all my travels I have only met two dancers I would put above him. . . .[1]

During rehearsals the actor who played the count was made to say:

> Then Count Wermuth entered. After a few silent compliments he sat down on the sofa and asked whether Madame had seen the new dancing master, who had arrived from Dresden. He was a Marchese from Florence. . . . The Count made a slight pause, as his memory failed him. He nimbly added, that on all his travels he had only met two dancers whom he would put above him . . . etc.[2]

Another device for inhibiting the identification of actor and character is the inclusion of all stage directions in the text spoken during rehearsals. For his production of *Antigone* at Chur in 1948 Brecht composed linking passages in hexameters, which the characters spoke during rehearsals and which transformed the tragedy into the recitation of an epic poem. In this production the actors who were not involved in the action sat in a semicircle at the back of the stage.

[1] Brecht, 'Der Hofmeister, Episierungen', *Versuche 11*, p. 67.
[2] ibid.

Brecht advised them that 'they could read, freely make small movements, put on their make-up, or leave the stage quietly'.[1]

Brecht also wrote *Practice Scenes for Actors*. These include 'parallel
scenes' by which the actors are to be made to see hackneyed classical
situations in a new – estranged – light (the murder scene in *Macbeth*
is equated with the pangs of conscience of a concierge's wife who has
broken off the head of a china statue belonging to the lady of the house,
and finally blames the deed on a passing beggar); and 'bridge scenes',
to be acted during rehearsal but omitted in performance (Hamlet
learns that Claudius has ceded a strip of land to Norway in return for
a trade agreement, which guarantees the sale of Danish salted herrings
to Norway; this puts him into the right mood to hear of Fortinbras's
expedition to Poland and explains his change of mind in 'How all
occasions do inform against me'). But as Brecht never tackled *Macbeth*,
Hamlet, or any of the other plays for which he wrote these practice
scenes, they remain expressions of his love of debunking and parody
rather than constructive contributions to the art of acting.

In his own work as a director with the Berliner Ensemble, Brecht
refrained from expounding his theories to the actors. For an author of
copious theoretical writings on the art of acting, he was surprisingly
empirical. Leading actors who worked with him found little difference
in his approach from that of other directors with a literary background, except that he was perhaps more patient and ready to listen
to suggestions than most. As one observer of rehearsals of the Berliner
Ensemble put it:

> In this theatre everyone is allowed to state his opinion. The actors
> make all sorts of suggestions to the director. The director is all
> ear and greatly praises the suggestions. But in the end it is done as
> the director wanted it in the first place. . . . Everything is given
> a trial: Mr K. is asked to insert an occasional grunt – 'oeh!'. But
> 'oeh' can be said with the most varied nuances. The most significant,
> the most comical 'oeh' will have to be found. Six different kinds are
> tried, and in the end perhaps the most effective 'oeh' has been
> discovered.[2]

In spite of Brecht's untheoretical approach it is astonishing that the
Berliner Ensemble's splendidly produced publication on its work,

[1] Brecht and Neher, *Antigonemodell 1948*.
[2] J. Ruehle, *Das gefesselte Theater*, p. 229.

Theaterarbeit, discloses that in the course of a survey of the views of the members of the company it became clear that 'the majority of the actors showed considerable uncertainty', when asked whether the Berliner Ensemble was using a special style of acting! This is explained as

> probably due to the fact that neither Brecht nor other directors of the Berliner Ensemble refer to Brecht's theoretical writings during rehearsals. For certain plays some practical hints from these works are made use of, but in Brecht's view the present state of the theatre does not permit their full application.[1]

Whether Brecht's theories were merely rationalizations of his intuition, taste, and imagination (which they almost certainly were), or whether they were the results of the application of ice-cold logic and deeply probing sociological analysis (as he sometimes claimed them to be), they have had a most stimulating effect in freeing the stage from a narrow and cramping convention and will certainly continue to play their part within the much wider movement for the renewal of the theatre.

Brecht, who loved the exotic and the 'vulgar', often drew attention to his debt to the oriental theatre of China, India, and Japan, and the folk theatre of Austria and Bavaria. These exotic and folk influences, however, should not lead one to overlook the large extent to which the Brechtian theatre represents a return to the main stream of the European classical tradition. As Jean-Paul Sartre has pointed out,[2] the 'Verfremdungseffekt', the idea that the playwright should not show characters or situations too familiar to the audience, was one of the basic principles of classical French tragedy. Racine anticipates much of Brecht's ideas in his preface to *Bajazet*:

> Les personnages tragiques doivent être regardés d'un autre oeil que nous ne regardons d'ordinaire les personnages que nous avons vus de si près. On peut dire que le respect que l'on a pour les héros augmente à mesure qu'ils s'éloignent de nous: *major e longinquo reverentia*.[3]

[1] *Theaterarbeit*, p. 412.

[2] J.-P. Sartre, 'Brecht et les classiques', *World Theatre*, Paris, No. VII (Spring, 1958).

[3] Racine, 'Bajazet, Seconde Préface'; Racine, *Œuvres* (Ed. de la Pléiade), vol. I, p. 548.

The same is true of the rejection of empathy as the basis of great acting. Diderot in his *Paradoxe sur le Comédien* foreshadows Brecht's demand for critical, 'cool' acting by condemning the idea that actors should be able to feel the emotions they portray, or even that they should be people of more than average sensibility.

C'est l'extrême sensibilité qui fait les acteurs médiocres: c'est la sensibilité médiocre qui fait la multitude des mauvais acteurs; et c'est le manque absolu de sensibilité qui prépare les acteurs sublimes. Les larmes du comédien descendent de son cerveau; celles de l'homme sensible montent de son cœur: ce sont les entrailles qui troublent sans mesure la tête de l'homme sensible; c'est la tête du comédien qui porte quelquefois un trouble passager dans ses entrailles; il pleure comme un prêtre incrédule qui prêche la Passion; comme un séducteur aux genoux d'une femme qu'il n'aime pas, mais qu'il veut tromper; comme un gueux dans la rue ou à la porte d'une église, qui vous injurie lorsqu'il désespère de vous toucher; ou comme une courtisane qui ne sent rien, mais qui se pâme entre vos bras.[1]

Brecht's most original contribution to the theory of the theatre – but also the most disputable – concerns the reactions of the audience. From Greek tragedy to Gerhart Hauptmann and Ibsen the audience was supposed to be *moved* by what was presented on the stage. Whether they were to believe in the play as real or artificial, to regard the actors as skilful mimics or suffering human beings, they were to feel pity with them and to identify themselves with the experiences of the hero. Towards the end of his life Brecht defended himself against the reproach that he wanted to banish emotion from the theatre altogether. But the emotions he wanted to produce were of an entirely different nature. The 'epic' theatre, he said,

in no way renounces emotion. Least of all emotions like the love of justice, the urge to freedom or justified anger: so little does it renounce these emotions, that it does not rely on their being there, but tries to strengthen or to evoke them. The 'critical attitude' into which it is trying to put its public cannot be passionate enough.[2]

[1] Diderot, 'Paradoxe sur le Comédien'; Diderot, *Œuvres* (Ed. de la Pléiade), p. 1041.
[2] Brecht and F. Wolf, 'Formprobleme des Theaters mit neuem Inhalt', *Theaterarbeit*, p. 254.

It is more than doubtful whether such emotions could ever be made to play a more than merely marginal part among the feelings engendered by the theatre. In his rejection of identification between audience and characters Brecht comes into conflict with the fundamental concepts of psychology which regards processes of identification as the basic mechanisms by which one human being communicates with another. Without identification and empathy each person would be irrevocably imprisoned within himself. Even the spectators of a sporting contest, whom Brecht so often invoked as the ideal of a critical audience, identify themselves with the contestants. And, of course, the use of the various 'estranging' devices in Brecht's theatre shows that he was aware of the constant need to counteract the powerful effect of these tendencies in the audience. In practice, he succeeded at best merely in reducing to some extent the emotional identification of the audience with his characters. He never succeeded in evoking the critical attitude he postulated. The audience stubbornly went on being moved to terror and to pity.

On the other hand, it is perhaps precisely this contradiction between the author's and director's intention and the audience's natural tendency to react, which creates the peculiar effect of the Brechtian theatre: the conflict between head and heart in the actors and in the spectators, the ambiguity created by the tug of war between the intended and the actual reaction of the audience gives depth to two-dimensional characters and sophistication to what was intended as naïve. If the audience were merely repelled by the rascality and baseness of the robber Macheath, they *might* conceivably leave the theatre convinced, as Brecht intended, of the corruption of bourgeois society. But in fact, while they are to a certain extent repelled by Macheath, they also identify themselves with him; while they are made to loathe his sentimentality they are also made to participate in it. And they leave the theatre by no means entirely convinced that bourgeois society is rotten, but having greatly enjoyed a poetical experience. And so Brecht's success lies in his partial failure to realize his own intentions.

Brecht believed that his 'non-aristotelian', 'epic' theatre was destined to become the theatre of the scientific age.

In an age whose science is able to change nature to an extent which makes the world appear almost habitable, man can no longer be described to man as a mere victim, the object of an unknown, but unalterable environment. . . . The world of today can be described to the human beings of today only as a world that can be changed.[1]

He thought that the 'epic' theatre which aimed at awakening the spectator's critical faculty, which concentrated on showing mankind from the point of view of social relationships, would serve as an instrument of social change, a laboratory of revolutionary enlightenment; in other words, that the 'epic' theatre was the Marxist theatre *par excellence*. But the chain of reasoning by which he arrives at this conclusion contains more than one weak link. A narrative theatre, he argues, can show far more than just the way people act and suffer. It is not compelled, as the conventional theatre is, to leave the conclusions entirely to the audience. It can provide sociological background material; it can comment on the action. By keeping the spectator in a critical frame of mind it prevents him from seeing the conflict entirely from the point of view of the characters involved in it and from accepting their passions and motives as being conditioned by 'eternal human nature'. Such a theatre will make the audience see the contradictions in the existing state of society; it might even make them ask themselves how it might be changed. But there is nothing in this particular *stage convention* which in itself would lead the public to a *Marxist* answer to this question. Of course, the characters, or the chorus, can be made to advocate Marxist solutions – but so can the characters in the conventional theatre, as innumerable Soviet propaganda plays, excellently acted in the tradition of Stanislavsky, amply prove. Brecht disliked and despised the openly propagandist play in the naturalistic convention. In his speech to the Fourth East German Writers' Congress in January 1956 he ridiculed plays in which 'the new' was being advocated through

the playwright giving a representative of 'the new' so much freedom of speech, that his point of view does in fact get the better of his opponent's point of view. But you must not forget that the representation of militant action on the stage, even from a set point of view, does not by itself automatically produce a militant effect. What we

[1] Brecht, 'Kann die heutige Welt durch Theater widergegeben werden?' (1955), *Schriften zum Theater*, p. 8.

must achieve is the creation of militancy in the audience, the militancy of the new against the old.[1]

But there is little evidence that Brecht's own, more subtle methods ever roused the audience to a militantly Marxist point of view. For the Brechtian theatre is a theatre designed to arouse indignation in the audience, dissatisfaction, a realization of contradictions – it is a theatre supremely fitted for parody, caricature, and denunciation, therefore essentially a *negative* theatre. That is why Brecht's plays conspicuously lack positive heroes, why the good characters are invariably crushed and defeated. Brecht believed that the audience's indignation with the existing order would necessarily and automatically lead them to support the Marxist alternative. But this belief presupposes a touching faith in the self-evident truth of the Marxist creed. What Brecht says, in effect, is: 'show the world in a critical spirit – and the audience will automatically see the need for a Marxist solution! It is enough to point out the contradictions in the existing state of society to make people clamour for Communism.' This is not only a *non sequitur* in theory, but has been shown to be one in practice. *The Threepenny Opera* ran for years in New York without turning the thousands of people who saw it into Communists. The East Berlin audience who followed the adventures of *Mother Courage* and saw poor dumb Katrin raped by the brutal soldiery knowingly compared what they had seen in the theatre with their experiences with the Russian soldiers, and concluded that in fact human nature had *not* changed. . . .

If Brecht believed that the 'epic' theatre was the truly Marxist theatre, the authorities of the Communist world certainly did not. The Brechtian theatre still only exists on the fringes of the Communist world, while the doctrines of Stanislavsky, the theatre of identification and illusion, remain the prescribed, official norm for actors, producers, and critics from Vladivostok to Prague.

Brecht's life-long struggle for the acceptance of his theories as those of the truly Marxist theatre (which is described in Chapter VII) finally led him to abandon the very name of the 'epic' theatre. His last theoretical essays, entitled *Dialectics in the Theatre*, foreshadow its substitution by the term 'dialectical theatre'. His disciple Manfred

---

[1] Brecht, 'Ausfuehrungen vor der Sektion Dramatik', 12.1.1956. Proceedings of the Fourth East German Writers' Congress, published in *Beitraege zur Gegenwartsliteratur*, 1956/I.

Wekwerth describes how he spoke of his theatre as a 'dialectical theatre' shortly before he died.[1] But in the introductory note to *Dialectics in the Theatre*, published after his death, Brecht merely says:

> The essays which follow suggest that the term 'epic theatre' may be too formal for the theatre we mean (and practise – up to a point). The epic theatre may be the underlying basis of these presentations, but it does not fully account for the way they show the productivity and malleability of society, which is the source of most of the enjoyment they provide. The term 'epic theatre' must therefore be regarded as inadequate, without our being able to offer a new one.[2]

[1] M. Wekwerth, 'Auffinden einer aesthetischen Kategorie', *Sinn und Form*, Second Special Brecht Issue, 1957, p. 265.
[2] Brecht, 'Die Dialektik auf dem Theater', *Schriften zum Theater*, p. 174.

Part Three:
Pitfalls of Commitment

Chapter VII

BRECHT AND THE COMMUNISTS

What meanness would you not commit, to
Stamp out meanness?
If, at last, you could change the world, what
Would you think yourself too good for?
Who are you?
Sink into the mire
Embrace the butcher, but
Change the world: it needs it!

BRECHT: *Die Massnahme*

No one could call the author of these lines a starry-eyed idealist, who did not realize the complexity of the moral dilemma that faces the artist and the intellectual who ranges himself in the Communist camp.

Did Brecht ever actually join the Communist party? Ruth Fischer, once a leading German Communist herself and the sister of Brecht's close friend, the composer Hanns Eisler, categorically states that he joined the party in 1930.[1] On the other hand, when the chief investigator of the Un-American Activities Committee in Washington asked him if he had ever applied for admission to the party, Brecht's reply was equally categorical: 'No, no, no, no, no, never!'[2]

This sixfold denial may well have been a sixfold deliberate lie; it may, in the narrowest, technical sense of the word, have been the truth. For in the case of artists who are unlikely to be very effective in the organizational work of the party and whose usefulness in attracting the sympathies of left-wing and liberal intellectuals is far greater if they are not too closely identified with the more sordid side of politics, the Communists often advise, or even order, their supporters not to join. But the technical detail of formal party membership hardly matters. What matters is that, with or without a party card, Brecht considered himself a Marxist; that he loyally supported the Communist cause and

[1] Ruth Fischer, *Stalin and German Communism*, Harvard University Press, Cambridge, Mass., 1948, p. 615.

[2] *Hearings Regarding the Communist Infiltration of the Motion Picture Industry*, Washington, 1947.

did all he could to put himself and his great talents at its service. There can be no doubt that he was ready, for its sake, to sink into the mire and to embrace more than one butcher.

Yet, as a moralist at heart, he remained aware of the delicate balance between ends and means involved in such a risky compromise and of the existence of a limit beyond which such a compromise could not go.

The party, on the other hand, accepted his support often without enthusiasm, and sometimes with an embarrassment bordering on bad grace. The freely offered adherence of an artist of world-wide fame and prestige is too great an asset ever to be lightly cast aside. Yet it is an asset that can all too easily turn into a liability, as in the case of André Gide, and, more than once, in that of Jean-Paul Sartre. Brecht never caused the party such embarrassment: he was only too conscious of the need for discipline and self-denial. But while he had no intention to defect, he made full and cunning use of the implied threat of possible defection. He carefully selected for himself the most advantageous position within the Eastern orbit, a position that was to secure him the material advantages of Communist patronage, while allowing him the maximum freedom of speech and movement.

With a theatre at his disposal in East Berlin, an Austrian passport in his pocket, and the copyright of his plays in the hands of a West German publisher, Brecht could dedicate himself to the pursuit of his political and artistic aims, without risking the fate that had overtaken so many of his fellow-artists who had been denied the opportunity of striking a bargain like his: Mayakovsky, Meyerhold, Tairov, or Pasternak.

But even after Brecht had succeeded in arriving at this arrangement, his relations with the Communist authorities remained complex and beset with many problems and dangers. For the story of Brecht's relations with the party, in spite of the deep craving that drove him towards this haven of orthodoxy and certainty, exemplifies the deep, fundamental contradiction between a creative personality, however willing and loyal, ultimately subject to the laws of its own inner being, and the party, an apparatus of power constantly shifting its tactics and demands behind a façade of rigidly unchanging dogma.

From his earliest youth Brecht was in revolt against the bourgeois world and the social order that had led to war. But, although he was briefly involved in the Communist rising at Augsburg at the end of the First World War, his attitude remained that of an anarchist, iconoclast, and radical pacifist, who was against authority of any kind.

Kragler, the soldier from the wars returning in Brecht's second play *Drums in the Night*, who refuses to risk his life by fighting for the Spartakists, expresses a violently unheroic attitude: 'I am a swine and the swine goes home.' Rather than fight for the ideals of the revolution he will settle down with his girl, even if she is pregnant by another man. 'I'll put on a clean shirt. I still have my skin. I'll grease my boots. The shouting will be all over by tomorrow morning, but I'll be in my bed tomorrow morning, procreating, lest I die out.'[1]

As so often with Brecht it is left unclear whether the author shares his character's view or not. When Brecht published his collected plays shortly before he died, the earlier Western edition contained *Drums in the Night* without comment. But for Eastern Germany he wrote a foreword, later incorporated in the reprints of the Western version, in which he argues that he had in fact intended Kragler as a negative, a comic character. 'But I did not succeed in making the audience see the revolution differently from the way "the hero" Kragler saw it. I did not yet have the technique of "Verfremdung" at my disposal.'[2] Brecht confesses that he thought of suppressing the play altogether. 'Only the thought that literature is part of history and history must not be falsified'[3] kept him from doing so. Instead he strengthened the play by inserting some reference to a more positive revolutionary who did fight for his cause and was killed.

But it is difficult to believe that Brecht had in fact intended Kragler as a negative character. In the first edition of *Hauspostille* there is a poem which shows that Brecht's contempt for fighting of any kind extended even to the Russian Revolution and Civil War. This poem, which has disappeared without a trace from later editions of *Hauspostille*, in spite of Brecht's professed conviction that literature belongs to history and history must not be falsified, is called 'The Red Army Soldier's Song'. This Red Army soldier feels even more bitter than Kragler:

> *Many we saw with tigers' teeth*
> *Behind the red, inhuman flag. . . .*[4]

[1] Brecht, *Trommeln in der Nacht. Erste Stuecke I*, p. 188.
[2] Brecht, *Stuecke I* (Aufbau Verlag, East Berlin), pp. 6–7.   [3] ibid.
[4] Brecht, *Hauspostille*, Berlin, 1927, p. 15.

The civil war was said to be a war for freedom,

> *But freedom, boys, it never came.*[1]

The Red Army soldier is thoroughly disillusioned:

> *When our body is all eaten up*
> *With its tired heart within,*
> *The army into cold, flat holes*
> *Will spit out our bones and skin.*
>
> *And with our body, hardened by the rain*
> *And with our heart, torn up by ice*
> *And with our bloodstained empty hands*
> *Grinning we step into your paradise.*[2]

These lines are not quoted here to score a point against Brecht: why should he not have gradually become converted to the Communist cause? But they are important as evidence that he did not, as he later tried to make it appear, and as the official legend now fostered in the Communist world proclaims, support the Russian revolution from the moment he heard of it. Arnolt Bronnen describes how he discussed the problem of Communism with Brecht in the winter of 1922–3. When Bronnen spoke about the need to change the world so that people need not starve any more, 'Brecht began to get angry. "What business is it of yours, if people are starving," he said. "One must get on, make a name for oneself, get a theatre to put on one's own plays!" He was not interested in anything else.'[3]

When Brecht was converted to Marxism in the late twenties, he was much attracted by its negative aspects. The anti-bourgeois and anarchist revelled in so savage and acute a diagnosis of the existing social order. This was Germany after the First World War, with its bloated and ignorant *nouveaux riches*, its stock-exchange gamblers and blackmarketeers, and all the prostitution and degradation that surrounded them. This was the world which George Grosz, Brecht's friend, depicted in his devastating drawings. And this world Brecht attacked with the weapon of his newly discovered Marxist analysis.

The Threepenny Opera is an essay on Proudhon's famous aphorism 'la propriété c'est le vol', and *Mahagonny* shows the capitalist system

---

[1] Brecht, *Hauspostille*, Berlin, 1927, p. 16.   [2] ibid., p. 17.
[3] *Arnolt Bronnen gibt zu Protokoll*, Hamburg, 1954, p. 112.

as a brothel town where everything is for sale and the only capital crime is lack of money. But if the Communist implications of these themes were clear to Brecht, they were not clear to the public (which either enjoyed the plays as rollicking near-pornography or attacked them as such); they were even less clear to the Communists themselves.

Die Rote Fahne, the main organ of the German Communist Party, criticized *The Threepenny Opera* for its 'lack of social concreteness'[1] while the theoretical periodical of the left-wing intellectuals *Die Linkskurve* referred to Brecht, in connexion with *Mahagonny*, as 'the spokesman of a resigned, sceptical petty bourgeoisie, which tries to cross the void of its own confusion by performing nihilistic balancing acts' [2] And, twenty-five years later, the Marxist author of the bulky East German study of the young Brecht, Ernst Schumacher, also condemned *Mahagonny*: for does this opera not err grievously in trying to expose the vices of capitalism by showing them being practised by lumberjacks – working-class men? It was a grave error on Brecht's part to have suggested that lumberjacks indulge in the capitalist sins of eating, drinking, and lechery. 'It may be true', Schumacher explains, 'that certain sections of the working class might under capitalism, and especially under imperialism, have an opportunity at times, and briefly, to indulge in "hedonism".'[3] But nevertheless Brecht should not have demonstrated the aberrations of capitalism on such men, who 'may be in possession of money for a while, but are not owners of the means of production'.[3]

Brecht soon abandoned his attempt at reforming society by holding up to it the mirror of its own vice and lechery. He became fascinated with the problem of discipline. The austere monastic side of Communism, its practice of self-denial and strict obedience had a magnetic attraction for the self-indulgent anarchist. Here was the rigid framework of order, which he instinctively felt he needed to counteract his drift towards amorphous emotions and nebulous formlessness. The nihilist needed a faith. He found it in the stark social logic of Marxism.

In the Lehrstuecke (didactic plays) and Schulopern (school operas) Brecht grappled with the problem of order, discipline, and submission: discipline within the party, submission to the inexorable laws of

[1] *Die Rote Fahne*, 4.9.1928. Quoted by Schumacher, p. 255.
[2] *Die Linkskurve*, Berlin, January 1931. Quoted by Schumacher, p. 279.
[3] Schumacher, p. 273.

history. These were the themes of the *Badener Lehrstueck* in which a group of transatlantic flyers are made to consent to their own death in the interest of technical progress, and the school opera *Der Jasager* (*He Who Says Yes*) which is based on a Japanese legend and shows the self-sacrifice of a boy who consents to die rather than hinder a party crossing the mountains. But, again, Brecht had not been specific enough: the critics saw these paeans to discipline and self-denial as expressions of Christian, Buddhist, or even Prussian military ethics, while the left-wing intellectuals were horrified. As one of them said about *Der Jasager*: 'this school opera cunningly infuses into the souls of young people a view of life containing all the wicked ingredients of reactionary thinking based on senseless authority. . . .'[1] Even the pupils of the left-wing Karl Marx School in Berlin who were to perform *Der Jasager* disagreed with its authoritarian ethics. Brecht, always open to change his mind, yielded to the criticisms and turned *Der Jasager* into a *Neinsager*. But this did not correspond to Brecht's yearning for discipline. And so he returned to the subject in his first real masterpiece, the didactic cantata *Die Massnahme* (*The Measure*).

Now for the first time he tackled the theme of Communism and Communist discipline itself. The moral problem of the conflict between ends and means is faced boldly and without fear of carrying it to its logical conclusion. The young comrade, whose heart has been too soft, who has failed to resist the temptation of helping the poor when the higher interest of the party lay in ignoring their suffering, must be killed. He sees the need for it himself and begs for death. The story is told and re-enacted by a group of party workers after their return to headquarters: each of them in turn plays the part of the young comrade, for he represents a part of their own nature, the part they have to suppress and kill in themselves. The 'control chorus', sitting in judgment on the party workers, approves of their disciplinary measure and praises them for having been hard.

The first performance of *Die Massnahme* was followed a few days later by a public discussion. According to an eyewitness

the Communists above all refused to admit that the killing of a comrade was a Communist practice. The Communist way was expulsion from the party, not the physical one of liquidation. The

[1] *Die Weltbuehne*, Berlin, 8.7.1930.

chairman of the meeting pointed out that physical death would be less tragic for the comrade . . . than expulsion.[1]

The party was horrified that Brecht had given the anti-Communist press the occasion of speaking about the 'murderous practices' of the Communist party, and the party organs strenuously denied that any such killing could ever happen in reality. *Die Linkskurve* attacked Brecht's lack of revolutionary experience:

> One feels that he does not draw his knowledge from practice, that he is merely deducing from theory. . . . The unreal analysis of the premises leads to a false synthesis of their political and artistic consequences. All this mirrors an abstract attitude towards the manifold and complicated store of knowledge, derived from experience, which the party possesses.[2]

In the light of these criticisms Brecht revised the text. But the second performance still did not satisfy the critics. *The Rote Fahne* admonished him:

> The author of *Die Massnahme*, Bert Brecht, must be told that knowledge of the theories of Marxism-Leninism is not enough, that the genius and wide reading of a writer cannot take the place of revolutionary experience and detailed day-to-day work in the movement.

But the heaviest attack came from Moscow itself. The central organ of the International Association of Revolutionary Writers, *Literatur der Weltrevolution*, published a long article by the German Communist theoretician Alfred Kurella entitled 'An Attempt with Inadequate Means' in which *Die Massnahme* was condemned on a number of counts. Above all, the young comrade would not have been killed because

> we can quote various examples how the Bolsheviks, and above all Lenin, took up the same position as the young comrade and acted accordingly: not to stop a spontaneous rising of the revolutionary masses by pointing with an air of wisdom to the teachings of the classics but to take it in hand and to lead it, even if it was to be assumed that it would end in defeat.[3]

[1] Thieme in *Hochland*, Munich, February 1932. Quoted by Schumacher, p. 367.

[2] *Die Linkskurve*, January 1931. Quoted by Schumacher, p. 367.

[3] Kurella, 'Ein Versuch mit nicht ganz tauglichen Mitteln', *Literatur der Weltrevolution*, Moscow, no. 4, 1931. Quoted by Schumacher, p. 361.

Brecht also erred because he postulated an opposition between reason and emotion, and therefore fell into the sin of idealism. 'The conflict between reason and emotion is a basic experience of the bourgeois intellectual, who is about to join the revolutionary proletariat.'[1] In fact, *Die Massnahme* was 'a typically petty-bourgeois, intellectualist piece of work'.[1]

In the end Brecht, who always considered himself a better Marxist than the party pundits, was vindicated by history itself. *Die Massnahme*, written in 1930, is an exact and horrifying anticipation of the great confession trials of the Stalinist era. Many years before Bukharin consented to his own execution in front of his judges, Brecht had given that act of self-sacrifice for the sake of the party its great, tragic expression. With the intuition of the poet he had grasped the real problem of Communist discipline with all its far-reaching implications. To this day *Die Massnahme* remains the only great tragedy on the moral dilemma of Soviet Communism.

Die Massnahme can, of course, not be performed in the Communist world. Ernst Schumacher goes to grotesque lengths in trying to expose the errors of the play as they appear to a present-day East German critic.

> If Brecht's description in *Die Massnahme* corresponded to an objective revolutionary situation [he writes] it would not be the young comrade who would be in conflict with party discipline, but it would be an historical situation in which the three party workers would have to be removed from the leadership as reformists and opportunists. . . . Such a removal of the three party officials as they appear in *Die Massnahme* would, in any case, be necessary as they are employing the young comrade for tasks which are obviously beyond him.[2]

In other words, Brecht had liquidated the wrong comrade!

Brecht himself reacted to all this in his own peculiar way. His French translator Pierre Abraham describes a conversation with Brecht in 1956 shortly before he died: Brecht spoke about his intention of writing a new preface to his didactic plays, in which he wanted to explain that these plays were not meant to teach anything in particular, but were merely 'limbering-up exercises for those athletes of the spirit

---

[1] Kurella, loc. cit. Quoted by Schumacher, p. 366.
[2] Schumacher, p. 365.

that good dialecticians must be. The question whether any particular judgment in them is well or ill founded is an entirely different matter, which depends on elements I have not introduced into these discussions at all.'[1] Anyone who knows Brecht's love of irony and leg-pulling will feel that he would have written this preface with his tongue in his cheek. In fact, it was not written. Instead, in volume five of the collected plays, published after his death, we find a very brief 'Note on the Didactic Plays' which refers to *Die Massnahme* as follows:

> The author has repeatedly refused to permit performances of *Die Massnahme*, as only the actor of the young comrade can learn from it and he only if he has also acted one of the party workers and taken part in the control chorus.[2]

As the notes of the first edition already expressly state that 'each of the four actors is to have the opportunity of showing the attitude of the young comrade and therefore each actor is to play one of the main scenes of the young comrade in turn'[3] his solemn reiteration of his original intention as an argument against performance of the play must surely be considered as an example of typically Brechtian irony and delight in mystification.

Whatever Brecht may have thought about the party's condemnation of *Die Massnahme* in the fifties, in the early thirties he displayed a degree of patience and loyalty truly remarkable in so openly professed a cynic. He continued to devote himself to the Communist cause with all the fervour of a new convert. Only occasionally he was driven to utter a mild criticism of the party's dogmatism. 'It is a mistake to believe,' he makes his Mr Keuner say in 1932, 'that a stupid thing can be refuted only by a clever argument. Many stupid arguments are merely put forward to refute stupid statements.' And Keuner goes on to explain that he feels that the party is frightening people away by knowing the answer to every question. 'Could we not, in the interests of propaganda, draw up a list of questions which we consider quite unsolved?'[4] Apart from such mild digs at the party stalwarts, however, Brecht did his utmost to help the cause: he fought like a lion to infuse

[1] *Europe*, Paris, January February 1957, p. 173.
[2] 'Anmerkung zu den Lehrstuecken', *Stuecke V*, p. 276.
[3] *Versuche 4*, p. 361.
[4] *Geschichten vom Herrn Keuner. Versuche 5*, p. 457. In later versions of this story the reference to 'stupid arguments' is omitted.

a more positively Marxist content into the film version of *The Three-penny Opera*. He wrote another film scenario, strictly on party lines, for *Kuhle Wampe*. And, above all, he produced a play which carefully embodied all the lessons from the party's strictures on *Die Massnahme*. If *Die Massnahme* had been criticized for its lack of concreteness and remoteness from the daily struggles of the ordinary party member, Brecht's adaptation of Gorky's novel *The Mother* was severely practical, concrete, and historical. Although Brecht did not follow Gorky very closely and continued the story to the eve of the October Revolution, he avoided all abstract argument and presented his audience with a primer of propaganda methods and revolutionary behaviour. And on the whole the German Communist Party approved of this effort; in spite of the somewhat patronizing tone of the main party organ *Die Rote Fahne*:

> This is a new Bert Brecht. He has escaped from the desert of bourgeois theatre business; he is fighting for the revolutionary working class. As yet he has not torn off all the shackles that bind him to his past. But he will. He must – soon.[1]

The Mother is Brecht's nearest approach to an orthodox Communist propaganda play: it is based on an accepted classic of Russian revolutionary literature, and apart from *Die Massnahme* it is his only play that deals directly with the Russian revolution or the Communist party. The reaction of Soviet party circles was therefore of particular interest to him. When it came, five years after the first performance of *The Mother*, it took a characteristic form.

In 1937 the Soviet monthly journal *International Literature* – in its English edition – published an article on Brecht by the Soviet dramatist Sergei Tretyakov. This essay, described as a chapter from Tretyakov's forthcoming book on banned German authors, gave a vivid sketch of Brecht's personality. It showed him as typical of those German intellectuals who spent their time arguing about abstract problems while the Nazis were about to take power, described how Brecht had only gradually freed himself from this bourgeois attitude, and how he had finally reached a definite proletarian standpoint in *The Mother*. But even this turned out to be a somewhat backhanded compliment.

---

[1] *Die Rote Fahne*, 19.1.1932. Quoted by Schumacher, p. 432.

At first sight [Tretyakov wrote] Brecht's *Mother* deals with the revolutionary development of Pelageya Vlasova, the Tver working woman. But this is misleading. It would be wrong to regard it as an historical play about a Russian working woman. Such an interpretation involves one absurdity after another.[1]

And Tretyakov enumerates a whole list of features of the play which would be quite unthinkable in Russia. And he continues:

Regardless of whether Brecht likes it or not I must mention the vividness of the teacher, the house-owner, the shopwoman, and the policeman in the play. The workers are hard to distinguish from each other; this is a general shortcoming of all Brecht's plays, which shows that he does not know the proletarian milieu intimately (this is a warning to him that he must get to know it so).[1]

Brecht is said to have been infuriated by this article, which managed to imply that *The Mother* was the only good thing he had ever written, thanks to a Soviet model, but at the same time suggested that this model had not been imitated well enough.

Tretyakov's proposed book on banned German writers never seems to have been published: he disappeared without a trace in the great purges. All his writings were banned in the Soviet Union until 1957.

The Mother was Brecht's last play to be performed on the German stage before Hitler came to power. The material and spiritual needs of exile drove Brecht closer than ever to the Communists. On the other hand, the struggle against the Nazis made it much easier to keep in step with them. The Communists became the allies of all anti-Fascists, and even anti-Nazi writers with liberal views could rally round them.

It is a sign of Brecht's uncanny shrewdness in these matters that he, who was an ardent and convinced supporter of the party and was eager to participate in its propaganda activities, should have resisted the temptation of settling in the Soviet Union. He accepted the editorship, jointly with Lion Feuchtwanger and Willi Bredel, of a German literary journal published in Moscow. But he performed his duties by mail from Denmark. The story is told – on very good authority – that in 1935 he went to Moscow to have a look at the place

[1] S. Tretyakov, 'Bert Brecht', *International Literature*, Moscow, May 1937.

and to decide whether he should make it his home. He looked round – and left after a few days. When he was asked why he had not stayed, he would smile and say: 'I could not get enough sugar for my tea and coffee.'[1]

The play *The Life of Galileo*, written in 1938–9, reflects his thinking on this point: Galileo has the choice between a life of relative freedom and hard work in earning his living as a teacher in the mercantile Republic of Venice or leisure and luxury in the service of the Medici in Florence, where papal influence is strong and he runs the risk of having his researches prohibited by the Inquisition. After Galileo has gone to Florence and been forced to recant, his pupils discuss this dilemma: '. . . he should never have left Venice', says one of them. 'There he could not have written his book,' retorts the other. 'And in Florence he could not publish it,' replies a third.[2]

This is a dilemma that Brecht faced more than once in his life: his Galileo went to Florence, the totalitarian country where he had the leisure to write his book at the cost of terrible suffering. Brecht stayed in Denmark, where he had to work hard to keep alive and lacked the chance of having his plays performed as he imagined them. It turned out to have been the wiser choice: the large majority of the German Communist intellectuals who had gone to Russia came to grief in the great purges. Brecht's friend Carola Neher, the Polly of *The Threepenny Opera* film, was among those who perished.

By the time he was faced with the need to leave Scandinavia the dilemma had temporarily vanished. In the spring of 1941 the Soviet Union and Nazi Germany were allies. Brecht went to America. In one of his poems he describes his situation in Finland in 1941 –

> . . . *with curiosity*
> *I scan the map of Europe. High up in Lapland*
> *Towards the Arctic Ocean*
> *I still see a tiny door.*[3]

As Herbert Luethy has pointed out, if one really looks at the map of Europe one will find that Finland has an immensely long eastern frontier with the Soviet Union. Brecht had not even thought of that

---

[1] E. W. White in *Life and Letters*, September 1935. The story has been independently confirmed by other, oral, sources.

[2] *Leben des Galilei. Stuecke VIII*, p. 162.

[3] '1941', *Hundert Gedichte*, East Berlin, 1951, p. 307.

country as a possible refuge. And what is even more astonishing: he published that poem in the East German edition of his verse in 1951!

Seven years after he had decided to go to the United States, Brecht was once more faced with the need to make up his mind: should he settle in Switzerland or Austria, an independent artist, struggling to get his plays performed according to his own ideas, or should he accept the offer of a theatre all his own in East Berlin, lavishly subsidized but dependent on the goodwill of an authoritarian state? It was not an easy decision. The long time he took over it and his trial period in Berlin show that he weighed the arguments for and against it most carefully. In the end he did accept.

And so the eternal rebel became the member of the ruling class of a rigidly organized, hierarchical society, the eternal outsider a member of the establishment. It was an interesting and a dangerous situation: Brecht's experiences provide an illuminating example of the strains and stresses that arise when an intellectual of high standing and strong personality sincerely tries to live and work in a totalitarian system.

To understand his reactions and development in this situation it is, however, important to keep in mind the nature of his own personal brand of Communist beliefs and the motives that had brought him to adopt them.

Contempt for bourgeois society, the bourgeois way of life, bourgeois respectability lies at the root of these beliefs. In Germany more than elsewhere the artistic temperament was driven into opposition to the established way of life. Respectable society was not only stuffy, stupid, and hypocritical, it was above all utterly without grace or wit; it was ugly and unaesthetic. The German intellectuals and artists of the Wilhelminian period used to dream of the wit and gay conversation, the *savoir-vivre* of France, the exquisite manners and beautiful country houses of England. The First World War confirmed the younger generation's contempt for the respectable Germany of their parents, which now stood revealed not only as crude and ugly but also incompetent and bankrupt.

Brecht's generation of young poets linked its contempt for this society with an utter rejection of its accepted standards of art or literature. Goethe and Schiller and all the other school-book classics filled these young men with disgust. The very language they used to express their idealistic sentiments seemed contaminated. Feuchtwanger describes how Brecht told him one day: 'When Horace expresses the most ordinary thought or the most trivial emotion, it looks magnificent. He worked in marble. We work with dirt.'[1]

The cheap Chauvinism of German patriotic literature turned young people like Brecht into violent anti-nationalists. Sentiments expressed in such vulgar, graceless language could not but be contemptible.

When the First World War broke out the ugliness of war-time propaganda and the horrors of physical suffering appeared inextricably linked in the minds of such sensitive intellectuals. The Austrian critic Karl Kraus, whom Brecht greatly admired, was their chief spokesman. To him the debasement of its language appeared as the expression of the moral and intellectual debasement of the nation.

If the ugliness of jingoist sentiments turned young Brecht into an anti-patriot, the horror of war made him a pacifist and the vulgarity and crudeness of the German post-war profiteers, the feverish parasites of the inflationary boom, inspired him with loathing for what he thought to be the capitalist system.

And so it was for aesthetic reasons that Brecht, like many sensitive German intellectuals of artistic temperament and tastes, was driven into opposition against the existing order of things.

In Germany after the First World War the picture of commercial society certainly was an ugly one. There the bull-necked, bloated financier, in his loud suit, his bowler hat, chewing enormous cigars in dreary night-clubs, listening to vulgar music, and leering at disgusting floor-shows, really existed. The horror of this picture left a lasting mark on Brecht's writing. It is the origin of his crude and over-simplified ideas about the nature of all business: again and again he equates finance or industrial enterprise with robbery, fraud, vulgarity, and violence. And this naïve idea of the nature of the capitalist system often mars his efforts to present a serious analysis of the evils of a commercial society, particularly when he transfers his vulgar German black-marketeers to London or Chicago, where they become completely unconvincing. But in the very special context of the Germany of the twenties these images did have a meaning.

These were the aesthetic roots of Brecht's furious negation of the existing order of things. He could not endure the ugliness and vulgarity of patriotic cant, the witlessness of respectable society, and the loath-

---

[1] L. Feuchtwanger, 'Bertolt Brecht', *Sinn und Form*, Second Special Brecht Issue, 1957, p. 106.

some cynicism of the *nouveaux riches*. And it is clear that his sensitivity was not only aesthetic. He also was basically a puritan and an idealist. When this moral sensitivity was shattered by the horrors of the war and the post-war era, it turned into a violent denial of all values. But in the long run so purely destructive and negative an attitude was bound to lead to disaster. Brecht needed a new core of positive belief.

Marxism, as Brecht understood it, provided such a framework: it allowed all these negative attitudes to crystallize into a positive pattern. And what was even more important to Brecht, it was aesthetically satisfying.

Marxism provided the dramatist in Brecht with a splendid picture of conflict, a ready-made tragic pattern of history. He was so taken with the grandeur of the historical conception of the Marxist classics that he tried to put the Communist Manifesto into hexameters on the pattern of Lucretius's *De Rerum Natura*. Although he abandoned the attempt after many years of strenuous effort, a long and impressive fragment was found among his posthumous papers:

> *Reading history you read of the deeds of great individuals*
> *Rising and falling like stars and the mighty march of their armies,*
> *Glory and ruin of empires. But to the classics*
> *History is, above all, the history of struggles of classes:*
> *For they see the nations divided and fighting as classes*
> *Riven within themselves: Knights and Patricians, Slaves and*
>   *Plebeians,*
> *Nobles, Artisans, Peasants – and now Bourgeois and Proletarians,*
> *Ever maintaining in motion the gigantic machine of production*
> *And distribution of goods, while they are fighting the age-old*
> *Fight to the death, the mighty struggle for power. . . .*[1]

For the anarchist Brecht, to whom the world had appeared utterly without sense or purpose, and the individual so completely alone that he made his hero say in *Im Dickicht der Staedte*: 'the infinite isolation of man makes even enmity an unattainable goal. . . . Yes, so great is this isolation that there cannot even be a struggle,'[2] the discovery of this great and simple pattern and purpose in history must have come as a tremendous relief.

But what excited him even more was the dramatic quality of the

[1] Brecht, 'Das Manifest', *Sinn und Form*, 1957 V, p. 293.
[2] Brecht, *Im Dickicht der Staedte, Erste Stuecke I*, pp. 291–2.

Hegelian dialectic. The coexistence of opposites, the merging of thesis and antithesis appealed not only to Brecht's dramatic sense but also to his sense of the comic:

> (Hegel) had the greatest comic talent among all the philosophers; only Socrates, whose method was similar, was his equal. . . . He had such a sense of humour that, for example, he could not even conceive of, say, order without disorder. . . . He denied that one equals one, not only because everything that exists is continually turning into something else, namely its opposite, but because generally nothing is identical with itself.[1]

For Brecht this ambiguity of all things, the idea that nothing is really what it seems, constituted the essence of drama and poetry. His ideas about the 'epic' theatre ante-date his discovery of the dialectic. But it is easy to see how the Marxist dialectic as he understood it must have confirmed and justified these ideas: the actor who impersonates the character and yet remains himself, the stage which represents reality and yet remains a stage, the characters who are themselves but can at a moment's notice be re-tooled into someone else, like Galy Gay in *Mann ist Mann*, they all fell into place within the framework of the Hegelian dialectic.

And if the despair engendered by the seeming absurdity of the human condition had led the young Brecht into a self-destructive attitude of complete moral anarchism, now that the world was seen to have a purpose, the force of this despair could be canalized into more positive channels. If the pattern and purpose of history were known, it was easy to submit to them. The self-destructive impulses could be turned outwards. If the heroes of *Baal* and *Im Dickicht der Staedte* drifted to self-destruction by yielding to blind impulses within them, the airmen of *The Didactic Play of Baden*, who have to perish, are redeemed by the knowledge that their fate has significance within the process of history:

> But you who consent and agree with the flow of things
> Will not sink back into the void. . . .[2]

The young comrade in *Die Massnahme* still yields to the impulse of pity, because he cannot endure the suffering inherent in the human

[1] Brecht, 'Fluechtlingsgespraeche', *Aufbau*, East Berlin, February 1958, pp. 181–2.
[2] Brecht, *Das Badener Lehrstueck*, *Versuche 2*, p. 145.

condition. But he also knows that he was wrong to be weak, that the inexorable workings of history cannot be hurried and therefore consents to his own liquidation.

The horror at the violence of war, which had led Brecht to despair, turned into the willing acceptance of violence as part of the workings of necessity. The little Salvation Army girl of *St Joan of the Stockyards*, driven to despair by the human suffering before her, tries to relieve suffering by kindness. But in the hour of her death she comes to the conclusion:

> *For only violence helps, where violence reigns*
> *And only men can help where there are men. . . .*[1]

It is easy to see how this austere, poetic version of the Marxist creed corresponded to the subconscious needs of a young man of deep sensibility whose world had been shattered by the spectacle of horrible human suffering. But it is equally clear that the chief value of this creed to him was that it dissolved the nightmare of absurdity, that it dispelled the oppressive feeling that life was ruled by vast impersonal and irrational forces; in the light of this redeeming creed human suffering no longer appeared as the outcome of a fate beyond human comprehension and incapable of being influenced by human endeavour; if history was merely the outcome of human struggles, and the laws that governed these were known, the fate of mankind could be controlled. Brecht's aggressive rationalism, his obstinate refusal to recognize the existence of psychological factors or areas of mystery in nature, is the reaction of a personality that had felt deeply threatened and disturbed by the irrationality of the world around it, and that therefore had to cling to its newly found belief in reason with grim determination. Hence Brecht's fear of emotion in the theatre and his constant insistence on the scientific nature of Marxism and of the 'epic' theatre based on it.

This preoccupation with the scientific certainty of the Marxist creed shows to what an extent Brecht really was an idealist of truly religious fervour behind the mask of cynicism and toughness he displayed. He never did much as a practical politician or party worker: during the Hitler period he had written some anti-Nazi plays and poems for broadcasting, had made a few speeches at international congresses of anti-Fascist writers, and even written one or two pamphlets that were

[1] Brecht, *Die Heilige Johanna der Schlachthoefe, Versuche 5*, p. 453.

smuggled into Germany. One of these, characteristically, was *Five Difficulties in Writing the Truth* (published behind the title-page of a booklet on *Hints for First Aid*), a highly theoretical piece of advice to other writers which reveals moral scruples of all kinds. No wonder that the professional Communists, preoccupied with the techniques of subversion and the exercise of power, thought little of so ineffectual a dreamer. For them the means were all; the ends had been thrust into the limbo of a Utopian future. For Brecht the relation between ends and means always remained a vital problem.

That is why the scientific character of Marxism was so important for Brecht. The means are only justified when they are based on the mathematical certainty that they will bring about the ends to be attained. Violence can only be accepted when it is based on an absolutely certain knowledge of the results, freedom can only be given up for a time, when it is certain that the State will really wither away in the end. Brecht had a horror of dogma, and therefore insisted that doubt, criticism, and free inquiry, the essential elements of the scientific attitude, must be the basis of Marxism. One of his pupils reports that during the rehearsals of *Galileo* in the last months of his life, whenever he came to the sentence 'My task is not to prove that I have been right up till now, but to find out *whether* I have been right,' 'Brecht regularly used to interrupt the rehearsal and to draw his pupils' attention to the fact that for a Marxist this was the most important sentence in the play'.[1]

As long as Brecht could believe in the scientific certainty of Marxism he was safe. Everything became very simple. Violence and dictatorship could be defended, as old Pelageya Vlasova defends them in *The Mother*:

> With freedom it is rather as it is with your money, Nikolai Ivanovich. Since I have been giving you so little pocket-money, you are able to buy much more. By spending less money for a time, you can spend more money later.[2]

That is how clear and simple things became as long as the truth of the doctrine remained inviolate. To one who had been driven to despair by the absurdity and chaos of the world, this certainty was of

[1] Kaethe Ruelicke, 'Leben des Galilei – Schlusszene', *Sinn und Form*, Second Special Brecht Issue, 1957, p. 284.

[2] *Die Mutter*, *Stuecke V*, p. 84 (this passage is not in the earlier version, *Versuche 7*).

the utmost importance. That is why for Brecht Communism, as he put it,

> . . . is not madness, but
> The end of madness.
> It is not chaos
> But order.
> It is the simple thing
> That is hard to accomplish.[1]

Yet Brecht was far too lucid and sceptical a person to have any illusions about the true nature of Stalin's régime in the Soviet Union. Brecht's great friend, the critic Walter Benjamin (1892–1940; he committed suicide while fleeing from Nazi-occupied France), has left us a vivid record of conversations he had with Brecht during a visit to Brecht's Danish home in the summer of 1938. On 28 June, 1938, for example, Benjamin noted: 'Brecht talks about his deeply ingrained hatred of priests, which he inherited from his grandmother. He drops hints that those who have made Marx's theoretical teachings their own . . . will always form a priestly camarilla.' On the same day Benjamin reports a conversation on Soviet literature and the bad Soviet poetry which flooded the issues of Das Wort, the Soviet German-language periodical, of which Brecht was nominally an editor. 'Brecht says, authors over there have a hard life. It is already considered a sign of ill will if the name of Stalin does not appear in a poem.'

On 29 July, 1938 Benjamin reports that Brecht was preparing an article against György Lukacs's views on 'socialist realism' and asked Benjamin whether he ought to take the risk and publish it in Das Wort. 'I told him I could not give him useful advice. "These are questions of power. You ought to ask someone over there. After all, you've got friends there [i.e. in the Soviet Union]." Brecht: "To tell you the truth, I have no friends there. And the Muscovites themselves have no friends – like the dead."'

Benjamin's reports of private conversations with Brecht are fully confirmed by fragments of a book which was published nine years after Brecht died – in 1965 – but which dates back to the late thirties:

[1] Brecht, Die Mutter, Versuche 7, pp. 26–7. When Brecht republished this song in East Germany in 1951 the lines about chaos and order had disappeared and been replaced by: it is not the *riddle*
but the *solution*.

Me-ti. Buch der Wendungen (*Me-ti. Book of Twists and Turns*). This consists of brief stories and thoughts, purporting to be the work of an ancient Chinese philosopher (there are echoes here of Confucius, Lao-tzu and the Book of Changes), but clearly referring to Brecht's own political and private experience. The posthumous edition even contains a key to the Chinese names. Lenin appears as Mi-en-leh, Marx as Ka-meh, Stalin as Ni-en, the Soviet Union as Su.

The book of Me-ti leaves no doubt whatever on Brecht's attitude to Stalin: 'Mi-en-leh (Lenin) believed before the great revolution that the workers would have to help the citizens to free themselves from the rule of the Emperor. . . . Later the workers, under his leadership, obtained power; but his successor, Ni-en, acted exactly like an Emperor. The backwardness of the country of Su, of which Mi-en-leh had always spoken, did after all show itself in this phenomenon. The great machinery (i.e. technology) was built up not by the citizens under people's rule, but by workers under the rule of an Emperor.' In another section Brecht deals with the show trials under Stalin: 'Me-ti expressed his disapproval of Ni-en (Stalin) because, in his trials against his enemies in the association [i.e. the Party] he demanded too much confidence from the people. He said: If I am asked to believe something which can be proven (without furnishing me the proof) that is tantamount to my being asked to believe something that can*not* be proven. Ni-en *might* have benefited the people by removing his enemies inside the association, but he *did* not prove it. By conducting trials without proof he has done damage to the people. He ought to have taught the people to demand proof. . . .'

That Brecht was equally disturbed by Stalin's influence on the Party and on the Marxist doctrine itself is shown by this passage from *Me-ti*: 'Under Ni-en's leadership industry without exploiters was being built up in Su and agriculture collectivised and furnished with machines. But the associations [i.e. Communist Parties] outside Su decayed. It was no longer the members who elected the secretaries, but the secretaries who elected the members. The guidelines were issued by Su and the secretaries were paid from Su. If mistakes were made, those who had *criticised* the mistakes were punished; but those who had *made* the mistakes remained in office. Soon the office holders were no longer the best members but merely the most servile. . . . Those who issued the orders in Su no longer learned any facts, because the secretaries no longer reported facts that might not have pleased them.

In view of these conditions, the best (members) were in despair. Me-ti deplored the decay of the great method [i.e. Marxism]. Master Ko [i.e. Korsch, Brecht's teacher of Marxism] turned away from it. . . . Outside Su all those who praised Ni-en's merits, even those which were undeniable, became suspect of corruption; inside Su all those who uncovered his mistakes, even those from which he himself suffered, became suspect of treason.'

When Brecht returned to East Berlin in 1948 he was well aware of the duality, the truly Hegelian contradiction, between his own ideals of Communism and the realities of life in a Communist country. In the thirties he had watched the fight against the *avant-gardists* of the Soviet theatre and seen the acceptance of the Stanislavsky method as the official style of acting in the Soviet Union. In his earlier theoretical writings he had never concealed his opinion of Stanislavsky's theatre as the antithesis of what a truly Marxist theatre should be. Nevertheless he had paid his tribute to the newly adopted formula of 'socialist realism'. But it had been a typically double-edged Brechtian tribute: in an essay on the *Range and Variety of the Realist Style* (1938) Brecht used Shelley's *Mask of Anarchy* as an example of realism – i.e. progressive political tendency – which was nevertheless clothed in the form of fantasy. From it he had drawn the conclusion:

> . . . we see . . . that realism is not a matter of form. Nothing is so bad in putting up models as to put up *too few models*. It is dangerous to tie the great concept of realism to a few names, and to gather together a few forms as examples of the only true creative method, however useful these forms themselves may be. . . . The truth can be concealed in many ways. It can be uttered in many ways. . . .[1]

A few months later Brecht felt that he ought to come out more clearly against 'formalism', but here again he kept his obeisance to the anti-formalist campaign, then raging in the Soviet Union, carefully balanced:

> The very salutary campaign against formalism has helped the productive development of artistic forms, by proving that social content is an absolutely decisive condition for such development.

[1] Brecht, 'Weite und Vielfalt der Realistischen Schreibweise', *Versuche 13*, p. 107.

Any formal innovation which does not serve, and derive its justification from, its social content will remain utterly fruitless.[1]

Which means that Brecht, while acknowledging the demand for social content (which he had never denied), insisted on his right to continue his experiments with form.

Brecht never concealed his contempt for the artistic standards of Stalinist Russia. Shortly after his return to East Berlin he created considerable embarrassment among a group of German actors in the Soviet-run artists' club 'Die Moewe' by declaring in a loud voice that he considered the performances of Soviet drama he had seen as downright *Kitsch*. And when he advised the Swiss journalist Gody Suter to read Soviet novels, he praised their social attitude but added 'As to quality – rather like Gerstaecker or Kellermann'[2] – both authors of highly popular novels whose names are synonymous with Kitsch among most German left-wing intellectuals. During his visit to Moscow in 1955 to receive the Stalin Peace Prize, Brecht told the Soviet critic Fradkin that the performances he had liked best among those he had been taken to see were Mayakovsky's *The Bug* and *The Bath* at the Satirical Theatre. Both these plays had been banned since the middle thirties, because they are savage and grotesque satires on Soviet bureaucracy. Fradkin adds that Brecht told him he considered the actor Yachnitski a perfect exponent of the epic style, because he left no doubt about the difference between his own personality and that of the character he portrayed.[3] A typically Brechtian way of expressing his contempt for the Stanislavsky method and the official style of the Stalinist era!

Brecht's first post-war visit to East Berlin had been preceded by a performance of *Fear and Misery of the Third Reich* (*The Private Life of the Master Race*) at the Deutsches Theater in January 1948. One of the party's main spokesmen in the field of theatrical criticism, Fritz Erpenbeck, had greeted this sequence of relatively un-Brechtian scenes with shouts of joy that Brecht had at last abandoned his 'in our view false theory of the epic theatre and the "didactic play"', his advocacy of which his friends had considered a tragic aberration in so talented

[1] 'Ueber reimlose Lyrik mit unregelmaessigen Rhythmen', *Versuche 12*, p. 147.
[2] Gody Suter, 'Brecht', *Tagesanzeiger*, Zurich, 1.9.1956.
[3] I. Fradkin, 'Bertolt Brecht', *Teatr*, Moscow, January 1956.

an artist.[1] So it must have been clear to Brecht that he was in for a hard struggle.

The East German authorities not only regarded the winning over of such a famous playwright as a major propaganda victory *vis-à-vis* the West; they also made a sincere attempt to win him over to their own – artistic – point of view. They spared no expense to give him what he wanted, and argued with him, patiently and at great length. Much of this went on behind closed doors, but sometimes it was found necessary to bring these arguments into the open. In the case of *Mother Courage*, for example, the text has been published of a discussion which Brecht had with the party's favourite playwright Friedrich Wolf (author of the well-known anti-Nazi play *Professor Mamlock*). Wolf very politely reproached Brecht with leaving the audience to draw its own conclusions from Mother Courage's fate. 'How can we activate our people to overcome that fatalistic attitude towards a new war?' Wolf asked, and added, 'I should have thought Courage *even more* effective if her words "Cursed be war!" had found a visible expression in action, if she had drawn the consequences from her experience.' In other words, the party would have liked Mother Courage to have been converted to an active political attitude at the end of the play, instead of continuing her old life as a victualler. Brecht's retort was: 'If Courage learns nothing – in my opinion the public can learn something by watching her.'[2]

From its own point of view the party was right: the East Berlin public regarded *Mother Courage* as a faithful picture of the horrors of war, including those of the Russian occupation. The brilliantly sarcastic things that are said in *Mother Courage* about great generals and field-marshals who bask in glory at the expense of the poor devils in the mud apply to the great Marshal Stalin with the same force as to Field-Marshal Tilly or King Gustavus Adolphus of Sweden.

But if Brecht was prepared for, and unperturbed by, this kind of criticism, the matter became more serious when his most openly Communist play, *The Mother*, was the target for similar criticism. This was a magnificent production. Helene Weigel gave a great performance and Caspar Neher had designed some highly effective sets. It looked like a great success. But a few weeks after the first night the Central Committee of the party launched a massive attack against it. At the

---

[1] F. Erpenbeck, *Lebendiges Theater*, Berlin, 1949, p. 281.
[2] *Theaterarbeit*, p. 255.

fifth plenary meeting of the Central Committee in March 1951 one of the highest members of the hierarchy, Oelssner, asked:

Is this in fact realism? Are these typical figures shown in typical surroundings? . . . In my opinion this is not theatre. It is a kind of mixture between Meyerhold and Proletkult. If a man as talented as Brecht could write a play that really hangs together, that is really composed, what a work of art we could get! Besides . . . there are scenes that are historically wrong and politically harmful.[1]

Here Brecht was bluntly asked to abandon his very own epic style. The mention of Meyerhold was ominous in view of what had happened to that unfortunate producer of genius. Another high party official, Hans Rodenberg, also reproached Brecht for holding wrong views of Marxism, but asked that Brecht should be reprieved:

Of course, we must give him more time. . . . Brecht is using up his old luggage at the moment . . . he needs time to find his feet. . . . Provided he had felt able to do so, he would surely by now have written a play about our own time. Our real criticism of Brecht will depend on the time it takes him to write this play, and what a play it will be! . . . We must give Brecht some time. We must not stop criticizing him, but we must criticize him as intelligently as he himself is intelligent.[1]

So Brecht was given a reprieve to allow him to write a play on a contemporary East German problem. He never wrote such a play and continued, to the day of his death, to produce his earlier works – the luggage he had brought with him from his exile.

One of these earlier works was *The Trial of Lucullus*, which caused the most widely publicized of Brecht's clashes with the authorities.

The Trial of Lucullus had been written in 1939 as a radio play and had been broadcast by a Swiss station. It shows the trial of the great Roman general after his death by a jury of shades in the underworld. It is a straightforward, and very moving, poem on the futility of military glory and conquest *sub specie aeternitatis*. Stravinsky is said to have at one time been interested in setting it to music, Roger Sessions based an opera on the English version, but it was Paul Dessau, whom Brecht had met in the United States and who had also

[1] Quoted in Ruehle, *Das gefesselte Theater*, pp. 238 ff.

gone back to East Berlin, who wrote the music for the new opera, which was to be performed for the first time by the East Berlin State Opera on 17 March 1951.

This was the period of the Korean war, and the Communist authorities were clearly perturbed when they heard that the new work was a condemnation of all war as folly and showed the futility of conquest, a sentiment that might have been appropriate when it referred to Hitler, but could scarcely appear very politic in the centre of Soviet-occupied Germany. The story goes that the Communist authorities wanted to stop the performance altogether, but because a great deal of money had already been spent on the production, a famous conductor, Hermann Scherchen, had been invited from the West, and the first performance of so important a work had been widely publicized, they decided to permit three performances before a strictly controlled, hand-picked audience of party stalwarts and members of the youth organization.

These young people, however, were not very interested in opera, and many of them sold their tickets to Brecht enthusiasts and intellectuals from East and West Berlin. As a result the plan misfired: instead of giving the new opera the planned cool reception which would have allowed the production to have been withdrawn as unsuccessful, the first-night audience received it with tremendous – and demonstrative – applause and cheers. The members of the East German Government, who had watched the performance with growing consternation, left in a huff and the two remaining performances that had already been billed were cancelled.

On the 22 March the party organ *Neues Deutschland* fired a veritable broadside against Brecht and his composer Paul Dessau. In an article headed '*The Trial of Lucullus* – the Failure of an Experiment of the German State Opera' they were taken to task for having produced a work which

does not correspond to reality. The world peace camp with its 800 million people, led by the Soviet Union, is not a court of shades, but has the very real power to subject all war criminals to a very earthbound kind of justice. What at the beginning of Hitler's war might have been understood as the expression of the uncertain political position of an exiled anti-Fascist writer appears in 1951 as a relapse into doubt and weakness the poet should have overcome long ago, particularly when, by the very manner of its staging, it is put forward as an authoritative comment on the current situation.[1]

The composer Paul Dessau was accused of cheap cabaret effects. A Western paper had compared his music to that of Stravinsky. And

Igor Stravinsky, a composer who lives in the U.S.A., is a fanatical destroyer of the European musical tradition. Anyone who follows such an example destroys his own talent. Dessau robs himself of the possibility of arousing the enthusiasm of the masses against a new war of conquest. A music that pours dissonances and intellectualist cleverness over its listeners confirms the reactionary part of the audience in its attitudes, and repels the progressive section. . . .[1]

The fury of this attack against the music of *The Trial of Lucullus* is reminiscent of the Nazis' campaign against 'decadent' music. In a later article in the party organ, directed this time mainly against the management of the State Opera, this point was put even more forcefully:

Take *The Trial of Lucullus* and look at the composition of the orchestra for this work. There are no violins. This most noble of all instruments, which can produce the most beautiful tonal patterns, is missing. Instead there is a piano doctored with drawing-pins and nine different kinds of percussion instruments, among them drums, large and small, and metal sheets that are banged with stones. . . .[2]

Brecht and Dessau were summoned to a discussion with the party leaders, which is reported to have lasted eight hours. When Brecht emerged from this marathon he said, with his usual ambiguity: 'Where else in the world can you find a government that shows such interest in, and pays such attention to, artists?'[3]

But he tackled the re-writing of the text with the good grace of a craftsman who puts in alterations according to the wishes and tastes of his employers. Yet on closer scrutiny these alterations do not amount to much: some passages are omitted for obvious reasons – for example:

---

[1] *Neues Deutschland*, East Berlin, 22.3.1951.
[2] *Neues Deutschland*, East Berlin, quoted in *Deutsche Zeitung*, 10.1.1953.
[3] Ruehle, *Das gefesselte Theater*, p. 243.

> *. . . they say, they are recruiting legionaries*
> *in the taverns by the Tiber, for the war against the West*
> *which is to be conquered. . . .*[1]

Other passages have been inserted to make a distinction between a war of conquest and one of national defence. The shades of Roman soldiers are now made to exclaim:

> *If only we had ceased*
> *serving the aggressor!*
> *If only we had*
> *Joined the defenders!*[2]

The title was changed from the excessively objective *The Trial of Lucullus* to the more clear-cut *Condemnation of Lucullus*. Dessau revised the music and replaced some of the Sprechgesang with arias that could have come from traditional grand opera.

To forestall any criticism that a trial by the shades of the departed was too unrealistic, at the first performance of the revised version on 12 October 1951 an inscription in large letters announced that 'the verdict of the court of the dead differs in no way from that of posterity'.[3]

But in spite of all these precautions the reception of the *Condemnation of Lucullus* by the official party organ *Neues Deutschland* was decidedly cool:

> It must be stated that the new version represents a distinct improvement on the original shape of the work, as a number of weaknesses have been eliminated. Nevertheless it must not be overlooked that it still lacks the real dramatic tension that would compel the spectator to participate and take sides. This is due to the fact that the defeat and annihilation of the conqueror takes place not in living reality, not as part of the real struggle of the progressive forces of the nations against their bloodsuckers but, as it were, posthumously, in the kingdom of the dead. . . . This brings the whole conception dangerously near to symbolism. . . .[4]

The music too, in spite of Dessau's changes, received a severe rebuke. After a few performances the *Condemnation of Lucullus* also

---

[1] Brecht, *Das Verhoer des Lukullus*, Scene 12, *Versuche 11*, p. 150.
[2] ibid., p. 159.   [3] *National Zeitung*, East Berlin, 19.10.1951.
[4] *Neues Deutschland*, East Berlin, 19.10.1951.

disappeared from the stage of the State Opera. It reappeared in the East German repertoire only after Brecht's death.

Shortly after the failure of the revised version to win the favour of the East German authorities, Brecht gave permission for *Lucullus* to be performed in Western Germany: in the original unrevised version and under its original title: *The Trial of Lucullus*! And at the same time he published the text of the opera in the eleventh issue of his *Versuche* – also in the original form, with the alterations attached as an appendix.

Friends who met Brecht at the time of the controversy about *Lucullus* unanimously report that he took to it like a duck to water and seemed to enjoy it all tremendously. He cheerfully entered into the intentions of the authorities, gladly admitted his political mistakes – and yet, at the same time, he did not make any really important changes, certainly none that altered the character of the work as a whole. The essential features that had been singled out as formalistic remained intact. The decision to publish both versions, and the permission to perform the original version in Western Germany, show Brecht's tactics: cheerful compliance, even subservience, in his dealings with the authorities on the one hand, stubborn persistence in his own essential convictions on the other.

There is a passage in *The Life of Galileo* that throws a good deal of light on Brecht's attitude in these matters: one of his friends is horrified by the grovelling tone of the letter in which Galileo solicits the favours of the Medici. Galileo replies:

> You think my letter too subservient? I ask myself: is it subservient *enough*? Not too formal, as though I lacked genuine devotion? . . . A man like me can get into a moderately dignified position only by crawling on his belly. And you know I despise people whose brains are unable to fill their stomachs.[1]

To make up for *Lucullus* and to prove their usefulness to the régime, Brecht and Dessau followed it up by producing one of the most blatant pieces of propaganda hack-work of their careers. It is a choral cantata *Herrnburger Bericht* (*Report on Herrnburg*), written for performance by youth groups during the East German World Youth Festival in the summer of 1951. The theme is an incident from the previous year, when West German police had tried to stop a large

[1] Brecht, *Leben des Galilei, Stuecke VIII*, pp. 53–4.

contingent of Western Communist youths from recrossing the zonal frontier in force. Dessau, who had been accused of failing to write music of propaganda value, produced a pastiche of folk-song to the accompaniment of such recognized popular instruments as accordions, guitars, mandolines, etc., and Brecht manfully tried to express politically acceptable sentiments.

> . . . Adenauer, Adenauer, show us your hand
> For thirty pieces of silver you sell our land,[1]

is a fair sample of the studied banality of this verse, which almost makes it appear intentional, as if designed to expose its absurdity. Yet Brecht no doubt meant it seriously enough. He was merely too good a poet to be able to write such stuff to order.

It is significant that Herrnburger Bericht was never published in its entirety by Brecht in the issues of his Versuche which appeared at regular intervals till he died, and that he did not include it in the collected edition of his plays or any of the various anthologies of his poetry published in his lifetime. Nor has Dessau published any of the 'Herrnburg' songs in his volume of Brecht songs, issued in 1957.[2] Although Herrnburger Bericht is still in print in East Germany, the publishers declare that it is not for export.

On the other hand, it was certainly for his Herrnburger Bericht rather than for The Trial of Lucullus that Brecht received the National Prize for Literature, First Class, from the East German Government in 1951.

But the fact that he was a national laureate and a member of the Academy of Arts did not exempt Brecht from further and even more serious attack. This was the last phase of Stalin's reign, a time of trials, purges, and terror. In the cultural field it was the period of the campaign against 'cosmopolitanism'. In East Germany this coincided with a return to violent Chauvinism, partly to win over the masses who were still largely conditioned by National Socialism, partly to lend weight to the propaganda line that East Germany represented the true spirit of the nation. Brecht had always been nauseated by German Chauvinism. He disliked the school-book view of the German classics. No wonder that he fell foul of the party line.

[1] Brecht and Dessau, 'Herrnburger Bericht', Neues Deutschland, East Berlin, 22.7.1951.
[2] Brecht and Dessau, Lieder und Gesaenge, East Berlin, 1957.

In Brecht's view the German people had to make a fresh start and to cut themselves loose from much of their tradition. He began to revive some of the classical plays of the German repertory with a view of showing the values they represented in a critical light, and of drawing the German public's attention to the moral and material squalor of their own past – *deutsche Misere* (German miserableness). Already in 1950 he had turned an eighteenth-century play *Der Hofmeister* (*The Private Tutor*) by J. M. R. Lenz into a vitriolic attack against the subservience of German intellectuals and schoolmasters to the whims of the rich and powerful: the hero of the play, Laeuffer, finds that his sexual instinct interferes with the performance of his duties as a private tutor, so he castrates himself to show his willingness to serve his master. The régime accepted this performance, one of the most brilliant ever put on by the Berliner Ensemble, with relatively good grace. The mad genius, Lenz, after all, had never been an acknowledged German classic. But when, in the following year, Kleist's *Zerbrochener Krug* (*The Broken Jug*) was put on to display the corruption and hypocrisy of rural life and the administration of justice in eighteenth-century Germany, this was considered to go too far: the honour of the nation was being dragged in the mud. And when Brecht went a step further by producing Goethe's *Faust* in its original form (*Urfaust*) the storm broke. *Neues Deutschland* attacked Brecht's young pupil Egon Monk, who had directed the play, for following in the footsteps of his master:

> The producer Monk copied models we have already encountered in *The Private Tutor* and *The Broken Jug*. They too were fatalistic and pessimistic pictures of static conditions; they had only one hero: 'German miserableness'. This expresses an attitude – an attitude in fact directed against Germany's cultural heritage, against Germany's national culture.[1]

What particularly shocked the national feelings of *Neues Deutschland* was the scene in Auerbach's cellar, in which the drunken students had been made to bawl out some German folk-songs.

> Never before have we seen a similar mockery of German folk-song on our stage! . . . Abandon your forced primitivism, your artistic economy of means, be not afraid to say yes to the best artistic products of our past and you will produce wonderful, great theatre.

[1] 'Weitere Bemerkungen zum Faust-Problem', *Neues Deutschland*, East Berlin, 27.5.53.

We feel we must say that the young members of the Berliner Ensemble, many of whom are very talented, are being led into a wrong direction by the methods and principles applied in the adaptation of the classics by Bertolt Brecht, the artistic director of the Ensemble.[1]

Such an attack was a serious threat not only to Brecht but to the continued existence of the Berliner Ensemble. It coincided with a second and perhaps even more serious threat: the campaign to make Stanislavsky's method the only style of acting permitted in East Germany.

In April 1953 a Stanislavsky Conference was held in East Berlin. Actors and producers from all over Eastern Germany were lectured on the absolute necessity to follow the Soviet style: 'The Soviet theatre is the most highly developed form of theatre in history,' said *Neues Deutschland* in an article on the conference, and went on:

> We are compelled to state here that the reprehensible under-estimation of the significance of the Stanislavsky method for the development of a German national theatre is the main reason why the fight against formalism and cosmopolitanism on the stage has not yet reached that sharpness of principle which alone can guarantee a decisive breakthrough towards socialist realism in our theatre.[2]

And if there was still any doubt against whom this was directed, the following passage removed it:

> Are there not – and we all know it, above all in our capital city – performances in which admittedly 'great theatre' is produced under the direction of great artists, but in which nevertheless formalism and its twin brother schematism look out from every nook and cranny, starting from the choice of plays, right down to the adaptation, the basic production idea, the production itself, the décor, and the method of acting?[2]

Helene Weigel tried to parry the blow by declaring in the course of the conference debates that there *were* some things in common between the Brechtian theatre and the Stanislavsky method: accuracy of observation, ensemble acting, truthfulness, naturalness, etc. But the party

[1] ibid.
[2] 'Fuer den Sieg des sozialistischen Realismus auf der Buehne', *Neues Deutschland*, East Berlin, 17.4.1953.

was far too acutely aware of the real situation to be taken in. *Neues Deutschland* replied:

> . . . Helene Weigel . . . may have been right in so far as there is always something of Stanislavsky anywhere in the theatre where work is done conscientiously, with artistic ability and craftsmanship, and on the basis of socialist convictions. . . . But in so far as the Berliner Ensemble tries to put into practice Brecht's theoretical views embodied in *Kleines Organon fuer das Theater* and his other writings, it is undeniably in opposition to everything the name Stanislavsky stands for. The two leaders of the Ensemble must surely be the last people to hide their heads in the sand when faced with these facts.[1]

Such language could not be ignored. Brecht promptly announced that he had already begun to study Stanislavsky. And Western newspapers were already speculating on the imminent demise of the Berliner Ensemble. Their prophecies proved wrong – the party critics themselves had been overtaken by the events. They believed that they were still following the party line. But the party line had already changed. For in the meantime Stalin had died and the thaw had set in.

Brecht's reaction to the death of Stalin was in character. While the official court poet, Johannes R. Becher, published a poem in which Stalin, now an immortal among immortals, was shown sitting on a bench with Lenin and Thaelmann listening to accordion music, and stalking through the picture gallery of Dresden with the great paintings bowing in reverence before him, and while most of the other members of the German Academy of Art indulged in similarly fulsome paeans of praise and gratitude, Brecht's contribution was strictly in prose:

> The oppressed of all five continents, those who have already freed themselves, and all those who fight for world peace, must have felt their heart-beats stop when they heard that Stalin was dead. He was the embodiment of their hopes. But the spiritual and material weapons he made exist, and so does the doctrine to make new ones.[2]

To a casual reader this may appear wholly in praise of Stalin. But on more careful examination it will be noticed that the statement

---

[1] *Neues Deutschland*, East Berlin, quoted in *Berliner Stimme*, 6.6.1953.
[2] *Sinn und Form*, 1953 II, p. 9.

confines itself severely to fact. It does not even say *why* the heart-beats of the millions stopped. To say that Stalin was the embodiment of hopes is an equally factual, and ambiguous, statement, and the last sentence openly stresses the need to develop the Marxist doctrine beyond Stalin. Once again Brecht proved his shrewdness in these matters. When the cult of Stalin was denounced his colleagues had to eat their words. The party pundits who had questioned Brecht's soundness as a Marxist were embarrassed, or in trouble. But he had struck a note that was exactly right.

Stalin's death threw the party authorities in Eastern Germany into confusion and disarray. While the attacks on cosmopolitanism and anti-Stanislavskians continued, some concessions were made to the masses who had become restive. On the 17 June 1953 the people of Eastern Germany rose in open revolt. For a few hours the régime lost control. Then Soviet tanks restored order.

On the 21 June the party organ *Neues Deutschland* published the following brief item of news:

> National Prize Laureate Bertolt Brecht has sent the General Secretary of the Central Committee of the Socialist Unity Party, Walter Ulbricht, a letter, in which he declared: 'I feel the need to express to you at this moment my attachment to the Socialist Unity Party. Yours, Bertolt Brecht.'

This piece of news was immediately picked up in Western Germany, where it aroused a storm of indignation. Many who greatly admired Brecht as one of the outstanding poets of the nation were rightly outraged at seeing Brecht so brazenly support a régime that had called out Soviet tanks to shoot down unarmed workers demonstrating against intolerable living conditions. His message seemed to be couched in such unequivocal terms that there could be no doubt about the meaning of this 'telegram', as it soon came to be called. Brecht had clearly lost the claim to be considered as anything but an obedient, unthinking follower of the masters who paid for his services by providing him with a theatre and a life of luxury, while the workers starved.

This indignation in Western Germany was no doubt justified. For once Brecht had been too clever. He still believed in the Marxist doctrine, he still believed that it could be put into practice in East Germany. He had thought he could use the opportunity for putting forward his criticisms of the methods of the régime in a carefully balanced letter. But, as the Swiss correspondent Gody Suter later reported,

> of that whole long clever piece of writing only the one sentence, which had been of no importance to Brecht, remained. The red pencil of the party line had destroyed his cunning design and mercilessly exposed the poet, and turned him, in the eyes of the West, into a loyal henchman of the executioners. His independent position, the platform of a kind of 'inner opposition', was suddenly revealed as a grotesque illusion; a well-aimed blow by the party's paw had smashed the reputation Brecht had built up for himself in long, patient efforts. It was the only time that I saw him helpless, almost small: when he eagerly pulled the tattered original of that letter, that he had obviously shown to many people, from his pocket.[1]

There can be no doubt that this version of the incident is correct. If any proof were needed it is furnished by an official East German publication. The organ of the German Academy of Arts, the periodical *Sinn und Form*, published a voluminous commemorative number after Brecht's death. This contains an excellent bibliography of Brecht's writings, compiled by Mr Walter Nubel of New York, but with the obvious co-operation of Brecht's own circle. This bibliography, which lists even the minutest contributions by Brecht to newspapers and periodicals, enters the famous message to Ulbricht, under number C.37c, as follows:

> (Bertolt Brecht to Walter Ulbricht.) *Neues Deutschland* (Berlin), No. 143, 21 June 1953. (On the occasion of the Berlin riots of 17 June 1953. *Final sentence of a letter*.)[2]

This, however discreetly it may be done, clearly puts it on record that the party distorted, and thereby virtually forged, the message of loyalty to Ulbricht which earned Brecht the detestation of many of his erstwhile admirers.

On 23 June 1953, two days after the publication of the truncated letter, another declaration by Brecht appeared in *Neues Deutschland*:

---

[1] Gody Suter, 'Brecht', *Tagesanzeiger*, Zurich, 1.9.1956.
[2] *Sinn und Form*, Second Special Brecht Issue, 1957, p. 560.

On the morning of June 17, when it became clear that the workers' demonstrations were being misused for warlike purposes, I expressed my attachment to the Socialist Unity Party. Now I hope that the provocateurs will be isolated and their network of communication destroyed, but that *the workers who demonstrated from justified discontent*, will not be put on the same level with the provocateurs, so as not to inhibit the very necessary exchange of views on the *mistakes which have been made on all sides*, from the very outset. (My italics, M.E.)

It is as though Brecht had demanded that his views which had been censored on 21 June should after all be published.

The commemorative issue of *Sinn und Form* contains other unmistakable indications of Brecht's attitude after the 17 June. It publishes a number of interviews with stagehands and technicians of the Berliner Ensemble who describe their experiences with Brecht. One of them is quoted as saying:

After the 17 June we had three workers' meetings. I put forward the view that many party officials had shown little interest in the needs and worries of the workers. I also said that the technicians had too little opportunity to qualify. . . . Afterwards (Brecht) firmly shook my hand and told me that what I had said had been particularly good; that I should have said it much sooner; and that one could not say these things too often.[1]

Even more revealing of Brecht's state of mind after the 17 June 1953 is a group of his poems dating from that period, also published posthumously in the special issue of *Sinn und Form*. One of these, headed 'Evil Morning', shows a state of deep malaise. The world looks stale and joyless. And why?

> *Last night I dreamed I saw fingers pointing at me*
> *As at a leper. They were work-gnarled and*
> *They were broken.*
> *'You don't know!' I cried*
> *Guiltily.*[2]

Another poem by Brecht which came to light after his death and which, though not included in any authorized publication of his works,

[1] '13 Buehnentechniker erzaehlen', ibid., p. 472.
[2] *Unwissende! schrie ich Schuldbewusst.* Brecht, 'Boeser Morgen', ibid., p. 341.

bears the marks of authenticity – Brecht's own incisive style and brand of wit – openly attacks the official interpretation of the June rising. The poem is called *The Solution*:

> *After the rising of the 17th June*
> *The Secretary of the Writers' Union*
> *Had leaflets distributed in the Stalinallee*
> *In which you could read that the People*
> *Had lost the Government's confidence*
> *Which it could only regain*
> *By redoubled efforts. Would it in that case*
> *Not be simpler if the Government*
> *Dissolved the People*
> *And elected another ?*[1]

The 17 June had revealed the depth of the hatred the masses felt for the régime. It left the party deeply shaken. Mistakes had to be admitted. And so the way was open for some freer speaking and criticism.

For Brecht this was an opportunity for putting forward some of the suggestions that had no doubt been contained in the censored letter to Ulbricht. The main target for his attack was the Staatliche Kunstkommission (State Commission for the Arts), the body that had been mainly responsible for the campaign against the Berliner Ensemble.

On 30 June the German Academy of Arts, of which Brecht was one of the most active members, passed a resolution containing a number of sharp criticisms of past cultural policy and putting forward some bold demands:

The artist's responsibility before his public must be restored. The artistic directors of theatres must be able to exercise responsibility for the choice of their repertoire, publishers for the literary output of their authors, juries of artists for exhibitions, etc. State organs should help the arts in every imaginable way, but refrain from administrative interference in matters of artistic production and style. Criticism should be left to the public.[2]

This amounts to a plea for the re-establishment of freedom of artistic expression. Brecht certainly played an important part in drafting this

[1] Brecht, *Gesammelte Werke*, vol. 10, p. 1009/10.

[2] 'Mitteilungen der Deutschen Akademie der Künste' in *Sinn und Form*, 1953/III–IV, p. 256.

resolution: a few days later he published a satirical poem which openly attacked the members of the State Commission for the Arts, who had attended a session of the Academy where they had practised the Communist ritual of self-criticism by vaguely admitting that they had made some mistakes:

> . . . *But when asked:*
> *'What mistakes?' somehow they could not remember*
> *Any particular mistakes, hard as they tried. Anything*
> *That was brought forward, had*
> *Not in fact been a mistake, for the commission*
> *Had, after all, suppressed only worthless things, and even these*
> *Not precisely suppressed, but only not fostered. . . .*[1]

A few days later the same newspaper printed a second poem of Brecht's, similar in style, which took the 'Office for Literature' to task for refusing paper for original works:

> *Welcome*
> *Are only works with ideas*
> *The 'Office for Literature' knows from the newspapers.*[2]

That these poems were published showed that the Government was about to jettison the discredited State Commission for the Arts. On 12 August the party's own organ *Neues Deutschland* published a contribution by Brecht which was even more outspokenly critical:

> . . . it cannot be denied that many of our artists were in many essential points opposed to our cultural policy. . . . I see the reason for this in that a great ideology was not put before the artists as a tempting offering, but forced on them like sour beer. The unfortunate ways of the commissions, their dictates, with their poverty of argument, their inartistic administrative measures, their 'vulgar-Marxist' language, repelled the artists (even the Marxists among them). . . . No new state can be built up without confidence in the future . . . but facile optimism is dangerous. . . . Prettification and complacency are not only the worst enemies of the beautiful, but also of political reason. . . . Art must strive to be widely understood. But society for its part must raise the level of the appreciation of

[1] Brecht, 'Nicht feststellbare Fehler der Kunstkommission', *Berliner Zeitung*, East Berlin, 11.7.1953.

[2] Brecht, 'Das Amt fuer Literatur', *Berliner Zeitung*, East Berlin, 15.7.1953.

the arts by an educational effort. The requirements of the population must be met – but in opposition to the demand for *Kitsch*. From the point of view of the administration and to suit the requirements of the officials available to it, it may be simpler to work out certain schematic patterns for works of art. Then the artists 'only' will have to put their (or the administration's?) thoughts into the required form and everything will be 'in order'. But the cry for living art will then be a cry for living things to fill coffins. Art has its own order.[1]

This was bold speaking and a passionate plea in Brecht's own cause. The 17 June had so deeply shaken the party that free speaking had again become possible for a time – and up to a point. Beyond that point irony was still necessary:

We cannot expect to reach the political level of the Soviet Union within a few years, however much its example mav help us. But taking our bearings from these models would be fruitless if we did not succeed in modifying them to correspond to our own specific conditions. We have, to put it bluntly, less of the new, more of the old. . . .[2]

And therefore, Brecht argued, there was a need to attack the wrong conceptions of the past – room for a general onslaught on the *deutsche Misere*:

Eager to turn to the future, we have too soon turned our backs on our immediate past. But the future will depend on our liquidating the past. . . . Our socialist realism must at the same time be a critical realism.[2]

A number of East Germany's intellectuals joined in this attack on the State Commission for the Arts. Foremost among them was Wolfgang Harich, one of the country's leading literary critics, and Professor of Marxist philosophy at East Berlin University. The Government yielded; the commission was dissolved and replaced at the beginning of 1954 by a newly formed Ministry of Culture, headed by Johannes R. Becher, the former Expressionist poet who had turned himself into a mass-producer of pastiche political folk-songs of

[1] Brecht, 'Kulturpolitik und Akademie der Kuenste', *Neues Deutschland*, East Berlin, 12.8.1953.
[2] ibid.

174

incredible banality. The Berliner Ensemble could move into its own house, the rebuilt Theater am Schiffbauerdamm.

In spite of his violent feelings about the pettiness and stupidity of the party's cultural bureaucrats, Brecht remained convinced that in theory there was no contradiction between the dictatorship of the proletariat and artistic freedom – at least for Marxist artists of his own stamp.

When Western newspapers gleefully reported his outbursts against the State Commission for the Arts he retorted – in a poem dated 1953 but not published during his lifetime –

> *Even the narrowest minds*
> *That harbour peace,*
> *Are more welcome to the arts than those friends of art*
> *Who are also friends of the art of war.*[1]

For Brecht the Eastern camp was the camp of peace. Like many other German intellectuals who had suffered at the hands of the Nazis Brecht had little faith in a genuine regeneration of the German people or in the creation of a German democracy. That is why he supported the ruthless dictatorship in the Soviet zone.

> For democracy you need democrats [he told one of his friends]; you can't simply decree or order democracy. . . . In the Kaiser's Germany the democrats sat at the bottom and the authoritarians on top. We have turned the whole structure upside down. Now the democrats sit on top, and the lower down you go the more authoritarian becomes the administration.[2]

In other words, in the Soviet zone a handful of democrats (i.e. Communists) had to rule with an iron hand a vast mass of Nazis, to which even the lower echelons of the administration belonged. The shortcomings of the régime could be explained by the presence of Nazis, and the authoritarian spirit, everywhere. In Western Germany, on the other hand, the mass of the people *did* have real freedom to choose their leaders, and Brecht was certain that for that reason the Nazi elements *must* be on top in the West, that freedom and democracy

---

[1] Brecht, 'Nicht so gemeint', *Sinn und Form*, Second Special Brecht Issue, 1957, p. 342.

[2] Karl Kleinschmidt, 'Wir sind der Mensch von Sezuan', *Neue Zeit*, East Berlin, 19.8.1956.

could only mean freedom for the militarists there. When, after the Korean war and the creation of an East German army, West Germany also prepared herself to rearm, his worst fears seemed confirmed: he worked indefatigably against West German rearmament and sent appeals to theatre people in the West and to the West German Parliament, made eloquent speeches at peace congresses and meetings, and argued heatedly with Western friends.

For this activity he was awarded the Stalin Peace Prize towards the end of 1954. In May 1955 he journeyed to Moscow to receive it in the Sverdlov Hall of the Kremlin. He returned – and deposited a large proportion of his 160,000 roubles of prize-money in his Swiss bank account, to the undisguised dismay and fury of the East German party stalwarts.

The abolition of the State Commission for the Arts may have eased the situation for Brecht and his theatre, but in essentials it changed little. The great success of the Berliner Ensemble at the Paris Festival of 1954 and the growing interest in the Brechtian theatre which it engendered throughout Western Europe certainly put its future out of danger: it had become too obvious a propaganda asset and any drastic action against it would have provoked too much adverse publicity. So the Berliner Ensemble was left in relative peace and freedom: Brecht continued to produce his old plays, with an occasional Soviet or Chinese Communist play thrown in, as well as from time to time a local party product. In January 1955, for example, the Berliner Ensemble produced a play by Johannes R. Becher, the new Minister for Culture, *Winterschlacht* (*Winter Battle*), a feeble attempt at putting the Hamlet theme into the setting of Hitler's Russian campaign. But the performance had bad notices in the party press: the hero had not been shown in a positive enough light. 'We have been reproached because young Hoerder was much more radiant in other theatres.'[1] Sometimes the official party organ *Neues Deutschland* ignored first nights of the Berliner Ensemble altogether, notably that of *The Caucasian Chalk Circle*. And Brecht's plays were not given a very good showing by the other theatres of the Soviet zone. At the Fourth East German Writers' Congress in January 1956, Brecht rather bitterly remarked: 'The theatres of the German Democratic

[1] Brecht, 'Einige Irrtuemer ueber die Spielweise des Berliner Ensembles', *Sinn und Form*, Second Special Brecht Issue, 1957, p. 253.

Republic are – regrettably from my point of view – among the few theatres in Europe that do not perform my plays.'[1]

And Brecht was still critical of the continued bureaucratic supervision of literary work:

> Young Dramaturgen (literary editors) of the Berliner Ensemble have adapted plays for amateurs. To make these plays available to amateur groups they must be published. But they cannot be published because the Office for Literature does not grant the financial aid required. This shows an astonishing lack of political instinct – I am not even speaking of artistic instinct. It is a scandal – among others.[2]

In the same speech Brecht returned to the general lack of initiative shown in the Soviet zone:

> You cannot have your revolutions made by ministries alone. This is a special feature of the *deutsche Misere* that we still have with us: that people are always looking at others. . . .[3]

By the time Brecht made this speech he had grown visibly weary – weary not only of the constant struggle against bureaucrats like those who tried to prevent the publication of his volume of anti-war photographs and quatrains *Kriegsfibel* on the grounds that it was 'too pacifist',[4] but more and more critical also of the ruthless oppression of the common people by the Government of the German Democratic Republic. He is known to have been bitterly critical of the administration of justice by the brutal and unsavoury woman minister, Hilde Benjamin, that *tricoteuse* of German Communism. He was equally violently opposed to the whole apparatus of secret police. informers, and concentration camps represented by the State Security Service (SSD), the Communist Gestapo. He particularly hated the then deputy head of this organization, Mielke (who has since become Minister of State Security).[5]

But in spite of his dislike for the terror and oppression and the constant arbitrariness of a petty bureaucracy, Brecht remained a

---

[1] Brecht, 'Ausfuehrungen vor der Sektion Dramatik', 12.1.1956; *Beitraege zur Gegenwartsliteratur*, East Berlin, January 1956, p. 153.

[2] ibid., pp. 153–4. [3] ibid.

[4] 'Brecht beinahe verboten', *Frankfurter Allgemeine Zeitung*, 19.11.1955.

[5] This account of Brecht's attitude is mainly based on information contained in a letter from Professor Alfred Kantorowicz to the author.

Marxist to the end. His touching, almost religious, faith in the truth of the Marxist theory sustained in him the hope, however diminishing a hope this became in the last months of his life after Khrushchev's denunciation of Stalin, that the terrible reality of Communist practice would in the end be superseded by a society based on Confucian friendliness and courtesy.

In conversations with his more intimate friends on the evils of the Eastern and the Western type of society, Brecht used to illustrate his view by a parable: A doctor in a hospital is faced with two patients equally horribly afflicted with venereal disease, equally repulsive from a moral point of view: an old lecher and a pregnant prostitute. If he has only enough penicillin to save one of these two patients, will he not *have* to save the woman, because there still might be a chance that she would give birth to a healthy child? In the same way, Brecht argued, the rotten Ulbricht régime must be regarded as possibly a transition to better things and must therefore be supported. At least this was a régime paying lip-service to the idea that society must be changed. . . . That was the hope to which he clung.

Wolfgang Harich, the brilliant young Marxist philosopher who had been Brecht's ally in the fight against the party's culture bureaucrats, categorically stated – in his manifesto against Ulbricht which later led to his being sentenced to ten years' penal servitude – that Brecht shared his opposition to the régime:

> Bertolt Brecht sympathized with our group up to the time of his death, and saw in it the healthy forces of our party. In our frequent discussions with Bertolt Brecht we could see how bitterly he felt about the existing conditions in the GDR.[1]

From all we know it is certain that this claim is correct. Brecht agreed with Harich's attitude to Marxism and the party:

> We do not intend to break with the Communist party. We don't want to become renegades like, for example, the ex-Communist Koestler. We don't want to break with Marxism-Leninism, but we want to free it from Stalinism and dogmatism and to bring it back to its humanist and undogmatic way of thinking. . . .[1]

Harich's group was ruthlessly dealt with after the Hungarian Revolution of October 1956. Would Brecht have been among those who were

[1] Harich's Manifesto quoted by *Frankfurter Allgemeine Zeitung*, 21.3.1957.

arrested and tried, like Harich, and among whom there were many of his pupils and friends? Probably not. He was far too cautious and unheroic to have left any clear evidence of his being implicated with such foolhardy young people. But he escaped the terrible moral dilemma the events in Hungary would have presented to him – a feeling of guilt far deeper than that engendered by the East German rising of 1953, which had caused him such guilty dreams. For with his usual uncanny sense of timing Brecht died ten weeks before the outbreak of the Hungarian revolution.

Brecht's attitude to the problem of freedom in a Communist society coincided with the views of the Communist intellectuals who supported Gomulka in Poland and those who belonged to the Petoefi circle in Hungary. In the last months of his life Brecht was working on a translation of *Poem for Adults* by the Polish poet Adam Wazyk – a violent attack on the inhumanity of the Stalinist brand of Communism. George Lukács, the great Hungarian Marxist literary critic and philosopher, who played an important part in the Hungarian revolution, was one of the main speakers at the memorial meeting in the Schiffbauerdamm theatre after Brecht's death. And among the obituary tributes published by *Neues Deutschland* we find one from another friend of his, the Hungarian playwright Gyula Hay, one of the leaders of the Hungarian revolutionary intellectuals, whose message already foreshadowed the coming events:

> We Hungarian writers have in recent times had particular occasion to reflect on how far literary progress can be linked with politics in our daily struggles. In my thoughts I have often turned to Brecht and from his works I have gained the conviction that a writer cannot and must not spare himself, when the truth is at stake; and that eventually the truth will not fail a writer who remains loyal to it. Posterity will learn a very, very great deal from him, more than can even be imagined today.[1]

These words sounded harmless enough in August 1956. In the light of subsequent events their meaning is all too clear.

Brecht's irony and amused contempt for the party apparatus made itself felt even after he was dead. Immediately the news became known, the authorities appointed a funeral committee to prepare for

[1] Julius Hay, 'Es ist unfassbar . . .', *Neues Deutschland*, East Berlin, 18.8.1956.

a sumptuous ceremony from which they might extract the maximum propaganda benefit. But Rudi Engel, the director of the Academy of Arts, produced a letter of Brecht's, dated 15 May 1955, which frustrated these efforts:

> In the event of my death I don't want to be made to lie in state or to be *exhibited* anywhere. No speeches are to be made at my funeral. . . .[1]

But the speeches had to be made. So the party arranged a special memorial meeting at the Schiffbauerdamm theatre for the day after the funeral. There Ulbricht himself, Becher, and many others had their say in spite of Brecht. But Brecht nevertheless had the last word: on the day after the ceremony Karl Kleinschmidt, a Protestant cleric, canon of Schwerin Cathedral – note Brecht's deliberate choice of a clergyman, though a party member – published his reminiscences of his last conversation with Brecht:

> It was a conversation as unsentimental and unpathetic as any I ever had with him and dealt with the obituary I should probably have to write when he died. He regretted, with a smile, that he would be unable to read it and all the other beautiful obituaries, in which posterity would breathe its sigh of relief. . . . 'You at least write a candid obituary!' he said. 'That will make a very original effect among my obituaries. . . . Don't write that you admire me! Write that I was an uncomfortable person, and that I intend to remain so after my death. Even then there are certain possibilities.' These were his last words to me.[1]

Brecht's relations with the Communist party exemplify the dilemma of his generation, the dilemma of so many left-wing intellectuals between the wars. The old social order had collapsed in 1918. Something new, they felt, must be put in its place. The ugliness of the post-war world, in Central Europe at least, drove the seekers for aesthetic and moral beauty into the arms of the left. The weakness and poverty of ideas of the liberal and democratic forces in Germany when faced with the menace of Hitler finally confirmed them in their belief that the Communists were the only positive answer to Fascism. In Brecht's

[1] *Neues Deutschland*, East Berlin, 17.8.1956.

[2] Karl Kleinschmidt, 'Wir sind der Mensch von Sezuan', *Neue Zeit*, East Berlin, 19.8.1956.

case the deeper structure of his complex personality also made it imperative that he should find some positive faith – a positive set of beliefs that would be compatible with his anti-bourgeois, anti-psychological, anti-religious bias, with his need for a rational, scientific explanation of the world. Once Communism had been made to form the hard core around which his personality had crystallized it became impossible to separate the two again.

And so while he was fully and intelligently aware of the excesses of Stalinism – and took good care to remain at a safe distance, well out of reach of the terror machine – he had to cling to the ideal image of Marxism he had built up for himself. The Marxist dialectic, with its comforting doctrine that progress proceeds along zigzag lines and that even errors already contain the seeds of their own abolition, made it easy for him to develop the peculiar split mind of the believer, who perceives the shortcomings of his idol and is yet happily able to ignore them completely.

Nor can it be said that Brecht's experiences in the West during his exile gave him a real chance to change his opinion on the sterility of bourgeois society and its neglect of the artist. His lack of financial or critical success seemed to confirm his most pessimistic view about the philistinism and contempt for values in a commercial society. Of course what he blamed the Western world for was his personal lack of success; but can he be expected to have realized that this was largely due to the language barrier and the strangeness of his views and background in countries with an utterly different tradition?

When the East offered him the most lavish means to put his ideas into practice, to work and to experiment to his heart's content, he accepted – after having made elaborate provision for his personal safety and prepared the avenues of retreat in case of necessity.

By accepting the East German Government's offer he put himself at the disposal of one of the most cruel and heartless régimes in history and must bear his share of responsibility for it. On the other hand, the factual evidence here quoted also shows that he was opposed to many of the least attractive sides of the régime, and that he actively fought it in his own cautious and unheroic way. His dilemma was the dilemma of the Hungarian writers, the Polish intellectuals, and all the other 'liberal' elements within the Communist world. They fight against what they consider to be distortions of the true ideal of social justice by petty bureaucrats, cancerous growths of the apparatus of power that should have withered away; and they cannot believe that such distortions should not be quite easily corrected. But in fact these features of Communism are not surface blemishes but its essence – and the party itself proclaims them as such by ruthlessly liquidating the elements that have dared to suggest their removal. It is the dilemma of Dostoyevsky's parable about the Grand Inquisitor transferred into the setting of another and even more implacable orthodoxy. That Brecht was fully conscious of this problem is shown by his remark, also quoted by Kleinschmidt in his obituary, about the consequences of the Twentieth Party Congress. He saw in it 'the first step towards a regeneration of Marxism from its total *ideologization* towards total *secularization*', which, to translate it from the purposely esoteric jargon into plain language, means that Marxism must lose its character as a totalitarian orthodoxy and should return to being a practical and empirical way of social change. This view is identical with that we have quoted from Harich's oppositional manifesto, the view which emerges from the writings and speeches of the Polish intellectuals of *Po Prostu* or those of the doomed Hungarian writers. Events have shown again and again that such hopes are of necessity an illusion. But for men as deeply committed with their whole personalities, with their whole past work and achievement, to the Marxist creed, to have realized that this is so would have amounted to spiritual and physical suicide.

It is nevertheless remarkable how far Brecht succeeded in keeping the dead hand of orthodoxy and Marxist conformism out of his work. Whenever he failed to do it, he failed as a writer – not only in propaganda hack-work he undertook with his tongue in his cheek, but also in more serious experiments of putting Marxism to work as an instrument for the understanding of the real world. In a play which has as many fine passages as *The Roundheads and the Peakheads* the Marxist explanation of Hitler's racial policies fails so lamentably that the whole play is invalidated: the racial theory is explained as a mere trick to deceive the common people, and the rich peakheads in the end fraternize with the rich roundheads. In other words, if this Marxist interpretation of Nazi policy had been correct, the rich Jews would have been spared by Hitler and would in the end have emerged as having been on his side all the time! In *Fears and Miseries of the Third Reich* the Marxist interpretation also completely vitiates Brecht's efforts at explaining a totalitarian system. His main charge against Nazism, apart from its military preparations, was that it created hunger and delivered the workers into the hands of the capitalists. In fact, the main strength of Nazism was that it gave the German people a semblance of prosperity in exchange for the loss of its liberties. And in this Hitler's totalitarianism was closely akin to that of the Communists. But in his greatest plays Brecht avoids these pitfalls. And when he deals with human problems on the basis of his marvellously keen eye for human nature and human behaviour the sociological bias of his Marxist standpoint only adds spice and interest. The real content of these plays, moreover, does not spring from the conscious level but from the creative subconscious of a great poet. These great plays may fail as Communist propaganda. They succeed as plays and poetry.

From its own point of view therefore the party cannot be blamed for treating Brecht's work with considerable reserve and caution. Brecht believed himself a better Marxist than the party. But the party had very good reasons to think differently.

Chapter VIII

THE COMMUNISTS AND BRECHT

> On est contre les formalistes! Moi, je suis aussi
> contre les formalistes – mais ils ne sont pas les
> mêmes.
> PICASSO[1]

> To live in a country without a sense of humour is
> unbearable; but it is even more unbearable in a
> country where you need a sense of humour.
> BRECHT[2]

In the summer of 1956, shortly before Brecht died, the Berliner
Ensemble received an invitation to give a number of performances in
the Soviet Union.

One of Brecht's Russian acquaintances, Joseph Yuzovski, later
described how the same post that brought him Brecht's letter with
this news also brought the announcement of his death. Brecht's letter,
Yuzovski says, expressed his gratification that 'after his plays had
passed across the stages of the world and had aroused such a lively
response from millions of spectators and so much passionate discussion
among theatre people, they were *at last* coming to Moscow. . . '.[3]

But Yuzovski also detected another note in Brecht's letter:

> . . . something that I had already felt in the spring of this year (1956)
> when I received a crate from Berlin, filled with his plays, books and
> other literature, together with a letter from him, asking me to
> acquaint myself with all this – as it was so little known here in
> Moscow. I understood the hint, the hidden allusion – with its
> amused kind of puzzlement that was without any reproach, but
> contained a certain bitterness nevertheless. And indeed! Do we

[1] Picasso, quoted by Max Frisch, *Tagebuch 1946–1949*, Frankfurt, 1950,
p. 300.
[2] Brecht, 'Fluechtlingsgespraeche: Ueber die Hegelsche Dialektik', *Aufbau*,
February 1958, p. 181.
[3] J. Jusowski, 'Brecht und sein guter Mensch', *Sinn und Form*, Second
Special Brecht Issue, 1957, p. 204.

know Brecht's work in all its variety, do we know the writer, who, without exaggeration, can be called the most significant dramatist of our time? Who of us knows him? Let us be honest – don't we really know him very little?[1]

However false the emphasis of this question may sound with its assumed air of innocence which naïvely seems to suggest that Brecht had been neglected by the Soviet public unaccountably, by some oversight – behind the heavy-handed question there stands a solid fact: until the time of his death Brecht, the most important Communist dramatist, was almost totally unknown in the Soviet Union. As a Soviet periodical put it after Brecht died:

> Brecht's dramatic productions have not been fortunate in the Soviet Union. Not one of his plays has ever been performed, save for a (not very successful) showing of *The Threepenny Opera* at the Kamerny theatre over a quarter of a century ago. It would be wrong to gloss over these facts. . . .[2]

A few of Brecht's more orthodox Communist works had been published in Russian translations and in German in the Soviet Union in the thirties, a few of his poems in praise of the party were known, occasionally his name would be mentioned in the newspapers in connexion with some peace appeal he had signed, but his importance as a literary figure and as an innovator of the theatre was certainly not appreciated, even among experts. Boris Pasternak, the great Russian poet, who was the Soviet Union's leading translator of German literature, once told a West German journalist:

> . . . that Bertolt Brecht had asked him to put into Russian the speech of thanks he made when he came to Moscow to receive his Stalin Prize (in 1955). He had done so without pleasure, and without pleasure had read the volume of Brecht's poetry which the German dramatist had in gratitude sent him. He had little affinity with poets who were above all else political. It was only when Helene Weigel brought her company to Moscow (in 1957) that he realized that he

[1] J. Jusowski, 'Brecht und sein guter Mensch', *Sinn und Form*, Second Special Brecht Issue, 1957, p. 204.

[2] *Inostrannaya Literatura*, Moscow, no. 12, 1956, quoted by Laqueur and Lichtheim, *The Soviet Cultural Scene 1956–57*, New York and London, 1958, p. 61.

had translated the speech of a great poet and that because of the selection made in an anthology published in East Germany, he had nearly missed knowing the work of a great poet.[1]

The then current edition of the *Great Soviet Encyclopaedia*, a monumental publication in fifty-one enormous volumes, mentions Brecht in a short article of only about half a column, 33 lines to be exact. In the first edition, published in 1927, before he had written even *The Threepenny Opera* Brecht had been accorded 34 lines, one line more than in 1951, when he had become one of the world's leading dramatists. This counting of lines is by no means as childish as it must strike Western readers, unacquainted with the rigidly hierarchical ways of Soviet Russia and with the part the *Great Soviet Encyclopaedia* plays in that society as the repository of all officially sanctioned knowledge. When a great man – like the late Lavrenti Beria – falls, subscribers to the encyclopaedia are officially asked to excise the pages devoted to him and to replace them by new matter just come to light on the Bering Sea. In such a work the precise number and order of the adjectives after the name of a politician denotes his exact order of precedence in the ranks of the party – and in the same way the fact that Brecht was only accorded 33 lines as against 77 for a poet like Aragon, or full 112 lines for the East German party's court poet, J. R. Becher, shows how low his stock stood in the Communist world in 1951, when volume six of the *Great Soviet Encyclopaedia* was printed. It is equally significant that the bibliographical note that follows this brief article only mentions one single Soviet study of Brecht – an article on German anti-Fascist writers published in a periodical in 1941.

Why should a Communist of Brecht's eminence be treated in such a way? In his obituary article Brecht's Russian friend Yuzovski also asks this question. He wraps up the answer in an account of a conversation with an eminent Soviet producer, whom he had asked why it was that *he* had never produced any of Brecht's plays. Without waiting for that eminent man's answer, Yuzovski himself anticipated it:

> I know that you will immediately say: the personality cult and its consequences in art! Administrative and bureaucratic tutelage – suppression of initiative – arbitrariness that eventually leads to closed minds.... That is indeed true. But don't you think the time has come when we should not merely talk about this state of affairs but *do*

[1] Gerd Ruge, 'A Visit to Pasternak', *Encounter*, London, March 1958.

something about it? Were not the revivals of *The Optimistic Tragedy* (an *avant-gardist* work by Vishnyevsky) and of *The Bath* (Mayakovsky's bitter satire on the party that had long disappeared from the Soviet stage) great successes after all this time? What would you have risked if you had dared to put on Brecht – which, between ourselves, wouldn't have been such a special risk even much earlier![1]

Whether in 1956, when Stalin was safely dead, Yuzovski thought that putting on a play by Brecht would not have been such a risk after all in Stalin's lifetime matters little. What matters a great deal for the record, however, is the implied admission that in Stalin's time an eminent producer did indeed think that to perform a play by Brecht was such a risk – or that at least he felt no desire whatsoever to put the matter to the test.

There can be no doubt about it: from the early thirties to the time of his death Brecht's work was virtually suppressed in the Soviet Union and the whole Soviet orbit except in the Eastern zone of Germany, where Brecht served his own very special purpose in showing that the rickety régime enjoyed the support of an acknowledged leader of German letters and as an advertisement for the achievements of German Communist culture towards Western Germany. Vast populations in the Communist sphere had to be guarded from contamination by the works of that selfsame great Communist master. For rebels and iconoclasts against the established order of things, like Brecht or Picasso, are considered useful as allies in the task of undermining it in countries where the Communists are in opposition. In the Soviet sphere itself, where the established order of things is a Communist one, such rebels are highly undesirable.

Brecht's conversion to the Communist cause as the embodiment of his hatred of bourgeois society had – ironically enough – taken place at the precise moment when the Communist party in the Soviet Union had begun to jettison the motley crowd of anarchist poets, futurist and abstract painters, and other reformers of the arts or ethics that it had gathered around it in the chaotic wake of the revolution. It was a rude disappointment for many of these intellectuals, not only among artists but also among champions of progressive education,

[1] J. Jusowsky, 'Brecht und sein guter Mensch', *Sinn und Form*, Second Special Brecht Issue, 1951, pp. 205–6.

believers in open prisons, and social reformers who preached free love and hundreds of other panaceas and regarded the party as the ideal instrument for the realization of their dreams. By the early thirties the revolution had been consolidated. The party began to rediscover the usefulness of the traditional supports of any established power. Gradually epaulettes and dress uniforms for officers were reintroduced, and officers had to be saluted again. Schoolchildren were deprived of the right to vote for the dismissal of unpopular teachers; divorce was made more difficult and free love was frowned upon. And so was experiment and innovation in the arts.

In 1934 Stalin's trusted lieutenant, A. A. Zhdanov, told the First All-Union Congress of Soviet Writers what their duty was. 'Comrade Stalin', he said, 'has called our writers engineers of the human soul.' Like any other technicians they would henceforth have to deliver the products assigned to them in the plan: concrete results in the field of party propaganda. But to write in the true Communist spirit alone was not enough. From now on the writers' work must be understood by all. For the masses know what they like, and they like only what they can recognize. So all art must be true to life – up to a point:

> The truthfulness and historical exactitude of the artistic image must be linked with the task of ideological transformation, of the education of the working people in the spirit of socialism. This method in fiction and literary criticism is what we call the method of socialist realism.[1]

Not realism – *tout court*, but *socialist* realism. The world, if depicted as it really was in the Soviet Union, might well appear too nasty. Therefore it had to be shown not as it was, but as it *ought* to be, and perhaps *would* be one day, when the new society had been successfully established:

> Soviet literature must be able to portray our heroes and to see our tomorrow. This will not be Utopian since our tomorrow is being prepared by planned and conscious work today.[2]

Any work that showed reality in too gloomy a light fell into the sin of 'naturalism'. But even more grievous was the opposite fault: formalism.

---

[1] A. Zhdanov, 'Speech to the First All-Union Congress of Soviet Writers 1934', in Zhdanov, *On Literature, Music and Philosophy*, London, 1950, p. 15.
[2] ibid., p. 16.

Formalism, like Trotskyism, is extremely difficult to define. According to the *Great Soviet Encyclopaedia* it is 'the attribution to form, or formal elements, of self-contained, primary significance to the detriment of content'.[1] Content here obviously means *representational* content, for even the most abstract painting does not entirely divorce form from content: even there the artist is concerned to tell us something – namely what he feels about certain shapes, colours, or textures. The pseudo-philosophical language of the *Great Soviet Encyclopaedia*'s definition of formalism can be reduced to much simpler terms: any work of art that lacks *political* content is condemned as formalist. And so is any work of art that conveys a political content in a stylized form. As one East German Communist newspaper once summed up its whole case against Brecht: Why is it that in his theatre the trees have no leaves? Or as the East German party's top expert on theatre matters put it:

> In (Brecht's) *The Mother* the didactic element becomes an end in itself – and that is formalism. The didactic element must lie in man, in action, in conflict, in everything that man on the stage thinks, and feels, and in the relations of men to reality and of reality to them, in the clash of contradictions and in their solution. These things must contain the didactic element, but it cannot be isolated from them.[2]

So even Brecht's most openly political and propagandist play was condemned as formalist, for the simple reason that it did not obey the crude convention of a purely representational theatre, where all the political propaganda was neatly wrapped up in the plot itself. Brecht detested this kind of theatre and all his life's work was devoted to its destruction. But the party had decided that the only method of acting and production that was truly Marxist was the Stanislavsky method of the Moscow Art Theatre. Brecht's whole theory is based on his conception that the theatre of Stanislavsky, by making the audience identify themselves with the characters, prevents them from seeing the world in a detached, critical spirit and is therefore un-Marxist and reactionary. But the party did not want the audience to be put into a critical frame of mind. It *wanted* them to be hypnotized and made

---

[1] *Bolshaya Sovietskaya Entsiklopediya*, vol. 45, pp. 314–15.
[2] Hans Rodenberg in a speech at the 5th Plenary Session of the Central Committee of the SED quoted by Schumacher, p. 573.

uncritical by having their emotions fully engaged in favour of the positive characters and against the negative ones. Brecht wanted to let them draw their own conclusions from a critical reflection on the play. The party wanted the audience to be left in no doubt as to any conclusion they should draw from what they saw. Brecht believed in irony and parody. The party wanted simplicity – the good characters wholly good, the bad ones wholly bad. But Brecht considered himself a better Marxist than the party officials.

This was a truly tragicomic conflict – a conflict born from the totalitarian fallacy that each political system must have its own philosophy in which every element logically follows from one great central principle: the one Communist creed determining its one Communist art, theatre, style of chess-playing, or gardening, right down to the most trivial activity. As there could only be one correct Communist policy line, there could only be one correct way of painting, theatrical production, or chess-playing. Any other style automatically became treason. On the altars of this fallacy the party sacrificed some of its greatest talents. What good was it to Meyerhold, one of the world's greatest producers, that he was a convinced and active supporter of the Communist party? Stalin had decided that only Stanislavsky's kind of theatre was truly Marxist. When Meyerhold persisted in working in his own style, he was denounced, deprived of his theatre, arrested, and finally disappeared. And he was only one among hundreds of artists who paid with their lives for not conforming to the wishes of the party authorities, while hundreds of others, who were less brave, had to do violence to their talents and inclinations by slavishly following the officially prescribed models.

Brecht had been far too shrewd to put himself into any such situation by accepting a position inside the Soviet Union in the early years of his exile. He knew only too well that he belonged to the same world-wide movement against naturalism in the theatre, as Tairov, Meyerhold, and so many other outstanding Soviet producers. As early as 1907 Meyerhold had advocated a theatre in which the audience 'never forgets for a minute that it is seeing actors who are playing and the actors never forget that an auditorium is before them, a stage beneath them and décor all along the sides',[1] the very principles of Brecht's anti-illusionist theatre. And it was Meyerhold who had

[1] V. Meyerhold in *Vesy*, January 1907, quoted by Gorchakov, *The Theatre in Soviet Russia*, Columbia University Press, 1957, p. 58.

demanded a style of acting without tremolo, tenseness, and emotional-ism and insisted on 'epic' calm, coolness, and ease of delivery[1] long before Brecht formulated the same ideas. And so as long as Meyerhold stood condemned as a formalist and his style was proscribed in the Soviet Union, Brecht's ideas too had to be played down. No wonder the Soviet producers and actors who got to know about them shunned his plays like the plague.

The contradiction between the propaganda requirements of the East German régime in its need to impress the West, and the official attitude of the inner core of the Soviet orbit, produced its own curious result: once Brecht's theatre was established in East Berlin to dazzle Western intellectuals it could not be concealed from visitors from the Communist countries either. The Berliner Ensemble became a point of attraction for visiting Communist intellectuals, and its ideas began to radiate throughout the Communist world.

It is characteristic that the first breach in the virtual ban on the Brechtian theatre throughout the satellite countries occurred in Poland, where Socialist realism with all its crudity and dullness had always been most resented. In 1952 the Berliner Ensemble was invited to perform *The Mother* and *Mother Courage* in a number of Polish cities. Another tour followed in 1954. Some of Brecht's plays were performed in Polish as the thaw gathered momentum after Stalin's death. The post-Stalinist renaissance in the Polish theatre is dated by Polish critics from the first appearance of the Berliner Ensemble in Warsaw.[2] Support for Brecht became synonymous with opposition against the vulgar creed of Socialist Realism. The authorities still uttered warning cries, but they were already tempered by the recognition of *some* merit, as we can see from this official directive to a theatre magazine:

> . . . Brecht does not . . . represent the art of socialist realism and therefore not even a special approach towards it, although in its own peculiar way Brecht's work has enriched and fructified the theatre of socialist realism. . . .[3]

[1] V. Meyerhold, *Teatr*, quoted by Gorchakov (see above), p. 58.
[2] Jerzy Pomianowski, 'Un Théâtre du Renouveau en Pologne', *Les Temps Modernes*, Paris, July 1958.
[3] Official directive to *Pamietnik Teatralny*, published by *Pamietnik Teatralny*, no. 1, 1955, quoted by Wirth, 'Beitrag zur Brecht-Rezeption in Polen', *Theater der Zeit*, East Berlin, December 1956, p. 6.

And the introduction to a Polish edition of some of Brecht's plays still warned the readers:

> In Brecht's theatre very different elements of diverse value are mixed together: here realism exists together with naturalism and both are subject to the influences of expressionism.[1]

Both naturalism and expressionism were still regarded as heinous crimes at that time (1953), but the revolt against the Stalinist categories was already stirring. A Polish Brechtian critic, Andrzej Wirth, later described the feelings of his friends about Brecht and the accepted standards of party aesthetics:

> The falsifiers of socialist realism had canonized a formal pattern that had been created by the bourgeois theatre of the nineteenth century. One need not be surprised that Brecht's art could not be accommodated within this rigid framework. Its formal means suddenly found themselves proscribed. Suitable terms were lacking, and so dreadful epithets had to be applied to it – expressionist, naturalist, symbolist. . . . It is typical that this odd kind of criticism from the left showed complete indifference to the plebeian content of Brecht's work, which one might surely have regarded as the essential element in any progressive play. . . .[2]

Here the Polish Marxist critic has seized the essential weakness of the anti-formalists who were so preoccupied with the question of form – the need for trees to have leaves – that they completely neglected the content, so that in fact the standard-bearers of anti-formalism stood themselves condemned as worshippers of external formal criteria. In the opinion of this Polish follower of Brecht this kind of criticism simply could not appreciate

> . . . the Socratic method which confines itself to the stating of questions, to undermining the established view of the problem and the awakening of creative doubt. This was a reflection of the general dogmatization of intellectual life which reduced the process of learning to a magical attitude, thereby completely frustrating the dialectical process as a genuine exploration of truth. It also showed

[1] Alfred Szczepanski, Introduction to three plays by Brecht, Warsaw, 1953, quoted by Wirth (see above).

[2] Andrzej Wirth, 'Beitrag zur Brecht-Rezeption in Polen', *Theater der Zeit*, East Berlin, December 1956, p. 6.

complete contempt for the public, the people who were seen as mere consumers of ready-made results rather than as participants in a process of discovery. The Brechtian conception of the educational role of art, based as it is on the conviction that a socialist revolution implies the intellectual activization of the masses, could never come to terms with the educational theory of the vulgarists, who never considered the people as worthy intellectual partners. The criticism of the vulgarists merely noticed the 'suspicious' formal aspects and immediately denounced these as having acquired absolute value (of an end in itself) without paying any attention to the function these formal elements had in Brecht's work. The discussion thus circled around the illusory problem, whether a play using expressionist, symbolist, or other means could be socialist. . . .[1]

In spite of the jargon in which all this is wrapped up, it is a devastating attack from the Marxist point of view on the advocates of socialist realism – that is, from that variant of the Marxist point of view which we know to have been Brecht's own. In Poland the revolution of October 1956 meant the collapse of the Stalinist doctrine of art. To many Polish intellectuals Brecht now became a symbol that a true socialist art of a different kind was possible. As Andrzej Wirth put it, in another essay on Brecht written at about the same time:

Today, in view of the crisis through which the art of the falsifiers is passing, Brecht's example assumes universal significance: for this experiment, carried out over many years, has proved the connexion between progressive trends in art and revolutionary ideas. . . .[2]

So in Poland Brecht had become the living proof that Communist art need not necessarily be modelled on Victorian oleographs and melodramas. But then Poland had undergone a second, anti-Stalinist revolution, which may have been cautious in the political field, but swept all before it in the arts and literature. In the Soviet Union the recognition of Brecht came far more slowly and was far more reluctant.

The thaw in the Soviet theatre which had set in gradually even before Stalin died had its ups and downs, advances and retreats: the

[1] Andrzej Wirth, 'Beitrag zur Brecht-Rezeption in Polen', *Theater der Zeit*, East Berlin, December 1956, p. 6.
[2] Andrzej Wirth, 'Ueber die stereometrische Struktur der Brechtschen Stuecke', *Sinn und Form*, Second Special Brecht Issue, 1957, p. 385.

monotonous insistence of the authorities that socialist realism should show only the positive sides of contemporary life had driven all conflict from the stage. Authors were afraid of showing anything in a critical light, lest they be dubbed 'naturalists' or 'bourgeois wreckers'. When this state of affairs led to a virtual boycott of the theatres by the public there were attempts to allow some negative features of Soviet life to be shown. Old satires like Mayakovsky's long banned plays reappeared, some bold new plays castigated the shady sides of Soviet life. But when these were felt to have gone too far their authors were severely taken to task. All these advances and retreats were closely bound up with the struggles for power of the post-Stalin era, the fall of Beria, and the rise of Malenkov, followed by the fall of Malenkov and the rise of Khrushchev. This is not the place to tell that intricate and depressing story. But it is relevant here to show how these developments appeared to Brecht and his theatre, whose future was intimately bound up with their outcome. One of Brecht's most brilliant and loyal young pupils, the producer Manfred Wekwerth (born 1929), whose entire outlook is based on Brecht's teaching, went to Moscow and Leningrad with the Berliner Ensemble in 1957. This is how he described the Soviet theatrical scene in an article published after his return:

Muscovites told us that their theatres had come dangerously close to stagnation around 1953. The repertoire, the style of acting, the lack of topicality had reached a stage where it was sufficient to see one theatre to know what all the others were like. The Moscow Art Theatre had become the only model. Regardless whether a theatre was presenting satire, historical plays, farce, or propaganda, the only standard was that of the great, lonely eminence of the Moscow Art Theatre. Only Obraztsov remained – with his puppets and his own theory. But all this had left the audience out of account. A certain theory about the theatre may have appeared vindicated, but the audience no longer came to the theatres. They often remained half empty, which means a great deal considering the Muscovites' proverbial love of the theatre. The situation changed rapidly towards the end of 1953. Here as in other fields people in Moscow talk about 'before' and 'after'. 'Before' all theatres played exactly like the Moscow Art Theatre – only worse. 'After' the Theatre of Satire developed its own style – within a matter of months. . . .

'After' the lost records of Meyerhold's productions were dug up and edited for study. 'After' Meyerhold was mentioned with Stanislavsky. 'After' the revolutionary discoveries of Tairov, the performances of the classical drama of the revolution (Vishnyevsky's *Optimistic Tragedy* and *First Cavalry Army*, etc.) were studied and used for new productions. 'After' the work of young Eisenstein was again studied. 'After' Okhlopkov repeated his famous production of the thirties, *Aristocrats* by Pogodin. . . .[1]

This description of the Moscow Theatre in 1957, seen through the eyes of one of Brecht's pupils and published in an East German periodical towards the end of 1957, sums up the feelings with which Brecht himself must have regarded the absolute sway of the Stanislavsky style that prevailed from the middle thirties to the middle fifties, and the relief and hope with which he and his followers watched the thaw. But even in 1957 Wekwerth registered his astonishment that Soviet theatre people knew practically nothing about Brecht's ideas.

About our discussions with Moscow theatre people much could be said. They certainly created a most fruitful confusion . . . the Moscow Dramaturgen (literary editors and readers of the theatres) who double as theatre critics heard with astonishment that the 'epic' theatre does not want to abolish the plot in plays. . . .[2]

In other words, the Moscow theatre experts, who had vaguely heard Brecht condemned as a formalist, imagined that in his theatre form and content had been so completely separated that no plot remained.

By the spring of 1957 a number of articles on Brecht had appeared in Soviet newspapers and periodicals, but most of these had been so mealy mouthed and dull that one can hardly blame the literary editors of the Moscow theatres for not having read them very carefully.

The first indication that the thaw which had brought back Mayakovsky's satires, Pogodin's *Aristocrats*, and Bulgakov's *Days of the Turbins*, and had even made it possible to mention Meyerhold again, extended to Brecht, came while he was still alive. In January 1956 the Soviet Union's official monthly of the theatre arts, *Teatr*, published a lengthy article on Brecht by the critic I. Fradkin, who had spent some time in

[1] Manfred Wekwerth, 'Anblick, Einblick, Ausblick. Bemerkungen zum Sowjet-Theater', *Theater der Zeit*, East Berlin, no. 10, 1957, p. 20.
[2] ibid., p. 23.

East Berlin and had come into contact with Brecht and his theatre there. This article is rather dry and tedious, accurate as far as it goes, yet not accurate enough to venture a mention of *Die Massnahme*. Its most interesting feature is the half-hearted account of Brecht's theory of the 'epic' theatre it gives, constantly hedging it round with safeguards that make it quite clear that the author of the article understands these views but does not share them:

> In opposing a theatre which saps the intellect and willpower of the audience, i.e. the contemporary decadent theatre, Brecht resorts to generalizations that go far beyond his own objective. Calling his 'epic' theatre the complete antithesis of the 'Aristotelian' theatre Brecht lays himself open to the reproach that he takes up an unjustifiedly sceptical attitude towards a significant part of the dramatic heritage and stage tradition of the past. On this point Brecht's position is not entirely clear – in any case this is not the essential feature of his theory: Brecht's main concern is with making the theatre a weapon for influencing the masses in a partisan spirit and teaching them ideas of a progressive revolutionary nature. . . .[1]

That is: Brecht is acceptable in so far as he wants to support Communist ideas and attacks the decadent bourgeois theatre – but not inasmuch as he is against the Moscow Art Theatre style of acting and production. In this respect his ideas have no relevance to the Soviet theatre:

> To the reader who knows the history of the Soviet theatre and the productions and discussions of the twenties, it is clear that much in the theoretical ideas of Brecht is not new, and in any case already superseded; much of it has already been tested, some of it accepted, some of it rejected by the experience and practice of the Soviet theatre. . . .[1]

These passages are quoted not so much for their own intrinsic interest, but as examples of the curiously naïve approach dictated to Soviet critics of undoubted intelligence and taste by the fears and taboos that surround them even in periods of thaw. With the utmost caution Fradkin approaches the dreaded centre of the problem, the wholly scholastic and verbal question whether Brecht can be called a realist.

> But is Brecht a realist? In this respect there is some room for doubt. Can a work be realistic in which the action happens among people

[1] I. Fradkin, 'Bertolt Brecht', *Teatr*, Moscow, January 1956.

of two imaginary races in a country not to be found on any map? (*Peakheads and Roundheads.*) Is it in accordance with the laws of realism to present a quarrel between two collective farms, in the course of which, against all the rules of agricultural co-operatives and against existing Soviet legal practice, the dispute is decided with the help of a ballad singer who tells the collective farmers an ancient legend? (In the prologue to *The Caucasian Chalk Circle.*) Can there be a trial of a dead man? (*Lucullus.*) But if these questions are put, what of such stories or plays as *Gulliver, Faust*, etc. . . .?[1]

And with the help of these examples of literature that was not banned in the Soviet Union even in the period of the most rigorous enforcement of socialist realism, Fradkin, heaving a sigh of relief, pronounces Brecht a realist – if only in the spirit of the eighteenth-century enlightenment:

> Just as Voltaire speaks about a Bulgarian army in *Candide*, or of a Princess of Babylon, so Brecht's Caucasus or his contemporary Setzuan have nothing to do with these regions in reality. . . .[1]

And as a follower of Swift, Voltaire, and Diderot, all recognized ancestors of revolutionary literature, Brecht just manages to secure the all-important epithet, 'realist'. In spite of the disavowal of the 'superseded' parts of his theories, he had secured something like approval. And so, when the time came for his obituaries a few months later, the Soviet press could, in good conscience, praise him not only as a staunch supporter of the Communist cause, but as an important dramatist and producer.

The visit of the Berliner Ensemble to Moscow and Leningrad was carefully prepared. In March and April 1957 three of Brecht's most important plays were published in translation: *Mother Courage, The Life of Galileo*, and *The Caucasian Chalk Circle* – little booklets with introductions and some notes, with a printing of 5,000 copies each, not a very large edition by Soviet standards. In April 1957 another important Soviet literary periodical *Zvezda* published a long study of Brecht by A. Dymshits. This article, which closely follows the pattern of Fradkin's pioneer effort, starts off with a pointed reference to the party's permission that foreign writers like Brecht could now be studied:

[1] I. Fradkin, 'Bertolt Brecht', *Teatr*, Moscow, January 1956.

In the message of greetings the Central Committee of the Communist Party of the USSR sent to the Second All-Union Congress of Writers, special stress is laid on how important it is that our artistic workers learn from, and master, the artistic experience of progressive artists in foreign countries. In the ranks of these Bertolt Brecht undoubtedly occupies one of the first places. His work as poet, dramatist, novelist, publicist, theoretician of aesthetics, and producer is received with the greatest attention; and his achievement which constitutes the pride and glory of German democratic culture must also enrich our literature and our theatre. . . .[1]

An imprecation like this unmistakably shows how conscious the writer still was of the daring of his action, that he had to reassure himself and his readers before he started out to discuss a writer who had been proscribed such a short while ago. This lengthy article also suppresses any mention of *Die Massnahme*, and even, whether by design or by mistake, attributes one of the choruses from that work, *Praise of the Party*, to *The Mother* – a clear sign that *Die Massnahme*, of which a Russian translation had existed in 1932, was no longer available in the Soviet Union. And again Brecht's theory of the 'epic' theatre is explained away as having been developed in opposition against the 'bourgeois decadent theatre', and therefore hardly relevant to current Soviet practice.

On the eve of the Berliner Ensemble's arrival in Moscow, Fradkin, as the leading exponent of Brecht in the Soviet Union, prepared the readers of *Sovietskaya Kultura*, the organ of the Soviet Ministry of Culture, for what they should expect – again almost as if to soften the shock awaiting them:

The directors, designers, and decorators of the Berliner Ensemble avoid the illusion of truth to nature and any naturalistically accurate rendering of the outward appearance of life. In their effort to explain reality correctly, in which they firmly occupy the standpoint of a determined realism, the Berliner Ensemble turn towards symbolism in the field of form (unfinished, suggestive décor, masks, etc.), and thus stimulate the imagination of the spectator. . . .[2]

[1] A. Dymshits, 'Bertolt Brecht', *Zvezda*, Moscow and Leningrad, April 1957, pp. 192 ff.
[2] I. Fradkin in *Sovietskaya Kultura*, quoted by *Neues Deutschland*, East Berlin, 9.5.1957.

And so the Berliner Ensemble came to Moscow. On the 8 May 1957 they opened at the Vakhtangov Theatre with *The Life of Galileo*. *Mother Courage*, *Pauken und Trompeten* (Farquhar's *Recruiting Officer*), and *The Caucasian Chalk Circle* followed. There was a good deal of applause, speech-making, and official receptions. The notices in the newspapers were generous while not displaying overmuch genuine understanding of what it had all been about, so that praise concentrated largely on the performances of the protagonists – Ernst Busch as Galilei, Helene Weigel as Mother Courage, Angelika Hurwicz as Grusche. These actors appealed to the Russian public's love for broadly human characterization. But the 'epic' theatre itself clearly made no headway with the authorities. This was finally made clear in a long review of *The Caucasian Chalk Circle* by S. Mokulski and B. Rostotski in the official organ *Sovietskaya Kultura*. After praising the progressive tendency of the play and pouring cold water on the genuineness of its Caucasian types, this article finally came to grips with the thorny problem of formalism. In a typically Soviet manner the whole question was made to centre on a purely external – formal – element: the use of masks for the negative characters. The two Soviet critics could not let this pass:

> Could not the basic idea of the inhumanity of the governor's wife have been expressed by subtler means? What gives us the right to ask this question is the experience of the Soviet theatre in the twenties and early thirties. We remember the disputes that raged at that time about the theory of the so-called 'attitude towards the character' and the practical experiments to put this theory into practice from the theatre of Meyerhold to TRAM.[1] We remember that the device of masks was more than once used in our theatres to express the relationship between the actor and the character he portrayed. The performance of the Berliner Ensemble reminds us of this and shows us once more that many experiments of our theatre have left their traces behind. . . . We must clearly ask ourselves if everything is equally valid and justified in this talented performance. . . .[2]

This article, which was headed 'The Contemporary and the Old

[1] Theatre of Working Youth – an *avant-garde* movement condemned by the party.

[2] S. Mokulski and B. Rostotski, 'Segodnyashnyeye i proidyennoye', *Sovietskaya Kultura*, Moscow, 18.5.1957.

Fashioned', shows one aspect of the lack of sympathy between Brecht's approach to the theatre and that of Soviet socialist realism. The use of masks obviously lacked realism. But Soviet socialist realism also dislikes an excess of reality. In an essay headed 'The Strength and Weakness of Brecht's Theatre – Notes of a Producer'[1] Boris Zakhava attacked the 'naturalism' of the Berliner Ensemble. Of course, he too began by paying the usual compliments. But while he stressed the thoughtfulness and directness of the productions he had seen, his enthusiasm had a distinctly soured air:

> One might quarrel with it (the Berliner Ensemble), one might not agree with some of the principles professed by this theatre, but it is impossible not to see that we have before us a theatre with a clearly defined creative personality.[2]

Zakhava, himself a well-known producer, objects to the coldness and lack of emotion of most of the performances he had seen:

> . . . recognizing the mastery and talent of Helene Weigel we cannot conceal the fact that for complete satisfaction we would have liked just one moment which would be filled with a powerful emotional upsurge, a creative outburst rising to the heights of great human feelings.[3]

But Zakhava not only disliked the coldness of the Berliner Ensemble's acting, he was appalled by its stress on the sordid side of life:

> Why was it necessary that Ernst Busch who plays the cook in *Mother Courage* should take off his dirty leggings and, sitting right in the foreground, should so carefully and with such visible pleasure rub them between his fingers? And why altogether should there be so many bare feet? To my puzzled question about this, one of our German guests replied by putting a counter-question: 'Would you want to put a brassière on the Venus of Milo?' Of course not! We should be indignant if anything prevented us from contemplating the magnificent body of Venus with delight – we despise all sanctimoniousness – but we should also be very much offended if someone wanted to paint the Venus of Milo in flesh colours. Let her stay white![4]

[1] Boris Zakhava, 'Sila i Slabost Teatra Brekhta', *Znamya*, Moscow, August 1958, pp. 160–6.
[2] ibid., p. 160.   [3] ibid., p. 163.   [4] ibid., p. 165.

It is clear that this is not just a criticism of details, but a basic divergence of tastes. On the one hand we have the respectable, Victorian sensibility of post-Zhdanov Soviet Russia, and on the other the bitter realism of the West European *avant-garde*. This becomes even more pointed in the Soviet critic's attack against one of the key-scenes in *Mother Courage* – the scene, in which poor dumb Katrin, Mother Courage's backward daughter, sacrifices her life to save the city of Halle from destruction. For Brecht the point of this scene obviously lay in the contrast between the dumb girl's inarticulate, almost animal, instinctive reaction and the conventional school-book idea of heroism. But the Soviet critic called precisely for this hackneyed, blimpish heroism in its purest form:

> ... in carrying out this heroic action, the actress Angelika Hurwicz, who plays the part, does not forget to emphasize Katrin's pathological state. And yet to what a pitch of emotion could the audience be raised, if in this scene of self-denying, fearless heroism Katrin's features could have been wholly free from the marks of mental sickness, and if this unhappy creature could have stood before us outwardly and inwardly transfigured.[1]

One might as well ask that Picasso's *Demoiselles d'Avignon* should be improved by the addition of faces borrowed from fashion photographs in *Vogue*.

These extracts from Soviet reactions to the visit of the Berliner Ensemble speak for themselves. It is not just a matter of official disapproval – although that element is certainly present – but also one of the irreconcilability of tastes. It may be that it is the Soviet theatre that is old-fashioned and the Western *avant-garde*, to which Brecht belonged, that is modern; or the Soviet critics may be right in regarding the styles of Meyerhold, Tairov – and Brecht – as reeking of the twenties, and therefore more old-fashioned than their own. But one thing is certain: in spite of all politeness and the sincere desire to understand what Brecht was after, Brecht's attempt to create a Marxist theatre simply could not be appreciated in the Soviet Union, at least among the circles in power in the State – and in the theatre.

In the period of the thaw under Khrushchev, Brecht's plays did reach the Soviet stage, at first in the outlying Baltic republics then, but

[1] Boris Zakhava, 'Sila i Slabost Teatra Brekhta', *Znamya*, Moscow, August 1958, p. 165.

not until 1959, in Russian, in Moscow, when *The Visions of Simone Machard* was performed at the M. N. Yermolova Theatre. In 1961 M. M. Strauch directed one of Brecht's great plays, *Mother Courage*, at the Mayakovsky Theatre. But he conformed to Soviet Russian rather than Brechtian methods of production by making the play into a naturalistic historical canvas and letting Mother Courage die a hero's death in the end, rather than trying to get back into business as Brecht had conceived the play. Since then there have been many productions of Brecht in the Soviet Union; *The Threepenny Opera* particularly has been widely produced, but the indications are that none of these productions is particularly Brechtian, with the sole exception of those by Lyubimov at the *avant-garde* Taganka Theatre in Moscow, where however they are reputed to incur the disapproval of the authorities.

In the satellite countries Brecht's theatre was allowed to make greater headway after he died. In 1957 *Mother Courage* and *The Good Soul of Setzuan* were performed in Hungarian in Budapest – as the papers pointed out, the first performances of Brecht in Hungarian since *The Threepenny Opera* had been produced there in the early thirties. And in 1958 the Berliner Ensemble went to Prague. On this occasion a Czech correspondent told East Berlin readers that since *The Threepenny Opera* had been put on immediately after the war in E. F. Burian's theatre 'D34', 'there has been silence about Brecht for almost ten years. Only the year 1955 brought a change. Czech theatre people remembered the importance of his work, and Brecht was rediscovered for the Czech stage'. But in spite of performances of *The Threepenny Opera* and *Mother Courage* in Prague, *Puntila* in Brno, and *Galileo* in Bratislava, the article says 'even among theatre artists the knowledge of Brecht's work is not yet deep enough, let alone the general public'.[1]

As Brecht was more and more transformed into a Communist saint and an establishment figure by East German propaganda in the years after his death, and as the thaw of the early sixties made him more acceptable in the Communist-bloc countries of Eastern Europe and he was more readily performed in Czechoslovakia, Poland, Hungary and Rumania, a paradoxical change in the public's attitude occurred. The younger generation, fighting for a new conception of Communism, 'Communism with a human face', began to associate Brecht with the

[1] Zdenek Eis, 'Brecht auf Buehnen der CSR', *Berliner Zeitung*, East Berlin, 26.4.1958.

official, old-fashioned, neo-Stalinist line. At the height of the 1968 revolution in Czechoslovakia the younger generation of Czechs and Slovaks openly rejected Brecht. This was the bitterest irony of all, for Brecht had always, behind the façade of Party loyalty he showed to the world, been a fighter for precisely that Communism with a human face. That, after all, was the reason why he was denounced as a formalist during the Stalinist and post-Stalinist period.

And in all fairness, from the party's own narrow point of view, Brecht was not only useless but potentially harmful. To the technicians of power who regard the arts merely as vehicles for propaganda, Brecht's claim that his work would help the Communist cause must have appeared absurd. Only two of his plays have openly Communist subjects. *Die Massnahme* which in its frankness about the use of force within the party was a propaganda catastrophe, and *The Mother*, a play so starkly didactic that the audience could not associate it with any real happenings in pre-revolutionary Russia. Such didactic drama was at best suitable for intellectuals who knew how to transfer abstract notions into everyday terms for themselves. Hence the party's attack on *The Mother* as formalism. All other plays by Brecht may be intended to prove Communist theses, but in the eyes of the party they must certainly be regarded as ineffective propaganda. *Mother Courage* and *Lucullus* are pacifism pure and simple and rather embarrassing in times when the Soviet Union is the strongest military power in the world. *Puntila* and *The Good Soul of Setzuan* describe the deep contradictions of human nature and the moral dilemma of being good in a wicked world. *The Caucasian Chalk Circle* preaches that things should be given to those who make the best use of them – a dangerous doctrine in any Communist country, where the waste and inefficiency of the authorities are in constant evidence. Apart from that, the prologue, intended to show the Confucian friendliness prevailing among the members of two rival collective farms in the Soviet Caucasus, is so clearly idealized that the Soviet critics hastened to protest that life in the Soviet Union was certainly not like *that*. *Galileo* deals with the problem of the freedom of scientific inquiry – also a very touchy problem in any Communist society. And as to the earlier plays – they are immoral, nihilist, and anarchist. Can the party be blamed for having so long discouraged performances of the works of such an author? In East Germany, where Brecht's adherence was a major political asset to the régime, his plays caused constant embarrassment to the authorities by provoking unnecessarily stormy applause at the more revolutionary passages, like the one in *The Mother* where the heroine says:

> *While you are still alive, do not say: never!*
> *The safe things are not safe.*
> *As it is, it will not remain.*
> *When the rulers have spoken*
> *The ruled will speak. . . .*[1]

This rousing poetry is dangerously ambiguous. From the party's point of view any useful propaganda has to be far more specific: such a passage would have to be made to speak not of rulers and ruled, but of wicked capitalists and their down-trodden slaves. Hence the constant nagging by the party authorities that Brecht's work was not *clear* enough, that it was too obscure, too highbrow, and made too many demands on the intelligence of the listeners. It is known that Brecht took these criticisms very seriously indeed. He wanted to be a poet of the people, as widely understood as possible. He constantly tried to make his writing clearer, to elucidate any obscurities. But he succeeded only in making it less clear. For his idea of clarity was entirely different from the party's. Being a real poet, he simply could not stoop down to pure, unadulterated platitudes and clichés, which are the only really clear language in the eyes of a party used to thinking in ready-made formulas and slogans. When in his *pièces d'occasion* Brecht did comply with the party's demands, his poetic genius vanished without trace. Even then, from the party's point of view, he proved completely useless: they already had a surfeit of bad political hacks. And he never delivered the play on an East German contemporary problem which the party demanded in the hope of extracting a really effective piece of propaganda from him. He is known to have been trying to write such a play – on the theme of the shock-worker who is resented by his mates for putting up the norms and lowering their wages. But he never finished it, and from what is known of Brecht's plan it is clear that the party would not have been very happy about it.

From the party's point of view therefore there remained only the propaganda value such a poet had in impressing the Western world: the original conception for the Berliner Ensemble, which in the first

[1] Brecht, *Die Mutter, Stuecke V*, p. 116.

four years of its existence possessed no permanent theatre of its own, was clearly that of a touring company, designed to spread the prestige of advanced Communist culture in the West. In the tensest times of East-West crisis the Berliner Ensemble could be seen in Western Germany, Austria, and France – a shop window in which the Communist camp, as it does so frequently, displayed goods not for sale within its own orbit. Brecht's case closely resembles that of Picasso: Picasso, who proclaimed himself a Communist, was held up as proof that the world's greatest talents are in the 'progressive' camp; he was even allowed to design a dove of peace, but he was rebuked when he produced a portrait of Stalin that was not a good likeness, and his works were consigned to the cellars of the Soviet museums until very recently. It is no coincidence that Brecht asked Picasso to design the curtain and the main poster for the Berliner Ensemble, nor that Picasso furnished him with highly 'formalist' designs. The difference, however, was that Picasso was so successful that he could afford to live and work in the West as his own master. Brecht was never successful enough in the Western world to gain similar independence to work and experiment in complete freedom from financial worries. So Picasso lived and worked in France, while Brecht, to get the means to work, had to accept the invitation to settle in East Berlin. To make effective use of Brecht the party had to give him the means to do his work according to his own ideas. By displaying that work to the West while barring it from its own orbit, the party thought that it was making use of Brecht for its own purpose. By accepting the party's lavish support and stubbornly sticking to his own ideas Brecht was equally firmly convinced that he was making use of the party to further his own artistic and political objectives. And so with mutual cynicism they mutually used each other. It was a curious arrangement. And who can tell which side had the best of the bargain?

Part Four: The Real Brecht

Chapter IX

THE USES OF COMMITMENT

I have feelings only when I have a headache –
never when I am writing: for then I think.

BRECHT[1]

Man lives by his head,
His head will not suffice.
You have a try! Your head will not
Feed more than a few lice.
  Because for this existence
  Man has not brains enough. . . .

BRECHT, *Song on the Inadequacy of Human Endeavour*[2]

Brecht was a professed, and aggressive, rationalist. From the time of his final conversion to Marxism in the late twenties he endeavoured to make his writing a scientific activity, a series of controlled experiments devoted to the elucidation of social relations, and to the transformation of society by producing strictly calculated, socially useful responses in the audience. The element of emotion was thus excluded both in the writer and in the public for whom he wrote.

The theory of the 'epic' theatre is based on this intention: the audience is to be confronted with a body of evidence from which it is to draw its conclusions in a critical, highly lucid state of mind. The emotions are to be involved only at a further remove. the critical analysis of the social facts, presented in the concrete form of living pictures, is to produce socially useful emotions such as indignation at injustice, hatred of oppressors, or an active desire for the overthrow of the existing social order.

This was Brecht's sincere intention. Yet the long and tangled story of his relations with the Communist party shows that those most qualified to evaluate his efforts in terms of their practical value as Marxist propaganda were far from convinced that he had succeeded

[1] Quoted by Ruth Berlau, 'Wie war Bert Brecht', *Magazin*, East Berlin, February 1958.
[2] *Dreigroschenoper, Stuecke III*, p. 111.

in achieving his aim. Nor would most Western observers have wanted to disagree with the Communist authorities. In Munich or Cologne, Paris or London, Brecht's own productions of his plays evoked anything but a wholly cerebral response. On the contrary: their success was due to their deep emotional impact on the audience.

For Brecht this was a tragic paradox; he always seemed to succeed in doing things he had never intended, to hit bulls-eyes on targets he never wanted to aim at, or, like Columbus, to discover continents he had not intended to reach. The plays he had written as ice-cold intellectual exercises contain far more than he himself consciously put into them. Behind the rational, propagandist surface there is always a layer of profound emotion, repressed, but all the more powerfully active. This repressed emotional content communicates itself to the deeper layers of the reader's or spectator's mind and is felt as a *poetic* quality. In fact, the tension between the poet's conscious aim and the subconscious, emotional content of his work of which he himself is unaware, is in Brecht's case the source of its poetic power.

Here lies the explanation for the contradictory emotions, the tangle of misunderstandings and misconceptions Brecht has aroused in so many different quarters. The divergence between his subjective intentions and his objective achievement was bound to puzzle and confuse both himself and his public. Those who responded to the poetical power of his work disliked his Communist intentions: those who agreed with his intentions were made uncomfortable by the actual effect. And Brecht himself was often enraged by the people who admired his work, and denounced them for liking it for the wrong reasons, while those he intended to please hurt him by rejecting it for reasons he could not understand.

This makes Brecht's case an illuminating example for the often noticed, but rarely so fully documented, phenomenon of the cleavage between an author's professed, conscious intention and its actual impact on the audience, a mystery which lies at the very base of all creative activity. Most writers and poets are aware of the mysterious mixture of conscious and subconscious processes by which their work is produced. The idea of inspiration, the mythical image of the Muse who dictates the finished poem into the poet's pen are attempts to describe them.

But if a poet like T. S. Eliot wisely acknowledges the mystery behind his own poetic activity, and therefore declines to explain what he *intended* his poetry to mean, Brecht obstinately refused to acknowledge that there was more in what he wrote than the rationally calculated effects he had wanted to achieve. This attitude, which sprang from Brecht's highly complex personality, had very curious results. As he refused even to consider the presence of subconscious emotional factors in his poetry, he could not and did not control it, so that the subconscious elements are, if anything, *more* clearly visible in Brecht's work than in that of poets who understand, and are therefore able to conceal, their subconscious impulses. In fact, as will be shown in the next chapter, the conflict between the rational and the instinctive was itself one of the main themes of Brecht's poetic work. His very denial of the emotional factor is an indication of his constant pre-occupation with this subject.

But the most obvious outcome of Brecht's refusal to admit the irrational was his blindness towards the real meaning and content of some of his best work. Unlike Pirandello's characters, who were in search of an author, Brecht was constantly faced with the problem of his characters running away from him and assuming an independent existence of which he strongly disapproved. The most clear-cut example of this curious state of affairs is that of *Mother Courage*.

Mother Courage was meant as a cautionary tale about the inevitable consequences of battening on war. Anna Fierling, called 'Mother Courage', is a camp-follower who in her small way helps the prosecution of the Thirty Years War by providing shoes, ale, and comforts for the soldiers. She was, in Brecht's conception, a negative, villainous character. Those who live by war must pay war its due. So Mother Courage loses her three children. Having sacrificed her family to her commercial instinct, she fails to learn her lesson. She continues her trade and, as the final curtain falls, she is seen dragging her cart across the stage to catch up with the advancing army.

Brecht wanted this last scene to arouse the spectator's indignation that such blindness and stupidity were possible. The public was to leave the theatre determined that something positive must be done to stop wars.

But when *Mother Courage* was first performed at the Zurich Schauspielhaus with Therese Giese, an actress of great power, in the title role, the public's response was quite different: they were moved to tears by the sufferings of a poor woman who, having lost her three children, heroically continued her brave struggle and refused to give in, an embodiment of the eternal virtues of the common people.

Brecht was furious. He re-wrote the play to emphasize the villainous side of Mother Courage's character. As he put it in a note to the text of the play in the ninth volume of *Versuche*:

> The first performance of *Mother Courage* gave the bourgeois press occasion to talk about a Niobe-tragedy and about the moving endurance of the female animal. Warned by this experience, the author has made some alterations for the Berlin performance.[1]

Having considerably underlined the villainy of Mother Courage, Brecht himself supervised the Berlin production, in which his own wife, Helene Weigel, also an excellent actress, but far less warm and motherly than Therese Giese and therefore more in line with Brecht's intention, played the title role. The Berlin production was a triumph. But how did the leading Communist critic, Max Schroeder, describe its impact? 'Mother Courage', he wrote, 'is a humanist saint from the tribe of Niobe and the *mater dolorosa*, who defends the life to which she has given birth with her bared teeth and claws. . . .'[2] Again, hardly anyone had noticed the villainy of Mother Courage, the profiteer who battens on war. Brecht himself admitted this but tried to explain it, not by any failure on his part to make himself clear, but by the obtuseness of the spectators who remained the slaves of long-established habits of emotion:

> Numerous discussions with members of the audience and many notices in the press show that many people regard Mother Courage merely as the representative of 'the little people', who are 'involved' in the war and 'who can't do anything about it', who are helplessly at the mercy of events, etc. A deeply ingrained habit induces the audience in the theatre to pick out the more emotional aspects of the characters and to ignore the rest. . . .[3]

The East German authorities also noted the lack of propagandist effect. While *Mother Courage* moved people to tears about the horrors of war, if the play had any lesson at all it was that all soldiers are beasts

[1] *Versuche* 9, p. 79.
[2] Max Schroeder, 'Verflucht sei der Krieg' (1949), reprinted in *Aufbau*, East Berlin, 1957, no. 1.
[3] Brecht, 'Der lange Weg in den Krieg', *Theaterarbeit*, p. 230.

(and the people of East Berlin automatically thought of Russian soldiers when it came to rape and rapine) and that nevertheless 'life goes on' and that the little man is eternally resilient. This was not a specifically Communist message, and so it was suggested to Brecht that he might make the end of the play more explicit. Mother Courage might make a little speech drawing a more positively Communist lesson, or she might do something which showed that she had at last realized that she would have to become politically active.

If Brecht had really been as cold a rationalist and propagandist as he professed himself to be, he could easily have yielded to these demands. In fact, he did nothing of the sort. However willing he had previously been to accept advice and suggestions for alterations from practically any quarter, in this case he refused. With a great display of casuistry he argued that it was *better propaganda* to leave Mother Courage unconverted, untaught, and unteachable.

No doubt Brecht himself was convinced that he was arguing on strictly logical and rational grounds. Yet his arguments clearly are nothing but the rationalizations of instinctive responses. With the sound instinct of the creative artist Brecht knew that the suggested alterations would simply have *spoiled his play*. The suggested change did not make sense to his poetic instinct, and so he was unable to accept it. Yet the deeper needs of his personality made it impossible for Brecht to argue on any other lines than strictly rational considerations of political, or propaganda, expediency. The poet deep within him always had to hide behind the Marxist.

The case of Mother Courage is by no means an isolated instance of Brecht's characters belying their author's intentions: the inhuman Finnish landowner Puntila, whose relapse into human feelings under the influence of drink was to emphasize his heartlessness when sober, conquered all audiences by his humanity and charm, while his hired man Matti, conceived by Brecht as a paragon of proletarian virtue, was disliked as the cold prig he is. Again Brecht fought vainly against this misunderstanding. 'In Zurich . . . most spectators had the impression of a sympathetic person with some evil moods when sober. . . . Practically all performances of the play in Germany, before and after the Berlin performance [where Brecht himself had tried to correct this wrong impression], suffered from the same mistake as the Zurich performance. . . .'[1] Galileo, whom Brecht had intended as a villain and

[1] 'Steckels zwei Puntilas', ibid., p. 22.

coward, who made science subservient to the State for centuries to come, was hailed by Soviet critics as a 'hero of science' bravely suffering for his convictions.

Not only single characters, however, made themselves independent from their author's intentions. Whole plays, conceived as arguments to prove one thing, turned out to prove something quite different. The school opera *Der Jasager* was to help the cause of socialism by showing the need to subordinate the individual's interests to those of the collective. But it was hailed by Prussian patriots as a masterly case for the maintenance of the old military virtues, so that Brecht had to reverse his argument and *Der Jasager* became *Der Neinsager*.

In the case of *Die Massnahme*, which derives from the *Jasager* and the *Neinsager*, the discrepancy between Brecht's intention and the play's real meaning is even more instructive: Brecht had wanted to write a propaganda tract designed to foster the stern virtues of discipline and unquestioning obedience among party members; in a scene of great poetic power the four party workers divest themselves of their private personalities before entering China, the country where they are to carry out their clandestine activities. As they don their masks, which symbolize the extinction of their private selves, the 'control chorus', the party's conscience, intones:

> He who fights for Communism must be able to fight and not to fight; to speak the truth and not to speak the truth; to render services and to refuse services; to keep promises and not to keep promises; to incur danger and to avoid danger; to be recognizable and unrecognizable. He who fights for Communism, has of all virtues only one; that he fights for Communism.[1]

But one of the four party workers cannot abide by these stern principles. His compassion for the suffering Chinese coolies leads him to disobey the party's orders. He is killed by his comrades. The control chorus agrees with the party workers' action and absolves them from all guilt.

The party's angry reaction to *Die Massnahme* has been discussed in a previous chapter. Brecht had intended to write a propaganda tract and had in fact written a sombre tragedy of great emotional intensity. The party did not want to admit that its members were faced with such fearful choices and such heavy risks. They denied the truth of the incident Brecht had depicted and asserted that such an occurrence

[1] Brecht, *Die Massnahme, Versuche 4*, p. 334.

was impossible. Yet Brecht's poetic intuition – as distinct from his understanding of party doctrine – proved itself in the most unexpected manner. A few years after *Die Massnahme* was first performed, the Stalinist terror followed it exactly in all detail. The 'control chorus' became a prophetic forecast of the arguments of the prosecutors and judges in the great show trials, and the accused at those trials confessed their errors and demanded their punishment in the same terms the young comrade had used when he asked to be shot and to be thrown into the quicklime in the higher interests of the party. Brecht's poetic intuition had laid bare the very essence of Stalinist Communism long before it had manifested itself in reality.

Today, half a century after Brecht wrote *Die Massnahme*, the play is as powerful, as vital, and as true as ever. And its meaning can be seen to be wholly independent of the author's conscious intention. What was written to boost the morale of Communist party stalwarts in the last years of the Weimar republic now stands revealed as one of the most powerful statements of the essence of the moral problem of Communism. The play, which is banned in the Communist world, could be performed anywhere outside it as a terrible picture of the party member's moral conflict, a devastating revelation of the tragic dilemma facing the adherents of a creed which demands the subordination of all human feeling to a dry and abstract ideal. The truth of a great poet's intuitive insight has transcended the author's conscious understanding of what he was doing.

This, of course, is by no means an unusual occurrence: Shakespeare, for example, may conceivably have intended Shylock as a piece of anti-Semitic propaganda. If so, his powers of characterization were too strong for his conscious intention. In any case, the immediate motives for which Shakespeare created the character have become irrelevant today, just as the political implications of *Richard II* or *Macbeth*, which may have played a considerable part in Shakespeare's approach to those plays, have lost any relevance for present-day audiences, whose attention is still held by the deeper human content of the plays in question.

This relative lack of importance of conscious political purpose in a poet's work, for which Brecht furnishes so many powerful and recent examples, has its implication on the much discussed problem of whether writers should or should not *commit* themselves to a political cause.

Of all the major creative writers of his age Brecht probably was the most wholeheartedly committed. Yet if his example shows anything, it shows that there is more to the act of commitment than the mere act of will, however wholehearted and sincere it may be, to throw in one's lot with a political party.

A really creative writer's power springs from sources that lie far below the sphere of conscious and rational thought. In committing himself, such a writer can only commit a relatively unimportant part of his personality. His commitment will furnish him with an incentive to write and it will influence his choice of subject-matter. But as to the substance of what he has to say, the political ties of such a major creative writer will remain relatively irrelevant.

All great writing must be true – that is, it must convey some truth about human nature or some aspect of reality. It must convey a genuine picture of the world as it is seen through the eyes of an important individual. As long, therefore, as the ideology or creed of a writer helps him in uncovering some aspect of the essential nature of reality, his commitment to it will be beneficial to his work. But as soon as the ideology concerned comes into conflict with reality – and most political ideologies, concerned as they are with some isolated and oversimplified aspect of reality, will do so sooner or later – a truly creative writer will have to break out of the narrow limits of the creed to which he has committed himself. By following his own intuition, which is nourished not only from his conscious but also from his subconscious perception of reality, he will inevitably come into conflict with the political ideology; that, for example, is the reason why Shaw's capitalists and millionaires tend to transcend his Fabian intentions, or why there is more to his *Pygmalion* than mere phonetics, more to his *St Joan* than mere anticlericalism. And that is also why Brecht's characters, though they were intended as black villains, so often emerge as poor struggling human beings who cannot but win the sympathy of the audience.

The more narrow a political creed, the less it corresponds to the real complexities of the world, the more difficult it will be for a creative writer to obey its dictates. Marxist dogma, in its midtwentieth-century Communist form, is so far removed from reality that it is practically impossible to make any literary work aiming at poetic truth to conform to it. Hence Brecht's inability to keep his work even remotely in line with the requirements of the party.

On the other hand, Brecht's commitment to Marxism and to the party did have a beneficial effect on his writing: it gave his anarchic and nihilistic tendencies a rigid framework of intellectual discipline. The inner tension created by this discipline, by the effort to repress the amorphous forces of his subconscious mind, gave Brecht's work its own peculiar spell, its tautness, poetic ambiguity, and depth. Had he set out by a conscious effort to make Mother Courage a latter-day Niobe, he would only have succeeded in producing a sentimental character – for Brecht had his sentimental, self-pitying side. But by following his rationalist, behaviourist conception, which denied the very existence of the deeper levels of human character and saw man as merely the product of the social environment he finds himself in at any moment, Brecht made Mother Courage a battlefield of contradictory impulses. Behind the rigid sociological framework the human side constantly reasserted itself: while the politician in Brecht piled on the social villainy, the poet in him drew on the subconscious feeling he had for the archetypal mother-figure, on his fund of pity – and sentiment – and cunningly smuggled these elements into the language, loading it with the subtlest overtones. And so in spite of Brecht's conscious and often declared intention of producing one-dimensional social schemata, the character he created has all the depth of a great tragic figure. And it is to this that the audience responds.

The act of *engagement* can therefore in Brecht's case be seen as having been of considerable importance in the mechanism of his creative process. It gave him the reason, the justification, and the incentive to work. But, on the other hand, Brecht's commitment to the Communist cause was, paradoxically, of little relevance to the ultimate significance, political or otherwise, of his work. His adherence to a political cause may have helped Brecht to write: it did not make him a very effective supporter of the cause, nor could it decisively influence the real content of his writing.

It is therefore difficult to agree with Herbert Luethy, who argues in his penetrating essay on Brecht[1] that his commitment to the Communist cause amounted to a *sacrificium intellectus*, because it decisively impoverished his creative talent. Brecht may have wanted to renounce his perception of the realities of human existence and character, and in that sense to abdicate the use of his own reason; he simply did not succeed in doing so. And even more paradoxically,

[1] Herbert Luethy, 'Vom armen Bert Brecht', *Der Monat*, West Berlin, May 1952.

while Brecht's conscious acceptance of Marxism, which he wrongly regarded as a supreme expression of scientific rationality, was wholly irrational, it allowed him to continue to follow his creative impulse and to produce plays, which, based as they are on his intuitive perception of reality rather than his consciously held beliefs, constantly belie the pedantic concepts of Marxism and give the audience a genuine insight into the dilemmas of the human condition.

Brecht's commitment was thus of importance mainly in stabilizing his tumultuous personality. It resolved the deep feeling of nihilism and despair which pervaded his early writings, canalized the destructive forces within him, and allowed him to rationalize his poetic impulse by giving it a purpose.

As long as he could believe that the devastatingly dark picture of the world he painted was helping people to realize the need to change the world, as long as he could believe that such a change was possible and even inevitable, he was safe from despair. Only by committing himself to a rigidly dogmatic faith in the inevitability of social progress could a writer, whose perception of the human condition was as pessimistic and devoid of saving grace as Brecht's, justify his own creative activity to himself.

If the foregoing analysis of the role of Brecht's commitment within the complex structure of his creative personality is correct, it will be clear that any analysis or critical evaluation of his work which does not go beyond the social purpose and political content of his plays will never be able to penetrate to the real springs of its poetic power and undoubted emotional impact. To understand the real significance of Brecht's work it is therefore necessary to go beyond the superficial level of his conscious political intention.

Superficially, most of Brecht's later plays deal with the iniquities of capitalism, the equation between business and crime, the injustice and brutality of a commercial society. But beneath this surface, behind the abrupt changes in style and subject-matter between Brecht's earlier and later works, there is a considerable unity in theme and imagery which links the exuberantly anarchic plays of his youth, the austerely didactic school operas and Lehrstuecke, and the broader historical or fairy-tale plays of his last phase. On closer analysis the whole of Brecht's work can be seen as reflecting his preoccupation with the same recurring basic problems, the same fundamental contradictions within himself, the same highly personal attitude to the world.

Chapter X

REASON VERSUS INSTINCT

> The conflict between reason and emotion is . . .
> the basic experience of the bourgeois intellectual
> about to join the revolutionary proletariat. In its
> idealistic approach to the problem (*Die Massnahme*)
> is a typically petty bourgeois, intellectualist work.
>
> ALFRED KURELLA, writing in *Literatur der*
> *Weltrevolution* (organ of the International
> Association of Revolutionary Writers)
>
> Moscow, 1931[1]

> Our arrangement is very simple: on the one hand
> we have the gooseliver, which (Galileo) insists that
> he must have, on the other hand is science, on
> which he also insists. So he sits between his two
> great vices: science and gluttony.
>
> BRECHT[2]

In one of his early poems, the *Ballad of Mazeppa*, Brecht describes
the execution of this Cossack Hetman, who, according to legend, was
tied to the back of a wild horse that was let loose in the desolation
of the endless Russian steppes and carried him to his death, headlong
across the wilderness.

In Brecht's poem Mazeppa's fate becomes an image of the human
condition; helplessly tied to a blind elemental force which carries us
along, the conscious part of ourselves is condemned to watch the skies
rush past as they change from light to darkness and back again to light;
waiting for the inevitable end, while the vultures already circle above.

This poem expresses one of Brecht's fundamental experiences: the
helplessness of man, his inability to influence the world around him.
It is an experience which recurs in many of his poems and plays. In his
early volume, *Hauspostille*, it is the basic theme behind the ballad

---

[1] Quoted by Schumacher, p. 366.

[2] Quoted by K. Ruelicke, 'Leben des Galilei – Schlusszene', *Sinn und Form*,
Second Special Brecht Issue, 1957, p. 287.

about the boy, Jakob Apfelboeck, who killed his parents and watched them decompose in the cupboard, without ever knowing why he had done what he had done, nor ever feeling any guilt; about the infanticide Marie Farrar, who brought a child into the world without knowing how or why it should happen, and killed it without knowing why. It is the basic theme also of *The Legend of the Dead Soldier* who is dragged to the wars, although he is already dead. And the same image of man, helplessly drifting along in a universe beyond his understanding or control, imbues Brecht's poems modelled on Rimbaud's *Bateau Ivre*: ships floating down mysterious rivers, their hulls slowly rotting away, decomposing bodies carried towards the sea. This also is the experience of life which Brecht expresses in his first play, *Baal*, whose hero is entirely at the mercy of his uncontrollable impulses and who sees himself flying through space on our planet exactly like Mazeppa on his horse:

> If you lie in the grass at night, you feel it in your bones that the earth is a sphere and that we are flying. . . .[1]

And in *Baal* too we find the image of drifting down a river carried along by a current

> . . . when you are carried along by a torrent, on your back, naked under an orange-coloured sky and you see nothing, but the sky as it turns purple and then black, like a hole. . . .[2]

This picture of the human condition is essentially one of passive acceptance; it matters little whether the bodies floating down the rivers are alive or dead, they drift along with equal helplessness. And if the living swimmer's body is not yet in a state of decomposition – it soon will be. The process of nature is seen as one of incessant birth and decay, with human consciousness powerless to break the eternal cycle. In *Baal* it is the *privy* which is proclaimed the true symbol of the human condition:

> *You see the meaning there of man's estate;*
> *Creatures that eat, while they evacuate. ... .*[3]

Man in fact is merely a vessel in which the process of decay takes place. In another of his most powerful ballads, *The Ballad of Cortez' Men*,

[1] *Erste Stuecke I*, p. 15.   [2] ibid., p. 28.   [3] ibid., p. 23.

Brecht depicts a party of conquistadors who are literally choked by the luxuriant growth of the jungle which has enveloped their camping place while they slept. Here, too, the blind forces of Nature smother helpless mankind.

Nature, the forest, and the sky thus stand for the forces of instinct and uncontrolled emotion which threaten his self-control: at a later stage of his development Brecht feared losing himself to Nature as he had lost himself in his youth, when his poetry reflected a complete merging of his self in the powerful process of vegetative growth and decay. His later poems often refer to the need to shut out the ecstasy of such feelings from a life which must be devoted to the pursuit of social betterment and the struggle against war and injustice. As Brecht's *alter ego*, Mr Keuner, puts it: 'We must make sparing use of Nature. If you spend your time in Nature without anything to do, you easily get into an unhealthy state – something like a fever comes over you.'[1]

In his early plays Brecht was still in the grip of this fever. With a mixture of horror and delight he yielded to the powerful lure of Nature and the dark, irrational call of subconscious compulsions: Baal is a poet, and his poetic gift is shown by Brecht as directly derived from his passivity. He is a poet *because* irrational forces are at work within him: his poetry pours from him without conscious effort on his part. And equally he cannot help seducing women; he cannot help becoming emotionally tied to his friend Ekart, the musician. When Ekart betrays him with a woman he cannot help killing him. In this Baal resembles the *poètes maudits*, Verlaine and Villon, whom Brecht so greatly admired. They too were vagabonds drifting through life because they were poets – and they were poets because they had to obey the irrational forces within them. Nor can there be any doubt that in writing *Baal* at the age of nineteen Brecht was describing his own experience.

The hero of Brecht's second play, Kragler, in *Drums in the Night*, though no poet, is also in the grip of an experience beyond his conscious control. He has been pressed into the army, has been kept a prisoner in Africa, and has come back to Germany. He is faced with the decision whether to join the revolutionary Spartakists or to marry his bride, pregnant by another man, and settle down to a life of passive mediocrity. He too chooses what instinct dictates rather than

[1] 'Herr Keuner und die Natur', *Versuche 5*, p. 457.

what reason would have demanded. He refuses to do anything about changing society and relaxes into a vegetative contentment. Kragler is no longer wholly representative of the author's own attitude. But while Brecht clearly feels some pangs of his social conscience, Kragler's choice nevertheless represents a victory of instinct over rational, premeditated action.

The two men, who are locked in battle in Brecht's third youthful play *Im Dickicht der Staedte* (the jungle of the great city of Chicago, being more elemental and relentless than the jungle that choked the men of Cortez), are even more completely in the grip of irrational impulses. Their love-hate relationship is wholly motiveless and inexplicable; they are driven along by forces entirely outside their control. And the author begs the audience not even to attempt to understand them: 'Do not wrack your brains as to the motive of this fight . . . but direct your attention towards the finish.'[1] But the finish of the fight merely brings the recognition of the complete isolation of man and his utter inability to control his own fate.

Self-destruction through the inability to resist subconscious forces within him is also the fate of Brecht's Edward II, who loses his kingdom and his life by his inexplicable infatuation with Gaveston, in Marlowe's original a nobleman, but in Brecht's adaptation a vulgar butcher's son devoid of any charm that might make the king's folly more easily understood on rational grounds. Edward also drifts towards his doom like a helpless piece of wood carried along a stream.

The hero of *Mann ist Mann*, Galy Gay, an Irish stevedore in a Kiplingesque India, is so passive a character that a trio of brutal soldiers can wipe out his individuality altogether; to replace a member of their platoon whose absence would give them away as temple-robbers, they change Galy Gay into the soldier Jeriah Jip. Man equals man – and human individuality can be wiped off like a coat of dust from a window-pane. A passport and a soldier's pay-book are more essential parts of a personality than memories or habits. The meek little pacifist Galy Gay is turned into a ferocious fighting machine which terrorizes whole populations. But his very fierceness is merely the outward sign of his passivity; he has been moulded like a piece of clay.

Brecht's early poems and the plays of his pre-Marxist phase thus reveal his basic attitude to life as that of a sensitive personality

[1] *Erste Stuecke I*, p. 194.

passively aware of being at the mercy of compulsions beyond conscious control; irrational impulses from within, powerful and inexplicable forces from without; Nature, the jungle of the great cities, the social conditions that determine man's character and way of life. The helplessness of the individual, moreover, is heightened to nightmare proportions by his inability to communicate with his fellow human beings. As Shlink and Garga, the heroes of *Im Dickicht der Staedte*, realize at the end of their fight to the death:

> Language is inadequate for communication. I have watched the animals; love, the warmth created by the proximity of our bodies, is the sole mercy in our darkness. But the contact of organs is the only possible contact. It cannot bridge the gulf of language. . . .[1]

This is the side of Brecht's nature which led Feuchtwanger to describe Proeckl, the character in his novel *Erfolg* closely modelled on Brecht, as deficient in social instinct and unable to develop genuine contact with other human beings.

All the characters in Brecht's early plays, not only Shlink and Garga, move through them like somnambulists or victims of post-hypnotic suggestion. But Shlink and Garga are particularly passive and unable to understand what it is that drives them to their ruin. As they cannot understand their own actions they cannot communicate with each other.

What does the fight between these men consist in? It opens with Shlink wanting to buy Garga's opinion about a book, and continues in a series of attempts by Garga and Shlink in turn to gain complete moral ascendancy over each other, to conquer the other's will, and bring him to submission. Their strange relationship which the author himself calls 'the inexplicable wrestling match of two men'[2] and which he begs the audience not even to try to understand is thus clearly a sexual one. Without knowing it, and probably without the author's knowing, Shlink and Garga are the victims of homosexual passion. But as the motivation of the action is repressed, the play is presented as a series of motiveless events – *actes gratuits*.

It is surely no coincidence that the term *acte gratuit* was first used by Gide, another writer deeply concerned with gaining mastery over, and coming to terms with, inexplicable and forbidden subconscious urges. Loss of contact with reality, inability to control events are

[1] ibid., p. 291.   [2] ibid., p. 194.

neurotic symptoms. They characterize an age of anxiety and neurosis. The visions of Kafka, the automatic writing and painting of the Surrealists, the dramatization of the absurd from Alfred Jarry and Apollinaire to Beckett and Ionesco are the expressions of such a loss of contact with the real world. The whole of Brecht's early work has close affinities with these writers.

Though it may be significant that three out of Brecht's early plays are concerned with the problem of homosexuality (*Baal*, *Im Dickicht*, and *Edward II*) the exact nature of the subconscious urge he sought to suppress is irrelevant. What matters for the understanding of Brecht's development as a writer and his deeply felt need for political commitment is merely the indisputable fact that his whole work is deeply concerned with the problem of the struggle between subconscious impulse and conscious control. In the early period the incomprehensible forces are presented as irresistible and the prevailing image is that of submission and drift; Mazeppa, tied to a wild, furious steed, rotting hulls of ships that drift down mighty rivers to a boundless sea, helpless bodies floating downstream are the dominant images.

But the passive acceptance of incomprehensible emotional forces was counterbalanced by an increasingly strenuous effort at rational, active self-control. Gradually the passive submission to instinct was resisted and gave rise to feelings of guilt and distaste. That is why the spectacle of an audience in the grip of emotional identification with the characters on the stage filled Brecht with feelings of physical disgust at so degrading an exhibition of lost self-control. That is why, as his friend George Grosz put it, Brecht 'clearly would have wanted a sensitive electric computer instead of a heart, and spokes like the wheels of a motor-car instead of legs'.[1]

The constant battle between subconscious impulse and the desire to establish complete control through the elimination of emotion by reason produced Brecht's deeply contradictory personality, which led his school-friend Caspar Neher to describe him as compounded of fire and water – *Hydatopyranthropos*.

To overcome the temptation to let himself drift along passively in the grip of emotion, Brecht had to become active, tough, cynical, and cerebral, to assume the public *persona* of a wholly rational, impersonal being. It is surely significant that in the whole canon of his hitherto published work there is not a single love poem addressed to a named

[1] George Grosz, *Ein grosses Ja und ein kleines Nein*, Hamburg, 1955, p. 181.

person. The nearest approach to it – *Erinnerung an Marie A.* – is a poem which insists that he remembers the girl in question only by virtue of the cloud which passed over them when he lay with her under a plum-tree. His feelings are forgotten. The image of a cloud remains. The extreme reticence of all love scenes in Brecht's plays has often been remarked on. In *The Caucasian Chalk Circle* Grusche and her soldier speak to each other in the third person as if afraid to address each other directly. The love scene between Paul and Jenny in *Mahagonny* takes place in a brothel, with a whole queue of men waiting outside and clamouring to be admitted. In *The Threepenny Opera* the love scenes are presented as grotesque parodies of petty-bourgeois sentimentality.

The ostentatious rejection of all sentiment and emotion led Brecht into the displays of arrogant rudeness which characterize his *enfant terrible* period, into his friendship with boxers, his interest in six-day cycle racing, and his onslaught on oversensitive poets.

But ultimately the irrational forces within him needed a stronger and more positive discipline; the discipline of political commitment.

Communism was particularly suitable for this purpose. It was itself supremely tough. It rejected the existing world with all its ugliness, cruelty, and absurdity. It provided a technique of self-control, discipline, and rational thought. It rejected all sentiment or emotion and claimed to be completely scientific. And it gave sense to a world which otherwise appeared devoid of meaning and purpose. That the claims of Communism themselves were basically irrational did not make its acceptance more difficult but, on the contrary, easier; a deeply irrational nature could best express itself in clinging to an irrational creed. For a personality so deeply tormented by inner contradictions could find immense satisfaction in the Hegelian dialectic, which described reality as constantly changing so that everything was both itself and its opposite and all contradictions were ultimately resolved.

The middle phase of Brecht's *œuvre* reflects the inner struggles inherent in the acceptance of such a creed, the submission of emotional impulses to conscious control according to scientific principles. In Brecht's plays of this period the problem appears as that of *Einverstaendnis* (consent, acceptance) and discipline. The airmen of the *Didactic Play of Baden on Consent* agree to subordinate their individual instinctive craving for life to historic necessity and are redeemed by dying in the cause of technological progress; the Japanese

boy in *Der Jasager* accepts the need to die in the interests of his companions: the young comrade of *Die Massnahme* agrees with the party's disciplinary measure and accepts his own liquidation to help his cause. All these are *hard, tough* decisions, brutally unsentimental. On the surface they are diametrically opposed to the passive drift of Baal, Kragler, Shlink, Garga, or Edward II. But on closer reflection this contradiction between the *soft* heroes of the early, exuberant plays and the *hard* heroes of the austere didactic works disappears. They are all brothers under the skin. The heroes of the hard plays are as passive as those of the earlier ones. The airmen of the *Didactic Play of Baden on Consent* submit and die; the boy of *Der Jasager* meekly suffers his sacrifice to ancient custom; and the young Communist of *Die Massnahme* resembles Baal or Edward II in being a victim of his inability to control his emotional impulses. The difference merely is that while the heroes of the early, soft plays drift to their death as casually as they sinned, the young comrade of *Die Massnahme* is deliberately put to death *as a punishment for having been unable to resist his emotional impulse.*

Henceforth the indulgence of one's emotions is linked with feelings of guilt. In *Mann ist Mann* the toughest character is the ferocious Sergeant Fairchild, nicknamed 'Bloody Five'. But this tough and hard character has one weakness:

> It is known throughout the whole army that when it rains he falls into a state of sensuality and changes inwardly and outwardly. . . . When it rains Bloody Five, the most dangerous man in the British Army, becomes as harmless as a milk-tooth. When he has one of his fits of sensuality he is blind for everything that happens around him.[1]

To end this unsatisfactory state of affairs and to regain complete self-control and manliness Sergeant Fairchild castrates himself:

> It is simple. Here is the solution. Here is a bit of rope. Here is a revolver. I know no mercy. Rebels are shot. . . . Girls will not cost me another penny after this. . . . I *must* do it, to remain 'Bloody Five'. Fire![2]

And so the cause of the trouble is removed. The root of instinctive impulse is torn out. Reason and self-control are re-established. Twenty-five years later Brecht returned to the same subject. In

[1] *Erste Stuecke II*, p. 196.   [2] ibid., p. 281.

Lenz's eighteenth-century tragi-comedy *Der Hofmeister* (*The Private Tutor*), which Brecht brilliantly adapted for the Berliner Ensemble, the hero, whose sexual impulse has interfered with the discharge of his duties as a teacher, takes the same remedial action.

The conflict between subconscious instinct and rational self-control is thus one of the main themes of Brecht's work. At times it takes the form of violence directed against the instinctive part of man's nature, at others it is mellowed into a gentler mood, like that of Schweik's friend Baloun who cannot restrain his boundless appetite. But it is always present, even if Brecht's own attitude towards the two warring sides of his nature changes. For sometimes it is reason which appears as the positive force and instinctive emotion which is seen as dangerous or evil, sometimes it is reason which is evil and emotion and instinct which are good.

In the bitter didactic play *The Exception and the Rule*, for example, the poor coolie yields to his positive emotion of compassion for a suffering fellow-being and offers his water-bottle to the thirsty merchant. The merchant, who has reason to believe that the coolie whom he has maltreated hates him, mistakes the gesture of compassion for an attack and kills the coolie. The judge at the trial accepts the evidence. He nevertheless acquits the merchant. To expect a human being to help his fellow creature in the hour of need is *unreasonable*. The merchant could not be expected to think that the coolie did not want to attack him. Kindness and compassion being the exception, inhumanity the rule, the coolie deserved to be killed. He was a victim of his kindly emotion. Reason, cold and hard, rules the world.

But in the *Rise and Fall of the City of Mahagonny* the pattern is reversed. There instinct and emotion stand for the chaos and wickedness of the self-seeking, greedy capitalist world. The hero Paul proclaims self-indulgence as the supreme law of Mahagonny. The result is intolerable chaos and Paul himself is condemned to death; those who follow the blind impulse of instinct must die.

It is interesting to see how Brecht has transformed his own conflict into the struggle between the old and new world order: here the mysterious forces of instinct, which had been represented by the image of the luxuriant virgin forest that choked the men of Cortez and later by the jungle of the great city of Chicago, have become the symbol of the greedy *laissez-faire* society of capitalism. Against it the forces of discipline and self-control are ranged under the banner of scientific Marxism and Communist party discipline.

The subjugation of one's own irrational impulses requires a violent effort. Self-restraint of this kind, projected outward, turns into violence. Brecht, though occasionally prone to violent outbursts, outwardly the mildest, most self-controlled man, was constantly preoccupied with the need for violence. The victory of reason could, for him, only be brought about by violent means. When chaos had been banished from the world, then there could be friendliness and Confucian courtesy, but first there must be violence; the violence of the Communist party workers in *Die Massnahme* against their young comrade, the violence of the hedonistic self-seekers of *Mahagonny*, and of the gangsters of *The Threepenny Opera*. Even the gentle Joan Dark, the *St Joan of the Stockyards* who believed in the God of love and Christian non-violence till events taught her better, dies with the demand for violence on her lips:

> *Therefore he who says down here that there is a God,*
> *And yet no God is visible,*
> *And being invisible will yet help them –*
> *His head should be beaten upon the paving-stones*
> *Till he die like a dog. . . .*
> *. . . For*
> *Only violence helps, where violence reigns – and*
> *Only men can help where there are men.*[1]

Violence is thus both evil and good: it is evil in the hands of the gangsters of *The Threepenny Opera*, the gold-diggers of *Mahagonny*, evil in the Tsar of the Chicago meat packers, Pierpont Mauler, but good in the hands of the Communist party, where it can be defended as being violence serving the end of abolishing violence. Nevertheless those who use violence are always seen with admiration by Brecht, just as he preferred the boxers and six-day cyclists to the whining bourgeois poets. It is the admiration for the strong man, the doer as opposed to the thinker, the Nietzschean hero, which pervades so much of German literature – an attitude born from the frustrations, the deep feelings of impotence of poets and philosophers in a country where intellectuals were traditionally classed as mere dreamers and excluded from any influence on the affairs of the real world. Marx's demand

[1] Brecht, *Die Hl. Johanna der Schlachthoefe, Versuche 5*, p. 453.

sophy should cease to be mere theory and enter the field of
action springs from the same source – and also naturally
the use of violence.

in the world be changed by violence? For Brecht, struggling
ue the forces of chaos within him, a positive answer to this
n was a desperate necessity. Violence could certainly change
rld for the worse – why then not also for the better? Brecht, as
tackled the problem from the negative angle. In his comedy
equals Man, written in the middle twenties, three greedy, wicked,
vulgar British colonial soldiers completely transform a harmless
: individual into a ferocious fighting man. They achieve this by
hods which foreshadow the brain-washing techniques of totali-
an society with an accuracy as uncannily prophetic as that with
ich Die Massnahme foreshadowed the Stalinist purge trials. Little
aly Gay is accused of some crime, till he feels an overwhelming sense
f guilt, condemned to death in a mock trial, induced to believe that
ae has been executed. Thereafter he willingly accepts his new identity:

> . . . Mr Bertolt Brecht will prove that one can
> Do whatever one wants to do with a man:
> A man will be reassembled like a motor-car tonight in front of you –
> fterwards will be as good as new. . . .[1]

ght of recent researches on the techniques of brain-washing,
intuitive anticipation of the essence and the methods of this
s early as 1924–6 is staggering. And once again what he
as an attack on the brutality of the existing social order
fact into a forecast of the reality of his own brand of totali-
sm. His argument that, if a man can be transformed by such
olent methods into something worse, he could also be made into
something better, was put into practice by the Stalinist 'social engineers'
with results as horrifying as those Brecht depicted in his play.

Does Brecht condemn the soldiers who brain-wash little Galy Gay?
Or does he admire them? Does he applaud the self-mutilation of
Sergeant Fairchild? Or is he repelled by it? Here as elsewhere in
Brecht's writings it is impossible to give a clear answer. What one part of
his personality approved, another condemned. The reader or spectator
can take his choice. Thus Brecht's success as a writer is largely dependent on the ambivalence of the images he uses – and this in turn derives

[1] Erste Stuecke II, p. 229.

from the particularly acute form in which he was involved i[n]
human conflict between reason and instinct. The ambiv[alence]
displays in his attitude towards the subject-matter of his v[...]
also reflected in the struggle between the exuberance of the [...]
and the austerity of the classical in the formal aspect of his wo[rk]
alternation between harshness and lyricism, banality and s[...]
simplicity, austerity and luxuriant imagery in his poetry and p[...]
the hall-mark of Brecht. Its most characteristic expression is h[...]
of parody. For parody in itself is ambivalent – it mocks and im[...]
at one and the same moment. The success of the songs in *The T[hree]*
penny Opera, for example, is largely attributable to this dual natu[re]
parody; the sentimental ballad of the pimp, or the mock-love duet [of]
Macheath and Polly allow us to laugh at the grotesqueness of s[uch]
emotions in such abject characters – at the same time they have t[he]
genuine force of true sentiment behind them. Parody enabled Brec[ht]
to be sentimental and to write love-lyrics without consciously yieldin[g]
to his emotions. It also enables the spectator to feel ironically superio[r]
and sentimental at once.

The ambivalence of Brecht's attitude, which springs from the duality
of a personality deeply divided within itself, also provides the clue to
the Brechtian style of acting: the denial of identification betwe[en the]
actor and the character produces a split image. The actor e[...]
the character and at the same time comments on it: in other w[ords]
shows the actions of the characters and simultaneously pre[sents the]
critical reasoning which might have stopped them from acti[ng as they]
do. Brecht wanted the actor to present a picture of man i[...]
his emotions, critically, yet helplessly, aware of their irratio[...]

The violence of Brecht's early conflicts within himself visibly abate[d]
from about the time when he finally committed himself to the Communist creed. Communism, or rather his own brand of it tailored to
measure to his personal needs, provided the focus around which he
could integrate the forces that pulled him in so many different
directions. The Hegelian dialectic gave an aura of rationality to the
most glaringly ambivalent attitudes and emotions: the Marxist claim
to scientific certainty made the most blatantly irrational promptings
of hatred and violence acceptable, and the Marxist condemnation of
the existing social order allowed him to indulge his blackest nihilistic
pessimism without having to give in to despair. And to a personality

so deeply aware of human isolation, so hard put to establish contact with others, the standardized imagery and collective aims of the party provided a redeeming illusion of being able to share in a great collective experience. As Pelageya Vlasova puts it in *The Mother*, a shared cause provides that 'third thing' which enables two human beings to communicate:

> . . . I
> Kept my son. How did I keep him? Through
> The third thing.
> He and I were two, but the third thing
> We had in common, pursued in common,
> United us . . .
>
> .   .   .   .   .
>
> How near were we to each other, when near
> This thing. How good were we for each other, near
> This good cause.[1]

Nor can it be coincidence that this mellowing of Brecht's attitude, the re-integration of his violently divided personality, dates from the time when a new type of character appears in his writing – the mother image. Until then a very large proportion of the female characters in Brecht's plays were whores and bawds, infanticides or ruined girls; the villainous brothel-keeper Leocadia Begbick, who appears both in *Mahagonny* and in *Man equals Man*, the women of Baal who are little more than objects of his sexual greed, all these female characters were seen with a mixture of hatred and contempt.

The dramatization of Gorky's *The Mother* and *St Joan of the Stockyards* introduce a new type of female character – the female revolutionary. But while Joan Dark is completely sexless, Pelageya Vlasova has the features of a real woman: her motherliness is both emotional and rational – and so is her revolutionary attitude, which is born of a mother's love for mankind, the desire to spread happiness. The same archetypal character, frequently played by Brecht's wife, Helene Weigel, reappears in a succession of Brecht's later plays: in *Mother Courage*, where the mother-image is overlaid by the camp follower's greed for profit and war-guilt, yet breaks through to the audience with elemental force; in *Señora Carrar's Rifles*, where mother-love emerges from selfishness with the readiness to sacrifice even one's children in

[1] Brecht, *Die Mutter*, *Versuche 7*, p. 48.

the fight against the class-enemy; in *The Good Soul of Setzuan*, where the only good human being is a prostitute but one with motherly feelings, ready to fight for her offspring, and in *The Caucasian Chalk Circle*, where characteristically the mother-figure is split into two: the physical mother and the spiritual mother, the woman who loves the child and the one who wants to use it for her own selfish ends. In trying to prove their claim to the child they are pulling it out of the chalk circle in different directions, threatening to tear it in half, just as the conflict of reason and instinct pulls the personality in opposite directions. But, characteristically, in this late play it is emotion not reason that wins the battle. And what is more, the foster-mother who loves the child lets it go so as not to hurt it. It is not violence but yielding that is awarded the prize.

For, once Brecht had accepted the discipline of his new creed and the threat of being overwhelmed by uncontrolled instinctive forces had receded, the emotional side appeared in an increasingly sympathetic light. It was as if the guilt-feelings which had originally been evoked by the temptation to succumb to subconscious urges had now been transferred to the other side: Brecht now felt guilty at having opted for a coldly rational and inevitably cruel ideology.

Frequently the conflict between reason and instinct is symbolized by split characters: in the ballet-cantata *The Seven Deadly Sins*, for example, the heroine Anna appears split into the instinctive, emotional Anna who dances and the rational, practical Anna who sings. Anna is a dancer who leaves her home in Louisiana with the object of earning enough money for her family to build a house. The natural instincts of a healthy girl, which, if followed, would impair her earning power appear as the seven deadly sins to her family and her rational self. Her love for a poor man which might keep her from selling herself to a rich lover is the sin of lust, her desire to eat rather than starve to keep her figure for the strip-tease act is greed, etc. Having resisted all these temptations Anna returns home with the money. In a commercial society instinct has to yield to calculation. Here instinct and emotion are seen as positive, cold rationality as negative.

This is also the theme of *The Good Soul of Setzuan*. The gods reward the kind prostitute with enough money to start a modest business, but to prevent her fellow men from exploiting her, kindly Shen Te has to assume the mask of a ruthless cousin, who drives the spongers out. Again reason and emotion appear as separate and contradictory aspects of the same personality. As to be wholly good means ruin, the ruthless, hard-boiled, rational part of nature must take command.

In Puntila the rational personality is sober, while the emotional, kindly side of his nature appears only when he is drunk. Shen Te is a good human being who has to be wicked to survive. Puntila is a wicked character who loses his villainy when he loses his reason. In both cases, as in that of *The Seven Deadly Sins*, reason is equated with the negative aspect of human nature. Here lies the main difference to Brecht's early period when he tended to reject the emotional side of human nature and called upon the discipline of cold reason to restore order when the emotions led to chaos. This change, however, is merely the result of lessened tension. The emotions, if followed, would still lead to ruin. In that sense they are still negative. But they are now seen as basically good rather than uncontrollable urges which threaten sanity itself. When Brecht was working his way towards the acceptance of Communist discipline he tended to reject the emotional side of man and to equate it with the chaos of the existing social order: after he had surrendered himself to what he regarded as a supremely rational creed, he depicted the rational side of his characters as an element of villainy in them – though one that is necessary for their survival in society. He, of course, always argued that after the victory of Communism this conflict between reason and instinct would disappear. But the fact remains that a practical approach to the problem of survival and success – such as the highly realistic tactics of Communism also demanded – is consistently shown in a negative light in Brecht's later work.

The conflict of instinct and emotion also colours Brecht's two most mature works, *The Caucasian Chalk Circle* and *The Life of Galileo*. In both these great plays one of the chief characters bears autobiographical features of the author. At last Brecht had found a way of portraying himself on the stage. The judge Azdak in *The Caucasian Chalk Circle* is a lecherous and immoral jester, yet, if only for the wrong reason, he does good. When civil war and public disorder sweep him into the seat of judgment, he dispenses justice, because he is ignorant of the law, and because he is corrupt enough not only to accept bribes but to cheat those who have bribed him. Because he follows his emotions he is a villain, but because he follows his native shrewdness and intuitive understanding of people rather than listen to the reasoning of lawyers, he does good. Whether he did it intentionally or not, Brecht has here drawn a masterly portrait of himself – a highly complex and contradictory character, servile and arrogant, shrewd and foolish, humorous and lewd, humble and conceited, familiar and yet distant – and a genius. Azdak is a battlefield of the conflict of instinct and emotion – but instinct wins every time: that is why Azdak is in the last resort a good man. He seldom achieves what he has set out to achieve, his plans are defeated by his instincts and intuition – just as Brecht's own poetical talent and intuition always got the better of his rational intentions.

Galileo too is a genius. He too is a lecherous and gluttonous man. But his most powerful instinct is curiosity. His greatest sensual pleasure is the pleasure of discovery. Here Brecht comes to the very core of the problem – the urge for knowledge, the most rational side of human endeavour, science itself, is shown as being merely another of man's basic, instinctive urges, just as deeply rooted in the irrational as the instinct for procreation. To be able to indulge this instinct Galileo is prepared to commit the meanest action: he cheats the Venetians by selling them the telescope he has not invented but merely plagiarized – clearly an autobiographical trait. He writes abjectly servile letters to the Medici whose despotism he despises. And with the physical cowardice of the sensuous man he recants his theories. In the earlier version of the play Galileo's action was made to appear excusable as a deliberate act of calculation and cunning: by recanting he saved his life and gained the time to complete his treatise which was then smuggled out into the free world. But shortly before Brecht died, as he put the final touches to the revised version of the play and conducted the rehearsals of the Berliner Ensemble, he had changed his mind – he insisted that Galileo 'must be shown as a social criminal, a complete rogue'[1] and told his actors:

Galileo is shown as a man who is right, one of the great heroes of the following five hundred years, who sweeps away all obstacles, but who then collapses and becomes a criminal. That is one of the great difficulties: to bring out the criminal element in the character of the hero. In spite of all, he is a hero – and in spite of all – he becomes a criminal. . . .[2]

[1] Brecht quoted by K. Ruelicke, 'Leben des Galilei – Schlusszene', *Sinn und Form*, Second Special Brecht Issue, 1957, p. 292.   [2] ibid., p. 294.

Hero and criminal – once again we encounter the duality of the Brechtian character. Galileo becomes a criminal because by his cowardice he has established the tradition of the scientists' subservience to the State – the tradition that, according to Brecht, reached its culmination in the production of the atomic bomb, which science put at the disposal of ordinary, non-scientific men, to serve their power politics. Galileo, the hero of science, thus becomes the embodiment of reason in all its splendour, ruined once more by its inability to overcome the base, instinctive, inarticulate side of human nature. The greatest of intellects, the personification of science itself, is thus as helplessly tied to the blind instincts of his subconscious nature, as poor Mazeppa is tied to the wild steed that carries him to his doom.

For the attempt to banish instinct and emotion and to live as a wholly rational being is foredoomed to failure. Although he strenuously denied it in public, Brecht knew that this was so. In one of his few really intimate, private poems, the magnificent sequence of *Four Psalms* (written in the middle thirties but published only after his death), he confessed it:

> *I am the most practical of all my brethren –*
> *And* my *head comes first of all!*
> *My brethren were cruel, I am the cruellest –*
> *And* I *weep in the night!*[1]

[1] Brecht, 'Der vierte Psalm', *Sinn und Form*, Second Special Brecht Issue, 1957, p. 141.

Chapter XI

BRECHT'S WORLD

I see the world in a mellow light: it is God's excrement. . . .

BRECHT, *Baal*[1]

It was very beautiful. . . . Everything.

BRECHT, *Baal*[2]

If the analysis attempted in the previous chapter of Brecht's life-long preoccupation with his own conflict between the forces of reason and instinct is accepted, his inability to conform with the requirements of a narrow political line will be readily understood. And it will be seen that far from being a mere left-wing, conformist *auteur du boulevard* as Eugène Ionesco has described him[3] – surely on the evidence of hearsay rather than a close reading of his plays – Brecht was as deeply concerned with the predicament of man and the irony of the human condition as James Joyce, Kafka, or the French Existentialists.

Brecht's picture of the world has a great deal in common with the sombre canvas of the latter school. Like Sartre or Camus, Brecht saw man determined by his social environment, his personality the mere product of changing outside circumstances.

It is of course no coincidence that Brecht – and the whole generation of German writers whose foremost representative he is, the only one likely to survive through the force of his language and the intensity of his poetic vision – anticipated the French Existentialists of the next generation. If their despair, their decision to 'commit' themselves, sprang from the experience of the French defeat of 1940, that of Brecht and his contemporaries was engendered by the German defeat in 1918. In each case the young intellectuals responded to a world in which the comfortable security of bourgeois standards and assumptions had been replaced by terror and violence, in a spirit of grim realism.

This ruthlessly realistic attitude was, in Brecht's case, akin to the

[1] *Erste Stuecke I*, p. 80.   [2] ibid., p. 98.
[3] Eugène Ionesco, 'The Playwright's Role', *The Observer*, London, 29.6.1958.

ruthlessness born of despair and wounded pride which led other, less sophisticated, members of his generation in Germany into the arms of Hitler. On the other hand, that tribal nationalist myth itself constituted the break-through of the forces of man's savage and irrational nature, that Brecht so dreaded in himself as well as in society. Yet, being of his time and generation, he sought to meet this threat by counter-measures which were tainted with the same poison: violence to stamp out violence. Hatred to eradicate hatred and to pave the way for sweet reason and friendliness. Totalitarianism to defeat totalitarianism. Evil to drive out evil.

His very failure to extricate himself from this dilemma is at the root of his success, and his significance, as a poet: being so deeply involved in the conflict, so deeply tainted with the evil of his time, he was able to give it full and valid expression. That is why plays like *Die Massnahme* or *Mann ist Mann* were not only prophetic forecasts of things unthought of when they were written but remain the most compelling and concentrated poetic statements of some of the fundamental preoccupations of our time.

Brecht's world is the empty universe through which Nietzsche's cry 'God is dead' resounds with terrifying and reverberating echo. 'The world is poor, and man is bad',[1] 'The meanest thing alive, and the weakest, is man'[2] – if these two statements sum up Brecht's opinion in his early phase, one of the foolish and impotent gods in *The Good Soul of Setzuan* repeats it in that much later play: 'The world is uninhabitable, you must admit that'[3] and the good soul herself, Shen Te, the motherly prostitute comes to the same conclusion:

> . . . He who helps the lost
> Is lost himself. For who could long
> Refuse to be wicked, when those die who eat no meat?
> . . .

And she asks:

> Something must be wrong with your world. Why
> Is there a reward for wickedness, why do the good receive
> Such hard punishment?[4]

[1] *Die Dreigroschenoper, Stuecke III*, p. 62.
[2] *Mann ist Mann, Erste Stuecke II*, p. 272.
[3] *Der Gute Mensch von Sezuan, Stuecke VIII*, p. 389.   [4] ibid., p. 402.

That virtue brings no reward and is in fact a sign of stupidity is a recurring theme. As Mother Courage puts it:

> If there is too much virtue somewhere, it is a sure sign that there is something wrong. . . . Why, if a general or king is stupid and lands his people in a mess, then they need desperate courage, a virtue. If he is too mean and recruits too few soldiers, then they have to be as strong as Hercules. And if he is slovenly and pays no attention, they have to be as clever as snakes, or else they are done for. They need special loyalty if he always asks too much of them. . . . All virtues that a proper country and a good king and general can do without. In a good country you need no virtues; people can all be quite ordinary, of middling intelligence and cowards, for all it matters. . . .[1]

And in that most bitter of all of Brecht's plays, *The Exception and the Rule*, one of the characters proclaims this philosophy:

> *Next to you someone is thirsty: quickly close your eyes!*
> *Plug up your ears: someone is groaning next to you!*
> *Restrain your foot: someone is calling for help!*
> *Woe to him who forgets himself! He*
> *Offers water to a man, and*
> *A wolf drinks!*[2]

The poor are mean and the rich are ruthless and cruel. Repeatedly Brecht demonstrates his thesis that the suffering poor, if given a chance to get on top, would be as greedy and heartless as the vulgar, rapacious business men he so delighted in putting before his audience. War is the natural state in a world peopled by men. And there is no justice. For all his love of court-room scenes (there is hardly a play by Brecht without one) he denied that man can be an honest judge of his fellow men. The possibility of a Solomonic judgment like that of *The Caucasian Chalk Circle* has to be explained by the very peculiar circumstances that bring a real rogue, Azdak, to act as judge. Only the very young and very simple have something like innocence: the two St Joans, Joan Dark of the Chicago stockyards, and Simone Machard, the little French girl who dreams of saving her country in 1940. And they are doomed because of their innocence and goodness. The only innocent and good character who wins in the end is the servant girl Grusche, in *The Caucasian Chalk Circle*, the mellowest of

---

[1] *Mutter Courage, Stuecke VII*, p. 88.
[2] *Die Ausnahme und die Regel, Stuecke V*, p. 226.

all the plays. But even she is warned against saving the helpless child: 'Terrible is the temptation to goodness!'[1] And life only continues because the mothers doggedly and irrationally persist in rearing their young.

This then is a vision of the world in the great tragic tradition of pessimism which has inspired so much of dramatic literature from Aeschylos to Seneca, from Shakespeare to the present day. It is a world sullied by the presence of evil, the blind workings of irrational forces, a world without God. In Brecht's plays the place of fate is taken by the inscrutable workings of the social order which moulds the life of the characters and tosses them into misfortune or happiness. Human personality is no longer an immutable essence but merely the product of the pull of social forces at any given moment. And human will is helpless against them.

That is the negative side of the picture. Again and again, in his later years, Brecht asserted that this, however, was only half the picture. On the positive side, he claimed, it was counterbalanced by the hope, the virtual certainty, of Communism. But invariably Brecht's plays have an elliptic construction: the negative side is presented at length and the world is shown to be a dreadful place. Sometimes at the very end there is a suggestion that all this must be, and could be, changed. Sometimes it is left entirely to the audience to draw this conclusion for itself. But the positive side is always merely postulated. It is never shown. The most positive play of all, *The Mother*, shows Pelageya Vlasova advancing in the van of the demonstrators of the October revolution, on the very threshold of the new order, but not a single step is taken inside it. Play after play depicts the horrors of the world *before* the revolution. Only a single scene, the prologue to *The Caucasian Chalk Circle*, is laid inside the promised land – a collective farm in Soviet Russia. And here Soviet critics have angrily disclaimed any resemblance to the real thing and pointed out that the way Brecht's Soviet collective farmers behave is pure fantasy. Brecht wrote *The Caucasian Chalk Circle* in the United States, where, it could be argued, he was out of touch with the realities of the Communist order. But in eight years in East Berlin he was unable to produce a single play on the realities of life in Communist Germany. There he had the experience on his doorstep. The authorities alternately begged and ordered him to try his hand. He did not succeed. Why?

[1] *Der kaukasische Kreidekreis, Stuecke X*, p. 174.

The answer is only too obvious: the positive side represents not a scientifically demonstrable truth, but merely a pious and touching hope, a hope, moreover, which was constantly belied by Brecht's own experience of the real world. He had escaped despair by attributing all the horror and disgust he felt to the social order of his time, while in fact what he attacked was not human nature under capitalism but his own personal experience of human nature itself. Analysis of his language shows that as a rule he is talking about *man, the world*, when he paints this pessimistic picture, only occasionally is there a qualifying clause: 'man in these circumstances', 'the world under this system', etc. But even then the truth of the proposition, that the world can be changed for the better, is never demonstrated. 'Change the world: it needs to be changed!' is an exhortation that runs through Brecht's plays like a refrain. But he never succeeded in convincingly demonstrating *what* he wanted the world to be changed into and *how* it could be changed. 'The Truth is concrete' was the slogan he displayed to his visitors in his work-rooms in Denmark and Hollywood. It is an aphorism which contains the essence of the dramatist's objective and justifies his labours: for science or philosophy can only generalize. The dramatist can put the truth in the only wholly convincing form because he creates a completely individual, concrete picture of reality. That is why it is, in Brecht's own terms, irrelevant what his political convictions were *outside*. his work. The truth can only be contained within the concrete action of his plays themselves. But these *never* give concrete evidence of the feasibility, or even the nature, of the Utopian state he aimed at. They are wholly negative: attacks upon the existing order.

In this, of course, Brecht is a genuine Marxist. For Marx and Engels themselves never presented a concrete picture of the world order they wanted to create. They too were essentially critics. They criticized the social system of their day in brilliant, witty, copiously documented and often unfair terms; they analysed the shortcomings of mid-nineteenth-century capitalism and proved to their own satisfaction that it was doomed to end in catastrophe. But when it came to defining the new order that was to take its place, their prophetic vision became a virtual blank. Brecht too is mainly a critic, brilliant in demonstrating the predicament of man, the iniquity of his institutions, somewhat naïve in exposing the details of the workings of business or high finance. But he has nothing concrete to offer when it comes to showing how a better system would work. The very violence of his demand for a change, his recurrent assertion that things cannot, must not, go on as they are at present, springs from this failure.

In fact, if we extract the meaning contained in his plays in the concrete, three-dimensional form of the artist's re-creation of reality, the result belies the facile optimism of Brecht's professed, and monotonously asserted, eschatological hope of a Marxist earthly paradise. For he constantly shows the weakness of man, his inability to deal with his problems according to his insight into what would be rational, his subjection to instinct and blind passion. Poverty, he never tires of demonstrating, breeds meanness and selfishness. But the rich too are mean and selfish. Why? Because they thrive on a wicked system, to which they too have to conform. Therefore the system must be changed. But, in Brecht's view, it simply cannot be changed slowly and gradually: only violence can bring about a really fundamental change. But violence is wicked. And wicked methods, as Brecht shows again and again, make wicked people. Brecht's creative power puts the proof of each of these propositions before us concretely and convincingly. And he is unable to suggest a way of breaking this vicious circle:

> Would you deny that the use of force debases him who resorts to it?
> No, I do not deny that.[1]

This brief exchange, which occurs in Brecht's last completed play, *The Days of the Commune*, sums up his dilemma. He could not solve it and was far too deeply imbued with the instinctive integrity of a real poet to bluff his way out by the empty rhetoric of a purple passage. After showing that the revolutionaries of the Paris Commune failed because their leaders were too idealistic, too tender-hearted to apply the terror in its ultimate ruthlessness, he cannot deny that violence itself is evil and begets evil. Whether Brecht was aware of the implication or not, it is clearly there. Lenin who *did* learn the lesson of the Paris Commune and did not shrink from violence landed on the other horn of the dilemma. And this is not the dilemma of capitalism. It is the dilemma of human nature.

Brecht's work thus fails, as the Communists rightly felt, in conveying the message of hope in man's redemption by a radical change in the social order, which he so earnestly and persistently sought to put into it. Yet the final effect of Brecht's negative picture of the human condition is not entirely one of despair. Again and again the hopelessness of man's lonely and senseless struggle is made bearable by its very

[1] *Die Tage der Kommune, Stuecke X*, p. 417.

acceptance by humble people who battle against the terrors of the universe in resignation and simplicity: Joan Dark, Simone Machard, Mother Courage, Schweik, Shen Te, Grusche, they all redeem themselves by their courage in the face of overwhelming odds.

One of the projects which occupied Brecht's mind but which he never completed was an opera, *Die Reisen des Gluecksgotts* (*Travels of the God of Fortune*), in which the Chinese God of Fortune was to come into the ruined cities after a great war to urge the people to fight for their happiness. He comes into conflict with the authorities and is condemned to death.

> And now the hangmen try their arts on this little god of fortune. But the poisons they administer taste delightful to him, his head, which is cut off, immediately grows again, he executes a dance of contagious hilarity on the gallows, etc. It is impossible to kill humanity's yearning for happiness.[1]

Paul Dessau, who was to write the score, reports: 'Happiness means Communism.'[2] But again this identification, which Brecht certainly believed in, remains an abstract one, confined to the author's private convictions, and does not appear to have been put into concrete terms. What the opera would have once more put before the audience was the apparatus of force and authority at grips with the unquenchable desire of humanity for redemption from the evils of the world.

But the little god, who cannot be subdued by the hangman, is also an image of non-violence: he shows that executions and coercive measures are bound to fail. Here Brecht, in sympathy with the Chinese God of Fortune whose tiny statuette he treasured, accepts the stoicism of the Orient. It is an attitude which recognizes the senselessness, the unreality of the world, but, having done so, reconciles itself to life and its everyday tasks. Long before he had discovered Confucianism and Taoism, Brecht had expressed similar sentiments; for example, in his early *Great Hymn of Thanksgiving*:

> *Praise the cold, the darkness and death down here,*
> *Look up from the ground:*
> *You are of no account*
> *And can die without fear.*[3]

[1] Brecht, 'Bei Durchsicht meiner ersten Stuecke', *Stuecke I*, East Berlin, p. 9.
[2] Brecht and Dessau, *Lieder und Gesaenge*, East Berlin, 1957, p. 20.
[3] Brecht, 'Grosser Dankchoral', *Hauspostille*, Berlin, 1927, p. 62.

This Taoist attitude of yielding to the flow of things, while recognizing its absurdity, coexisted in Brecht's mind with, and below, the doctrine of the class struggle and the gospel of the violent transformation of the world. This in fact is the passive attitude, the yielding to emotion, the abandonment of reason he so feared in his youth, transformed into a mellow and profound philosophy.

And so Brecht, the prophet of rational planning by violent methods, is also the author of a poem like *The Legend of the Origin of the Book Tao Te Ching during Lao Tzu's Journey into Exile*, where he preaches the wisdom of patient non-violence. For –

> . . . *the movement of the softest water will*
> *Conquer in time the powerful hard stone.*
> *You understand: hard things are overcome. . . .*[1]

And in one of his late, epigrammatic poems Brecht speaks of the Japanese mask of an evil demon on his wall, whose distorted features show –

> . . . *how strenuous it is to be evil.*[2]

Behind the loud, frenzied demand for violent change, dictated by the ruthless, cold process of scientific reasoning, therefore, there always lay a yearning for the quiet, passive acceptance of the world as it is, with all its harshness and absurdity. The more he forced himself into the strait-jacket of discipline and purposeful activity, the more deeply he longed for the warmth of self-oblivion and self-abandon. Brecht's work as a producer called for a style of relaxed ease. He abhorred the cramped features and strenuous movements of violent acting. And the favourite image of his early poems is that of the swimmer who is carried down the river, gently drifting. But such was his nature that his passive moods gave way to yearnings for self-control and self-domination by discipline and strenuous activity. Powerful attractions and revulsions propelled him in different directions, and his poetry is the resultant from this highly complex parallelogram of forces. No wonder that it does not move in the direction his lucid, calculating intellect had planned.

This is the reason for the bewildering complexity of Brecht's

[1] Brecht, 'Legende von der Entstehung des Buches Taoteking auf dem Wege des Lao Tse in die Emigration', *Hundert Gedichte*, East Berlin, 1951, p. 112.

[2] Brecht, 'Die Maske des Boesen', ibid., p. 309.

artistic impact. Behind a surface of deceptive simplicity his work reveals layer after layer of surprising intricacy and depth. The Polish critic Andrzej Wirth has spoken of the 'stereo-metric' construction of Brecht's plays, which always move on several levels of time, space, and narrative method at once. But the real secret of this three-dimensional effect lies not in any formal principle of construction but in the inner tensions and contradictions within the author's mind, conscious and subconscious. It seems that such deep conflicts within a personality are among the conditions without which major creative work cannot be produced, that such work must spring from the constant and painful clash between the different levels of the artist's personality. For only thus can there be more in a work than its creator consciously put into it. Only thus can it mean different things to different men and reveal new aspects to each succeeding generation.

But to Brecht himself, who could not suffer the idea that he was not wholly in control of his own activity, the obvious divergence between his intentions and the effect of his work on the public must have been truly tragic.

He wanted to be a writer for the common people, as easy to understand as fair-ground comics, but the simpler he tried to be, the more complex his work became, so that only intellectuals could appreciate it; he wanted to serve the cause of the revolution, but was regarded with suspicion by its recognized standard-bearers, who reviled him as a formalist and banned him as a dangerous, defeatist influence; he wanted to arouse the critical faculties of his audience, but only succeeded in moving them to tears; he wanted to make his theatre a laboratory of social change, a living proof that the world and mankind could be altered, and had to see it strengthen his public's faith in the enduring virtues of unchanging human nature. He had to witness his villains acclaimed as heroes and his heroes mistaken for villains. He sought to spread the cold light of logical clarity – and produced a rich texture of poetic ambiguity. He abhorred the very idea of beauty – and created beauty.

Yet such is the paradox of the creative process, that, had he succeeded in his objectives, he would merely have been a flat and boring party hack. He failed – and became one of the most puzzling, one of the most hotly debated, but also one of the most important writers of his age.

Part Five: for Reference

Section A

A SHORT CHRONOLOGY OF BRECHT'S LIFE

1898	10 February. Born at Augsburg.
1904–8	Elementary school, Augsburg.
1908–17	Realgymnasium, Augsburg.
1914	17 August. Brecht's first contribution to a newspaper, a short prose sketch, published in *Augsburger Neueste Nachrichten*.
1917	Starts reading Medicine and Natural Science at Munich University.
1918	Called up for military service as a medical orderly. Writes his first play *Baal*.
1919	Continues his studies at Munich University while acting as drama critic of *Der Volkswille*, Augsburg.
1920	'Dramaturg' at the Munich Kammerspiele.
1922	29 September. First night of *Drums in the Night*, Munich. 3 November. Marries Marianne Zoff in Munich.
1923	9 May. First night of *Im Dickicht*, Munich. 8 December. First night of *Baal*, Leipzig.
1924	18 March. First night of *Edward II*, Munich. Autumn. Moves to Berlin.
1926	26 September. First night of *Mann ist Mann*, Darmstadt.
1927	*Hauspostille* published. Summer. First version of *Mahagonny* (setting of poems from *Hauspostille* by Kurt Weill) performed at Baden-Baden. 22 November. Divorced from Marianne Zoff.
1928	23 January. First night of *Schweik*, adapted by Gasbarra, Leo Lania, and Brecht, in Piscator's production. 31 August. First night of *The Threepenny Opera* at the Theater am Schiffbauerdamm. December. Awarded first prize in *Berliner Illustrierte* short story competition for *Die Bestie*.

1929	Summer. First performance of *Flug der Lindberghs* and *Badener Lehrstueck* at Baden-Baden Music Week.
	10 April. Marries Helene Weigel.
	31 August. Failure of *Happy End*.
1930	9 March. First night of *Rise and Fall of the City of Mahagonny* at Leipzig.
	17 and 20 October. Hearings of Brecht's lawsuit against the company producing the film version of *The Threepenny Opera*.
	10 December. First performance of *Die Massnahme* by Arbeiterchor Grossberlin.
1932	15 January. First performance of *Die Mutter*.
	March. Brecht's film *Kuhle Wampe* banned.
1933	28 February. Leaves Germany.
	Spring. Vienna, Switzerland, France.
	June. *Die Sieben Todsuenden* at Théâtre des Champs-Elysees, Paris.
	Settles in Denmark.
1935	June. International Writers' Congress, Paris.
	November. Visits New York to attend performance of *The Mother* by the Theatre Union at the Civic Theatre.
1936	Becomes co-editor of *Das Wort*, Moscow.
	4 November. First performance of *The Roundheads and the Peakheads*, Copenhagen.
1937	17 October. First performance of *Señora Carrar's Rifles*, Paris.
1938	21 May. First performance of *Furcht und Elend des Dritten Reiches* (seven scenes under the title '99%'), Paris.
1939	Summer. Leaves Denmark for Stockholm.
1940	Moves to Finland.
	19 April. First night of *Mother Courage* at Zurich.
	3 May. U.S. Consul at Helsinki issues visa for the United States.
	11 June. Leaves Vladivostok aboard a Swedish ship.
	21 July. Arrives San Pedro, California.
1942	May. Performance of five scenes from *Furcht und Elend des Dritten Reiches* by refugee actors in New York.
	Film: *Hangmen also Die*.

1943   4 February. First night of *The Good Soul of Setzuan* at Zurich.

9 September. First night of *The Life of Galileo* at Zurich.

1945   Co-founder of German publishing house Aurora Verlag in New York.

7 June. *The Private Life of the Master Race* (English version of *Furcht und Elend*), first performance at Berkeley, California.

12 June. *The Private Life of the Master Race* opens in New York with Albert Bassermann.

1947   30 July. English version of *The Life of Galileo* with Charles Laughton opens at Coronet Theatre, Hollywood.

30 October. Brecht before the Un-American Activities Committee, Washington.

November. Returns to Europe.

7 December. *The Life of Galileo* opens in New York.

1948   February. *Antigone* at Chur (Coire), Switzerland.

5 June. First night of *Herr Puntila und sein Knecht Matti*, Zurich.

22 October. Arrives back in Berlin to prepare production of *Mother Courage* at Deutsches Theater.

1949   11 January. *Mother Courage* opens at Deutsches Theater.

Spring. Returns to Zurich.

Autumn. Foundation of Berliner Ensemble. Brecht settles in East Berlin.

8 November. Berliner Ensemble opens with *Puntila*.

1950   April. Application for Austrian nationality granted.

October. Produces *Mother Courage* at Munich.

1951   17 March. *The Trial of Lucullus* withdrawn after one performance at Berlin State Opera.

12 October. Revised version of *Lucullus – The Condemnation of Lucullus –* at Berlin State Opera.

8 November. *Mère Courage* produced by Théâtre Nationale Populaire at Paris.

1952   The Berliner Ensemble tours Poland: Warsaw, Cracow, Lodz, etc.

1953   17 June. Outbreak of the East German rising.

21 June. Publication of Brecht's message of loyalty to Ulbricht (First Secretary of SED).

1954   March. The Berliner Ensemble takes over the renovated Theater am Schiffbauerdamm.

15 June. First night of *The Caucasian Chalk Circle*, ignored by party organ, *Neues Deutschland*.

July. Berliner Ensemble at Paris International Festival (*Mother Courage*).

1955   26 May. Receives Stalin Peace Prize in Moscow.

June. Berliner Ensemble at Paris International Festival (*The Caucasian Chalk Circle*).

1956   14 August. Dies of coronary thrombosis.

27 August–11 September. Berliner Ensemble in London.

Section B

A DESCRIPTIVE LIST OF BRECHT'S WORKS

In the following pages the reader will find brief outlines of the character and content of Brecht's writings, together with basic facts concerning the time of composition, first performance in the case of plays, and an indication where they can be most readily found in published form. Where translations into English exist, and are accessible, they are also listed. But these bibliographical references lay no claim to completeness. For an indication where full bibliographical details can be found, see the section 'Bibliography'.

Poems

The principal volumes of poetry or cycles of poems published individually in Brecht's lifetime are:

Augsburger Sonette

Some poems from this cycle of juvenilia exist in manuscript copies. Brecht described them as 'just pornography'.

Bertolt Brechts Taschenpostille (published 1926)

Bertolt Brecht's Pocket Breviary, privately printed in an edition limited to only twenty-five copies, is, except for one poem, identical with

Bertolt Brechts Hauspostille (published 1927)

A German critic once called this 'Domestic Breviary' the devil's prayer-book. It is divided into five sections or 'Lessons': (1) Intercessions; (2) Spiritual Exercises; (3) Chronicles; (4) Mahagonny Songs; (5) Little Book of Hours of the Departed. Three more personal poems are appended as a final section 'Of Poor B.B.'. There are fifty poems in the book. Some of these Brecht had already used in his first plays, others he used in later plays. They include the ballads of *Baal*, *The Legend of the Dead Soldier*, which is sung in *Drums in the Night*, many of the songs in *Mahagonny* and *The Threepenny Opera*, etc. The poetry of *Hauspostille* derives from the folk-ballad and the French cabaret *chanson* as well as from more strictly literary models like Villon or Rimbaud. Its mood is one of passive acceptance of Nature with its sensuous beauty and its horror, and of pity for all poor and helpless creatures.

Lesebuch fuer Staedtebewohner (published in *Versuche 2*, 1930)

Described as 'Texts for gramophone records', the ten poems in this 'Primer for City-dwellers' deal with the loneliness and lovelessness of the individual lost in the stone jungle of the great cities.

Die Drei Soldaten (published in *Versuche 6*, 1932)

The Three Soldiers, a 'children's book' with twenty-five illustrations by George Grosz, consists of fourteen stories in verse. Three soldiers of the First World War refuse to die and return to the cities. They want to help the poor and down-trodden. But to accomplish this aim they *kill* all those poor people who suffer from the consequences of the post-war crisis. They thus want to induce the poor and down-trodden to cease to accept unbearable conditions. The three soldiers are eventually revealed to be personifications of 'Hunger', 'Accident', and 'Cough'. When they get to Moscow, where there are neither poor nor down-trodden people, they themselves are killed. The book is intended 'to provoke the children to ask questions'.

Gedichte, Lieder, Choere (published Paris, 1934)

A collection of poems and songs that were set to music by Hanns Eisler. Apart from the choruses and songs from *The Mother* and *Die Massnahme* it contains mainly political poems written at the height of the economic crisis and the struggle against Hitler.

Svendborger Gedichte (published London, 1939)

A collection of poetry written in the years of exile in Denmark. It includes a good deal of political verse of an ephemeral nature (Kriegsfibel – anti-war quatrains; Deutsche Satiren – satirical poems written for broadcasting), but also some of Brecht's most outstanding narrative poems: *Der Schuh des Empedokles* (*The Shoe of Empedocles*); *Legende von der Entstehung des Buches Taoteking auf dem Weg des Laotse in die Emigration* (*Legend on the origin of the book Tao Te Ching during Lao Tzu's Journey into Exile*); *Gleichnis des Buddha vom Brennenden Haus* (*Buddha's Parable of the Burning House*), etc., as well as Brecht's most significant personal statement: *An die Nachgeborenen* (*To Posterity*).

Chinesische Gedichte (published in *Versuche 10*, 1950)

Nine poems from the Chinese, seven of them based on English versions by Arthur Waley, the two others being based on modern Chinese poems by Mao Tse Tung and Kuan Chao.

Studien (published in *Versuche 11*, 1951)

Eight 'studies' in sonnet form, which elucidate – or debunk – literary masterpieces ranging from Dante's *Beatrice* and Shakespeare's *Hamlet* to Kant's *Metaphysics of Manners*.

Die Erziehung der Hirse (published 1951)

The Nurture of Millet, a long poem of fifty-two stanzas based on a Soviet propaganda story on how an old Tartar peasant, following the precepts of Michurin and Lysenko, so improved the yield of millet that he made a vital contribution to the Soviet victory in the Second World War. One of Brecht's rare attempts to write a propaganda poem in the Soviet tradition and to extract the lyrical possibilities from the statistics of increased yields per hectare. Paul Dessau has set *Die Erziehung der Hirse* to music.

Buckower Elegien (published in *Versuche 13*, 1954)

Six short poems written at Brecht's country retreat at Buckow, some of them in his late epigrammatic manner, modelled on the Japanese *haiku*. The cycle is, however, known to consist of a larger number of poems than the six published in *Versuche 13*.

Gedichte aus dem 'Messingkauf' (published in *Versuche 14*, 1955)

Didactic poems on the theory of the 'epic theatre'. (See below under 'Essays and Theoretical Writings'.)

A number of posthumous poems were published in

Sinn und Form, Second Special Brecht Issue, 1957.

They include some autobiographical poems from the thirties, among them the remarkable sequence

Vier Psalmen (*Four Psalms*), written in the middle thirties, four prose poems in Biblical language with a surrealist imagery quite unlike any of Brecht's other writing and reminiscent of St John Perse.

Equally impressive is a group of Brecht's last poems:

Aus Letzten Gedichten which includes his melancholy reflections from the time of the East German rising (1953).

While some of these volumes or cycles of poems are difficult to obtain, the three volumes of Brecht's selected poetry are easily obtainable. These are:

Hundert Gedichte (East Berlin, 1951; fifth amended edition, 1958)

This selection is heavily biassed towards Brecht's political output and does not do justice to his full range as a poet.

Brecht: Gedichte (Reclam, Leipzig, 1955)

Another East German selection in the famous cheap paper-back series of Reclams Universalbibliothek (no. 7996/97). This too is a politically biassed selection. Some of the poems have been ruthlessly mutilated or altered.

Bertolt Brechts Gedichte und Lieder (Frankfurt, 1956)

Edited by Brecht's friend and publisher Peter Suhrkamp, this is by far the best anthology of Brecht's poetry available.

Plays and Other Stage Works

BAAL

Written: 1918.

First performance: Leipzig, 8 December 1923.

Baal, a loosely constructed sequence of twenty-two (in another version twenty-one) scenes, preceded by the ballad 'Choral vom grossen Baal' ('Hymn of Great Baal'), tells the story of an ugly, asocial, vagabond poet. Baal is an amoral being who blindly follows his instincts. He has a fatal attraction for women whom he ruthlessly discards when he is tired of them. He spends his life in a variety of Bohemian occupations (cabaret artist, owner of a merry-go-round), but mostly in taverns, where he sings his songs to the guitar. He acquires a friend, the composer Ekart. When he finds Ekart making love to a waitress he kills him in a fit of jealous rage. He flees from the police into the forests of the north, where he dies among the woodcutters.

    Baal is a chaotically brilliant play in the tradition of German *Sturm und Drang*, Buechner and Wedekind. Its magnificently exuberant language expresses a passionate acceptance of the world in all its sordid grandeur.

TROMMELN IN DER NACHT (Drums in the Night)

Written: 1918.

First performance: Munich, 29 September 1922.

A comedy in five acts.

Berlin 1919: Kragler, a soldier returning from the war after years of captivity in Africa, finds his fiancée engaged to a repulsive profiteer. During the engagement party, held at the Piccadilly Bar, while the shooting of the Spartakus rising can be heard from the street, Kragler appears like a ghost from the past and demands his girl back. Anna, who is pregnant from her affair with the shady profiteer, still loves

Kragler but cannot bear to tell him what has happened and sends him away. As the drums of the doomed revolutionary rising reverberate through the night, Kragler errs through the streets, pursued by Anna, who does not want to lose him after all. Kragler is about to join the Spartakists when Anna finds him, confesses her disloyalty, and asks forgiveness. Kragler hurls abuse at her, but then nevertheless decides that he prefers a comfortable life with his bride, however shopsoiled she may be, to death as a revolutionary, however heroic. 'Every man feels best in his own skin,' he says, 'I am a swine and the swine goes home!'

Drums in the Night is to be played in simple sets, over which the backdrop of the city appears. A huge red moon hangs like a Chinese lantern from the flies and symbolizes the atmosphere of doom which pervades the play. The auditorium is to be decorated with anti-romantic slogans.

Drums in the Night was one of the first of a long line of plays about returning soldiers. It is still one of the best.

In the collected edition of his plays, published after Brecht's return to East Berlin, Brecht tried to offset the anti-revolutionary cynicism of his hero by introducing some references to a young revolutionary who does fight for the cause and dies a hero's death. But hardly anyone would have noticed this amendment if Brecht had not specially drawn the readers' attention to it in his introduction. The play remains a violent rejection of all heroic cant, whether militarist or revolutionary.

IM DICKICHT DER STAEDTE (In the Jungle of the Cities)

Written: 1921–3.

First performance: Munich, May 1923.

Eleven scenes, sub-titled: 'The Struggle of Two Men in the Giant City of Chicago'. Original version called *Im Dickicht*.

This is an attempt to write a play about a fight without motive. The public is specially asked not to wrack its brains about the motives of the wrestling match they are about to watch, but to savour it like a sporting contest and to concentrate on the *style* of the opponents.

Chicago 1912: Shlink, a middle-aged, well-to-do timber merchant, a Malay from Yokohama, becomes obsessed with a desire to dominate the will of young Garga, a clerk in a lending library. Garga refuses to sell his opinion about a book, and from this opening move the strange duel between the two men develops. Shlink seeks to gain possession of Garga's soul. Garga refuses to be bought, cajoled, even to be won over by gratitude, when Shlink makes him a gift of his thriving business. He revenges himself by concluding a fraudulent deal in Shlink's name which must lead to Shlink's disgrace as a swindler. But when Shlink is about to be arrested, Garga to shame him takes the blame and goes to prison himself. He deposits a letter with a newspaper, to be opened shortly before his release is due, which accuses Shlink of the rape of Garga's sister (who is in fact deeply in love with Shlink) and is certain to lead to his being lynched. As the lynching mob approaches, Shlink and Garga face each other and realize that man's loneliness is so great that not even a fight like theirs can establish real contact between human beings. 'If you crammed a ship full of human bodies till it burst, the loneliness inside it would be so great that they would turn to ice . . . so great is our isolation that even conflict is impossible.'

This strange play anticipates the plays of Beckett, Ionesco, and Adamov, which it resembles by its insistence on the impossibility of communication. Garga speaks in long passages lifted from Rimbaud's *Une Saison en Enfer*, and in many ways the relationship between him and Shlink resembles that of Rimbaud and Verlaine. The setting is a fantastically exotic dream-America, and there are a number of complicated side-plots involving Garga's sister and wife and a number of Chicago gangsters.

Im Dickicht der Staedte is one of Brecht's most difficult but also one of his most intriguing creations.

LEBEN EDUARDS DES ZWEITEN VON ENGLAND
(Life of Edward II of England)

Written (in collaboration with Lion Feuchtwanger): 1923–4.
First performance: Munich, 18 March 1924.
A history – after Marlowe.

Marlowe's *Edward II* very freely adapted. The plot has been concentrated and coarsened so that the relationship between Edward and Gaveston, which Marlowe treats with a certain amount of discretion, becomes an openly homosexual infatuation. The effect aimed at is that of the crude vitality of an old broadsheet ballad or an historical 'panorama' as it was displayed at country fairs. Captions giving the place and exact (though freely invented) date of the action and other devices of the 'epic' theatre are used. The language of the play is a rough, highly irregular form of blank verse of great vigour and poetic impact.

The story of Edward II's love for Gaveston, his war with the barons, his capture and execution, and the revenge of his young son upon his murderers is, however, told without any political or social moral, but merely as an illustration of the futility of human ambition and the blind turnings of the wheel of fortune.

GOESTA BERLING

The Prologue to a planned stage version of Selma Lagerloef's novel was published in the periodical *Das Kunstblatt*, Potsdam, January 1924. It is described as based on an adaptation of the novel by E. Karin and is written in rhymed couplets. Other fragments of this adaptation are preserved in the Brecht Archive in East Berlin.

DIE HOCHZEIT (The Wedding)

Written: in the early twenties.
First performance: Frankfurt, 11 December 1926.

A one-act play in the slapstick tradition of Bavarian folk comedy. The wedding reception in the newly married couple's apartment. The bridegroom boasts that he has made the furniture himself. But he has made it badly. As the veneer of gentility fades from the proceedings and the guests lose their party manners, one piece of furniture after the other collapses. The resulting recrimination reveals that all is not as it seems. The bride is already pregnant, the bridegroom suspects her of infidelity, etc. But as the guests depart peace is re-established. The lights go out and as the curtain falls the bridal bed is heard to collapse with a mighty crash.

This unpretentious play, which was a complete failure at its performance in Frankfurt, also foreshadows the 'pure' theatre of the fifties.

DER BETTLER ODER DER TOTE HUND (The Beggar or The Dead Dog)

Written: 1919.

This one-act play consists, according to Schumacher, of a dialogue between a king and a blind beggar. The beggar hurls abuse at the king and disconcerts him by revealing the loathing of the common people for the meaningless antics of the mighty. For the blind beggar a dead dog is more important than the mighty king and all his futile activity.

ER TREIBT EINEN TEUFEL AUS (He Exorcizes a Devil)

Written: 1919.

Another one-act play in the style of Bavarian folk comedy. A village wooing is constantly disturbed by the girl's parents. The lovers in their attempts to elude these intrusions end up on the roof of the house.

LUX IN TENEBRIS
Written: 1919.

The last in this group of early one-act plays deals with hypocrisy in matters of sex. In a brothel street, Paduk, a shady entrepreneur, has set up an exhibition on venereal disease, which, though it pretends to be intended to combat immorality, is in fact visited by a clientele no less prurient than that of the brothel opposite. The brothel-keeper, Madame Hogge, reveals that Paduk himself is a former *habitué* of her establishment, seeking revenge for having been thrown out. In the end Paduk, after making a vigorous speech against vice, is won over by an invitation to avail himself of the facilities of Madame Hogge's institution, becomes a partner in it, and closes his anti-vice exhibition.

KALKUTTA, 4. MAI (Calcutta, 4 May)
Feuchtwanger's play *Warren Hastings, Gouverneur von Indien* (written: 1915, published 1916), revised by Feuchtwanger and Brecht in 1925.
English translation: Warren Hastings (in *Feuchtwanger: Two Anglo-Saxon Plays*) by Willa and Edwin Muir. Martin Secker, London, 1929.
A colonial history in four acts.

Warren Hastings appals the Commissioners of the East India Company, sent out to investigate his conduct, by the ruthlessness and cynicism of his methods. But though he is cruel and corrupt, he is not out for personal gain but to fulfil his civilizing mission. Brecht's hand can be seen clearly only in the song 'Surabaya Johnny' (sung by Warren Hastings's mistress, Lady Marjorie Hike), which he used again in *Happy End*.

MANN IST MANN (Man Equals Man)
Written: 1924-5.
First performance: Darmstadt, 26 September 1926.
The transformation of the porter Galy Gay in the military barracks of Kilkoa in the year one thousand nine hundred and twenty-five. A comedy.

The scene is a fantasticated India based on Kipling's *Barrack Room Ballads*. Galy Gay, an Irish dock-worker in the port of Kilkoa, a mild little man who cannot say no, goes out to buy a fish for supper. He encounters three British soldiers who have been trying to rob a pagoda, and have lost the fourth member of their squad in the process. They would be discovered as the wanted temple thieves if they failed to produce the fourth man, so they decide that Galy Gay must be transformed into the soldier Jeriah Jip. One man, they argue, is as good as another and human personality can be taken apart and reassembled like a motor-car. With the help of the canteen landlady, Leocadia Begbick, the great transformation scene is set in motion. As each phase is announced like a circus act, poor Galy Gay is first involved in an illicit business deal, made to feel guilty, apprehended, sentenced to be shot, put through a mock-execution, and as he re-awakens from his faint his mind is such a blank that he consents to pronounce the funeral oration for Galy Gay. Having been persuaded that he is Jeriah Jip, the soldier, he takes part in the campaign against Tibet and captures the frontier fortress single-handed. A side-plot shows the consequences of being too attached to one's personality: Sergeant Fairchild, nicknamed 'Bloody Five', is a fierce warrior and great disciplinarian. But whenever it rains he succumbs to his sensuality and cannot resist the seduction of women. To avoid disgracing himself and to keep his honourable nickname he castrates himself.

Mann ist Mann marks the turning-point in Brecht's development from the anarchic nihilism of his youth to social awareness and didacticism. The theme of the play is the malleability of man, the possibility of social engineering. With amazing intuition Brecht grasped the essence of later brain-washing techniques.

DAS ELEPHANTENKALB (The Baby Elephant)

Written: 1924–5.

An interlude for performance in the foyer during the interval of *Mann ist Mann*. This short surrealist extravaganza is an attempt at creating a kind of side-show based on pure clowning. The actor of Galy Gay appears as a baby elephant accused of having murdered its mother. Although the mother is proved to be alive, and the baby elephant is proved not to be her child, the case against it is found proven.

This short play also anticipates the 'anti-theatre' of thirty years later. Moreover, being the outcome of almost completely free association, it gives a fascinating insight into Brecht's subconscious mind.

DIE DREIGROSCHENOPER (The Threepenny Opera)

Written: 1928.

First performance: Berlin, Theater am Schiffbauerdamm, 31 August 1928.

Ballad opera.

Music by Kurt Weill.

This free adaptation of John Gay's *Beggar's Opera* with ballads inspired by Villon and Kipling is the only play by Brecht that has achieved real popular success.

Although it has been transferred into a fantastic late-nineteenth-century Soho, the main line of Gay's plot has been kept: Polly, the daughter of Peachum, the king of the beggars, still marries the robber Macheath. Peachum, who disapproves of the match, still wants his son-in-law to be hanged. But the chief of police is now called Brown, nicknamed Tiger Brown, and has served with Macheath, 'Mac the Knife', in the Indian Army. Being in Macheath's pay, and his friend, Tiger Brown has to be blackmailed into having him arrested by the terrible threat that hordes of disgusting beggars will otherwise mar the coronation of a young queen which is about to take place. Macheath is warned to leave London, but the force of habit is so strong that he cannot give up his usual Thursday afternoon with the whores of his favourite brothel at Turnbridge [*sic*]. He is arrested, but escapes with the help of Lucy, Brown's daughter, another of his bigamous wives. Again he goes to the brothel, and again is arrested. This time there is no escape. Already he stands on the scaffold, the noose round his neck. But this is opera, not real life. A mounted messenger arrives with the queen's pardon, the award of a country house, and a pension of £10,000 per annum. Lest we forget, however, that such things do not happen in real life, the play ends with a solemn chorus imploring mankind to forgive all malefactors.

HAPPY END

Written (in collaboration with Elisabeth Hauptmann): 1928–9.
First performance: Berlin, Theater am Schiffbauerdamm, 31 August 1929.
A musical play.
Music by Kurt Weill.

This attempt to cash in on the success of *The Threepenny Opera* was billed as an adaptation of an American short story by 'Dorothy Lane', which never existed.

Set in Chicago before the First World War, *Happy End* describes the efforts of a Salvation Army girl, Lilian Holiday, to save a group of gangsters, led by a mysterious lady in grey, 'The Fly'. To win the gangsters' confidence Lilian has to conform to their tastes, to sing seductive songs, and to lure one of the gangsters into a *tête-à-tête* in order to prevent him from taking part in a robbery. Eventually the gang, who are being hotly pursued by the police, decide to join the Salvation Army.

This musical play, which contains some of Brecht's most effective jazz lyrics, was a complete failure. The plot is curiously similar to that of the much later American musical *Guys and Dolls*, based on Damon Runyon's story, *The Idyll of Sarah Brown*, which first appeared in *Collier's* (1933).

DER FLUG DER LINDBERGHS (The Flight of the Lindberghs).

Written: 1928–9.
First performance: Baden-Baden Music Week, summer 1929.
Didactic radio play for boys and girls.
Music by Kurt Weill and Paul Hindemith.

Lindbergh (who is impersonated by a chorus, to avoid any suggestion of individual hero-worship) describes his famous flight, while the American newspapers discuss his chances of success; fog, snowstorms, and weariness try to defeat him. He meditates on the significance of his adventure: it is a battle against the primitive forces of nature and will sweep the idea of God from the heavens. When he arrives at his destination, his achievement is greeted as a triumph of the forces of enlightenment.

FATZER 3

Written: *c*. 1930.
Two scenes from an uncompleted play *Untergang des Egoisten Johann Fatzer* (*Downfall of the Egoist Johann Fatzer*).

This curious fragment deals with the efforts of Fatzer, the leader of a group of army deserters in the last stage of the war, to secure a quantity of black-market meat for them. He persuades a soldier to let him have part of an army consignment of beef, but when the soldier appears at the meeting-place they have agreed on, Fatzer fails to turn up. The other members of Fatzer's group cannot recognize the soldier. One of the members of Fatzer's band is Keuner, the hero of Brecht's anecdotes, *Geschichten vom Herrn Keuner*. The Fatzer fragment is followed by a poem, entitled *Fatzer, Komm* (probably 'Commentary on Fatzer'), which deals with the need to change the social order.

AUFSTIEG UND FALL DER STADT MAHAGONNY (Rise and Fall of the City of Mahagonny)

Written: 1928–9.
First performance: Leipzig, March 1930.
Opera.
Music by Kurt Weill.

Unlike *The Threepenny Opera*, which is a ballad opera, *Mahagonny* was designed for performance in opera houses, although Weill wrote it for an orchestra of only about thirty 'specialists'.

A group of shady characters, on the run from the police towards the goldfields of the north, decide that it would be more profitable to establish a business which takes money from the gold-miners rather than dig for gold themselves. Led by the widow Leocadia Begbick, the canteen landlady from *Mann ist Mann*, they build the city of Mahagonny, where the hard-working men of the world will be able to buy any pleasure they may desire.

Four such men, woodcutters who have spent seven years in Alaska, arrive: Paul, Heinrich, Jakob, and Joe. But they are not happy. There are still too many restrictions and regulations. In a moment of terrror, when an approaching hurricane is almost certain to bring death and destruction to Mahagonny, Paul has an inspiration. He discovers the real principle of happiness: the abolition of *all* restrictions. Everything must be permitted. When the hurricane mysteriously spares Mahagonny, Paul's discovery becomes its supreme law: love-making, eating, fighting, and drinking become the sole duties of the citizens. But self-indulgence leads to ruin: Jakob, the glutton, eats himself to death; Joe, the fighter, is killed in a boxing bout; Paul, who has found fleeting love in the arms of the prostitute Jenny, spends all his money on drink and incurs a large debt. He is arrested and tried on a number of charges. Of most of these he is acquitted. But for the greatest crime of all he is sentenced to death: lack of money. In the electric chair he realizes that the society he has created was founded on greed: 'The joy that I bought was no joy and freedom for money was not freedom.' As he dies processions of the inhabitants march and counter-march across the stage, carrying posters which proclaim the helplessness and chaos of such a society. The final chorus is a cry of despair: 'We cannot help ourselves – or you – or any man.'

Mahagonny is a powerful symbol of the *laissez-faire* society of the late twenties and its feeling of helplessness in the face of the great economic crisis. It also proclaims Brecht's conviction that art should not just sell pleasurable emotion but serve the improvement and instruction of man.

DAS BADENER LEHRSTUECK VOM EINVER-STAENDNIS (The Didactic Play of Baden on Consent)

Written: 1928–9.
First performance: Baden-Baden Music Week, summer 1929.
Music by Paul Hindemith.
A short oratorio with an interlude of clowning.

Four airmen, who have tried to cross the Atlantic, have crash-landed. They do not want to die and ask mankind for help. The two choirs ('skilled choir' and 'mass choir') debate the question: 'Does man help man?' The evidence produced in the course of the debate includes pictures of men killing men in this century and a scene between three clowns: a giant clown, Herr Schmitt, complains that various parts of his body hurt. The two other clowns cure his ailments by sawing off the limbs in question, until in the end, with arms and legs and even his head torn off, Herr Schmitt is completely dismantled. The conclusion: man does not help man. The four airmen will have to die. The pilot refuses to accept the necessity of his extinction. The three mechanics, however, accept the choirs' instruction that death can only be overcome by consent to the inevitable necessities of history. The pilot who has clung to his individual desire for life and glory is annihilated. The three mechanics are redeemed, for 'you who have consented to the flow of things will not sink back into nothingness'. Violence and death cannot be overcome by palliatives. Only when a just world order is established will violence disappear.

An obscure but significant work.

DER JASAGER (He Who Says Yes)

Written: 1929–30.
First performance: Berlin, 1930.
School opera. Based on the Japanese No Play *Taniko*, translated by Arthur Waley.
Music by Kurt Weill.

A remote village. The schoolteacher is about to leave for a journey across the mountains. He has to bring back medicine to fight an epidemic. A boy whose mother is ill joins the party: he wants to consult the doctors in the town about her ailment. During the journey the boy falls ill. The expedition will have to be abandoned, if the boy is ·not to be left by himself in the wilderness. According to an ancient custom he is asked whether he consents to being left behind. He answers Yes, but asks to be killed rather than to suffer a slow death. He is thrown into the abyss.

DER NEINSAGER (He Who Says No)

Written: 1930.

A revised version of *Der Jasager*, in deference to criticisms made by pupils of schools that had performed that opera.

The teacher's expedition is no longer a journey to obtain medicine against an epidemic, but a journey of exploration. Nor is the need to kill the boy when he falls ill the outcome of circumstances. An old custom demands that anyone abandoned in that spot *must* be thrown into the abyss. This time, however, the boy refuses to consent to die. He rejects the old custom: 'I see the need for a *new* custom, which must be established at once: the custom of thinking afresh in every new situation.' The teacher and his party recognize the force of this argument and turn back, taking the boy with them.

DER BROTLADEN (The Bread Shop)

Written: 1929–30.

This unfinished play, a forerunner of *St Joan of the Stockyards*, deals with helpless humanity overwhelmed by the elemental force of economic crisis, which strikes like a hurricane. Meininger, the owner of the breadshop, asks his caretaker, the widow Queck, to order a load of firewood for him. When his bank calls in his mortgage, Meininger disowns his order and the poor woman is faced with ruin. A Salvation Army girl, Miss Hippler, and a Communist, Washington Meyer, try to help her, while a chorus of unemployed comments on the action.

Der Brotladen deals with trivial events in heroic language, particularly during a scuffle involving the unemployed, which is presented in Homeric idiom as 'the Battle of the Breadshop'.

DIE HEILIGE JOHANNA DER SCHLACHTHOEFE (St Joan of the Stockyards)

Written: 1929–30.
First performance: Berlin radio, 11 April 1932.
First stage performance: Hamburg, 30 April 1959.

This long play, which contains a good deal of parody of German classical drama (Schiller's *Maid of Orleans*, Goethe's *Faust*, etc.), tells the story of Joan Dark (i.e. d'Arc), a simple girl belonging to 'The Black Straw Hats', an evangelical organization modelled on the Salvation Army. Trying to alleviate the misery of the working people in the stockyards of Chicago, she learns that unemployment and misery are caused by the machinations of Pierpont Mauler, the canned-meat king, who is waging a life-and-death struggle with his competitors. Joan seeks him out, recognizes him – as St Joan recognized the Dauphin – and tries to persuade him to help the suffering masses. Mauler is strangely touched by the girl's innocence. But he wants to show her

that the poor are wicked and not worthy of her efforts. Joan is shown the wickedness of the poor, but realizes that they are wicked only because of their poverty. The meat packers want to use 'The Black Straw Hats' to divert the attention of the unemployed from their plight. Joan drives them out of the temple, but is expelled from 'The Black Straw Hats'. She decides to share the sufferings of the unemployed until Mauler consents to reopen the canning plants. The Communists want to persuade the other workers of the city to join them in a general strike. They send out messengers. Joan offers to carry one of the letters. But when she realizes that the Communists will not hesitate to use violence, she has doubts and fails to deliver her letter. The strike collapses. Mauler has smashed his competitors and is reopening the factories. But Joan, worn down by the privations she has taken upon herself, is dying: with her last breath she proclaims her newly found conviction that the world cannot be improved without violence. But the meat packers and 'The Black Straw Hats', who want to use the touching story of Joan's martyrdom for their pious propaganda, drown her last words with their pseudo-religious claptrap (modelled on the final scene of the second part of Goethe's *Faust*) by which she is canonized as the valiant little St Joan of the Stockyards.

Although the long scenes of stock-exchange intrigues give a grotesquely naïve picture of the workings of capitalism, *St Joan of the Stockyards* is one of Brecht's finest achievements.

DIE MASSNAHME (The [disciplinary] Measure)

Written: 1930.

First performance: Berlin, 10 December 1930, by the Arbeiterchor Grossberlin (Greater Berlin Workers' Choir).

Music by Hanns Eisler.

Labelled by Brecht a 'didactic play', *Die Massnahme* is a dramatic cantata performed by four soloists (one woman, three men) and chorus. The chorus represents the conscience of the Communist Party (hence: Kontrollchor – control chorus). The four soloists are a group of party workers (agitators) who have returned from an illegal mission in China (the time is the 1920s) and report the liquidation of a member of their group. The 'control chorus' invites them to act out what has happened, before it can pronounce judgment on *the measure* they felt compelled to take. The four agitators then report the incidents which led to their decision in dramatic form, playing all the parts – and *each in turn* taking *the part of the young comrade*, who was killed.

At the last party house before the frontier the four agitators asked for a guide who knew the country. The young comrade was assigned

this task. Before they started on their journey the party workers solemnly pledged themselves to efface their previous personalities. This descent into anonymity, a solemn, almost religious act ('the extinction'), is symbolized by the masking of their faces.

Inside China the young comrade's inability to control his emotion has four times endangered the illegal party work of the agitators: instead of exploiting the hardships of the coolies pulling the rice boats on the river, he found a way of alleviating their plight and thereby delayed their revolt; unable to bear seeing another man arrested for distributing illegal leaflets for which he himself was responsible, he attacked a policeman, alerted the authorities, and frustrated the party's propaganda work; sent to negotiate with a local capitalist who might become an ally in the fight against the imperialists, he was so revolted by the man's vileness that he broke off the talks; and lastly he could not bear to see the sufferings of the starving unemployed. In defiance of the party's order he led their premature rising and thereby disclosed his identity as an emissary of Moscow. This is symbolized by his tearing off his mask.

The agitators, whose continued illegal work depended on their not being recognized, had to protect themselves. The young comrade had to disappear without a trace. He himself saw that there was no other way out, confessed his errors and asked to be liquidated. So they shot him and threw his body into a chalk pit, where the quicklime was sure to obliterate its traces.

Having listened to this account, the control chorus acquits the four agitators of any guilt and signifies its approval of the measure they have taken in the interest of the party.

Die Massnahme is a work of severe purity, grimly austere, but without doubt one of Brecht's best works. Years before the great Soviet purge trials it expressed the essential nature of Stalinist Communism. Owing to Brecht's uncannily penetrating intuitive grasp of the realities of the problem of totalitarianism, the play transcends its author's conscious intention and becomes a classical statement of its basic dilemma.

DIE AUSNAHME UND DIE REGEL (The Exception and the Rule)

Written: 1930.

First performance: Paris, 1947 (in French).

Music by Paul Dessau.

This short didactic play tells the story of a merchant who is trying to cross a desert in Asia at great speed in order to beat a competitor. He

ruthlessly drives his coolie porter. In the waterless desert, when their supplies are running low, the kindly coolie offers the merchant some water he has secretly hoarded in his flask. The merchant mistakes the gesture for an attack upon his life and kills the coolie. At the subsequent trial it is established that the coolie only wanted to help. The judge, however, finds that the coolie had every reason to hate the merchant, so that the latter could not expect an act of kindness from him and was justified in interpreting the coolie's gesture as an attack. The merchant is acquitted as he acted in legitimate self-defence. For in our world an act of kindness is an exception, hatred and violence the rule by which alone we can regulate our conduct.

DIE MUTTER: Leben der Revolutionaerin Pelagea Wlassowa aus Twer. (The Mother: Life of the revolutionary Pelageya Vlasova from Tver)

Written: 1930–2.
First performance: Berlin, 12 January 1932.
Music by Hanns Eisler.

This very free adaptation of Gorky's novel, which continues Gorky's story that ends in 1905 to the eve of the October Revolution of 1917, intentionally neglects the psychological and sentimental aspects of the characters. It is intended as a primer of revolutionary method and gives a wealth of practical demonstrations of effective action and propaganda. Pelageya Vlasova at first disapproves of her son's revolutionary work, but gradually, to protect him, she is drawn into it: she learns to read and write, converts the neighbours, carries the message of the party into the countryside. Her son is shot. But she continues the good work. On the eve of the October Revolution she marches in the van of the striking munitions workers.

The Mother is written in a dry, puritanical style: even the songs and choral passages are strictly didactic. But the central figure nevertheless emerges as a human being: dignified, sly, stubborn, and heroic.

DIE RUNDKOEPFE UND DIE SPITZKOEPFE (The Roundheads and the Peakheads)

Written: 1932–4.
First performance: Copenhagen, 4 November 1936.
Music by Hanns Eisler.

A long parable play about Hitler's race theories, based on the plot of Shakespeare's *Measure for Measure*. The land of Yahoo is threatened by a rising of the poor tenant farmers. The Viceroy is persuaded to meet the crisis by handing over power to Angelo Iberin, a demagogue, who promises that he will deal with the situation. He proclaims the racial superiority of the Roundheads over the Peakheads, and thus confuses the clear-cut social issue which lies between rich and poor. The rich landlord de Guzman has seduced the daughter of his tenant, the peasant Callas. As a Peakhead he is accused of having ruined the honour of a Roundhead and sentenced to death. But when the father of the girl claims his rights as a Roundhead and takes possession of a team of horses belonging to de Guzman, the laws of property are upheld by the court. Isabella, de Guzman's sister and a novice in a convent, learns that she might save her brother's life by spending the night with the commandant of the concentration camp where her brother awaits his execution. She pays Nanna Callas, who has become a prostitute, to take her place. De Guzman's lawyers persuade old Callas, who is in debt to his landlord, to take de Guzman's place under the gallows. The Viceroy returns and uncovers the substitutions: despite the race theory the poor among the Roundheads are still at a disadvantage, being poor. But the racial issue has diverted the attention of the poor, and thus led to the defeat of the revolutionary movement. The country can now safely plan an attack against the land of the Squareheads.

DIE SIEBEN TODSUENDEN DER KLEINBUERGER (ANNA ANNA) (The Seven Deadly Sins of the Petty Bourgeois (Anna Anna))

Written: *c.* 1933.
First performance: Paris, June 1933, by 'Les Ballets 1933'.
Music by Kurt Weill.
Choreography by Georges Balanchine.
Ballet cantata.

The story of two sisters, both called Anna, who are aspects of the same personality. Anna I (the singer) represents her rational self; Anna II (the dancer) her emotional, instinctive nature.

Anna leaves her home in Louisiana to earn enough money for the building of a house for her family. As the ballet proceeds the house gradually rises in the background and the family is seen and heard admonishing Anna to work harder. Anna is a dancer. To make money she has to avoid committing the seven deadly sins of commercial society, which in fact represent the healthy instincts of her nature: she must not eat, lest she grow fat (greed); she must not love the man she wants (lust) but the one who pays; she must overcome her pride and exhibit herself in strip-tease shows, etc. Having resisted these temptations Anna can return to Louisiana, where the money she has earned has given her family a home.

DIE HORATIER UND DIE KURIATIER (The Horatians and the Curiatians)

Written: 1934.
First performance: Halle, 26 April 1958.
Music by Kurt Schwaen.
Didactic play.

This short and rather arid piece deals with dialectics and tactics. To distract their people's attention from internal social conflicts, the Curiatians attack the Horatians. As in Chinese classical theatre, whole armies are represented by single actors, who carry little flags on their shoulders to symbolize their strength. Each time a unit is destroyed, a flag is discarded. The course of the struggle demonstrates the principles of Marxist dialectics (identical actions have different values in differing circumstances) and of Marxist tactics (the weaker Horatians tire their attackers by hasty retreat and then beat their three detachments one by one. 'The flight was an attack.').

FURCHT UND ELEND DES DRITTEN REICHES (Fear and Misery of the Third Reich)

Written: 1935–8.
First performance: selected scenes under the title '99%' in Paris, May 1938.
An English version (*The Private Life of the Master Race*) (17 scenes) by Eric Bentley at Berkeley, California, 7 June 1945. New York, 12 June 1945.

Twenty-eight scenes of varying length, four of which have never been published, describing various aspects of life in Hitler's Reich: the brutality of the concentration camps, the struggle of the Communist underground movement, anti-Semitism, Goebbels' propaganda, etc. Among the most effective episodes are 'Rechtsfindung' ('Justice'): a judge is at a loss how to decide a case of robbery in a Jewish shop; 'Die juedische Frau' ('The Jewish Wife') in which a Jewish woman decides to leave her non-Jewish husband to save his career; 'Zwei Baecker' ('Two Bakers'), a short scene in a prison yard where one baker is in prison because he has adulterated his bread, the other because he *failed* to adulterate his under a *new* Nazi law; 'Der Spitzel' ('The Informer') in which a schoolboy's parents are terrified because they cannot trust the boy not to denounce some anti-Nazi remarks of theirs, etc.

These playlets are written in a rather un-Brechtian, naturalistic convention. They show his ability to write in a conventional style, but also his limitations outside his personal manner.

DIE GEWEHRE DER FRAU CARRAR (Señora Carrar's Rifles)

Written: 1937.

First performance: Paris, October 1937.

Play in one act, based on Synge's *Riders to the Sea*.

Teresa Carrar's husband, an Andalusian fisherman, has been killed in the Asturian rising. Now, at the height of the Spanish Civil War, she is determined to keep her son Juan out of the fighting. Señora Carrar's brother, a worker who is in the Republican Army, comes to ask for a cache of rifles hidden in the house by her late husband. She violently defends her decision to keep out of the war. But one cannot remain neutral: fishermen bring the body of her son, who has been machine-gunned while fishing. A nationalist gun-boat fired at him, merely because he wore a workman's cloth cap. Teresa Carrar herself goes out to fight against Franco.

Brecht notes that this play is written in the 'Aristotelian' convention. It is effective theatre and gives great opportunities to the actress playing Señora Carrar.

MUTTER COURAGE UND IHRE KINDER (Mother Courage and Her Children)

Written: 1939.

First performance: Zurich, 19 April 1941.

Music by Paul Burkhard (for Zurich performance); by Paul Dessau (for Berliner Ensemble).

A chronicle of the Thirty Years War.

Mother Courage is a character in Grimmelshausen's seventeenth-century picaresque writings, but Brecht has used only the name. Anna Fierling, nicknamed 'Mother Courage', is an itinerant trader who follows the Swedish and Imperial armies with her covered wagon, selling the soldiers shoes, shirts, brandy, etc. She has three children, each from a different father: two sons – the daring Eilif and the slow but honest Schweizerkas ('Swiss Cheese') – and one daughter – Katrin, who has been dumb and mentally retarded since a soldier hit her as a child, but who nevertheless is a motherly, tender-hearted creature.

Mother Courage lives by the war, so she must pay the war its due.

One by one she loses her children. Schweizerkas becomes paymaster in a Swedish regiment. When the Imperialists overrun its camp he hides the regimental cashbox. Too honest to betray his trust, he has to die. Mother Courage could save him, if she sold her wagon. But she haggles too long about the price. Schweizerkas is shot. Eilif has become a hero, when he requisitioned a herd of cattle during a siege. He repeats his exploit during a brief period of armistice and is executed as a looter. Poor dumb Katrin, disfigured by the assaults of lecherous soldiers, overhears a plan to take the town of Halle by stealth. She cannot bear the thought of women and children being killed, rouses the town by beating a drum, and is shot by the soldiers. Mother Courage is left alone. Determined to continue trading, she wearily pulls her cart to catch up with the army.

Written in the forceful, coarse language of its period, *Mother Courage* is rich in brilliantly observed characters: the Protestant chaplain, who escapes capture by disguising himself as Mother Courage's tapster and handy-man and discourses in elevated language; the Dutch cook, who lives with Mother Courage for a while, offers to marry her when he inherits a tavern in Utrecht, but leaves her when she insists on taking her dumb daughter with her; the harlot Yvette, who ends up as the wealthy widow of an Austrian colonel, etc.

Brecht insisted that Mother Courage herself was a negative character, a profiteer who sacrifices her children to her commercial instinct and cannot learn from her experience. But the audience never fails to be moved by her fate.

DAS VERHOER DES LUKULLUS (The Trial of Lucullus)
Written: 1939.
First performance as a radio play, Beromuenster, Switzerland, 1940.
   As an opera, with music by Paul Dessau: first version, Berlin, 17 March 1951; second version, under the title *Die Verurteilung des Lukullus*, Berlin, 12 October 1951.

The Roman general Lucullus has died. A judge and jury of the nether world examine him to decide whether he should be admitted to live on among the shades – or condemned to complete extinction. He points to his fame and achievement as a victorious soldier. But of all this nothing has remained except the suffering he caused. Only his cook testifies for him: he has introduced the cherry-tree into Europe. But that is not enough.

The first version of the opera was banned by the Communist authorities because it condemned all wars without distinction. The second version includes passages which make it clear that war waged against aggressors is laudable and heroic.

LEBEN DES GALILEI (Life of Galileo)

Written: 1938–9. English version (in collaboration with Charles Laughton), 1947. Third, revised version (in German), 1954.

First performance: Zurich, 9 September 1943. Second version, Beverly Hills, 30 July 1947. Third version, Cologne, April 1955.

Music by Hanns Eisler.

In the final version the play has fifteen scenes, but in the Berliner Ensemble performance the last scene is cut.

1609: aged forty-tive, Galileo lives with his daughter Virginia, his housekeeper Mrs Sarti, and her little son Andrea, already a promising pupil of the master. He earns a meagre living in the service of the Republic of Venice as a lecturer at the University of Padua. Galileo is an unscrupulous and sensuous man who does not hesitate to claim that he has invented the telescope when he has merely copied a Dutch invention. As the Venetians pay him too badly and allow him no time for research he accepts the invitation of the Grand Duke of Florence to move to his domains. Though the freedom of Venice may be lacking there, at least he will have leisure to pursue his observation of the stars through his new telescope.

Galileo has proved that the earth is not the centre of the universe. But although the Pope's own astronomer, Clavius, confirms his findings, the Inquisition forbids him to publish them. For eight years Galileo is silent. When a new Pope, Urban VIII, a mathematician known as an enlightened mind, ascends the throne, Galileo sees a chance that the new science will be accepted. But the Grand Inquisitor persuades the Pope that such discoveries would undermine the basis of the Church's authority. The Pope agrees that Galileo be shown the instruments of torture.

22 June 1633: Galileo's pupils, among them Andrea Sarti, grown to manhood, refuse to believe that Galileo will recant his teaching. The tolling of the bells announces that he has recanted. He enters, a broken man. Andrea cries out: 'Pity the country that has no heroes!' Galileo replies: 'No. Pity the country that needs heroes!'

Years later: Galileo lives in the country, under close surveillance by the Inquisition. His daughter, whose fiancé has broken off the engagement because of Galileo's views, is now an old maid who nags him incessantly. Galileo, nearly blind, obsequiously spends his time listening to readings from pious tracts. Andrea Sarti, disgusted at the old man's cowardice, visits him before leaving for Holland. When Galileo hands him the completed manuscript of his *Discorsi*, which he has written secretly, Andrea's contempt changes into admiration. Now he understands why Galileo recanted – to gain the time to complete his great work. But Galileo will not accept this view. He sees himself as a criminal, whose cowardice has set the pattern for centuries to come. He has made science the servant of authority rather than asserting its right to transform the world for the benefit of mankind.

Andrea smuggles the *Discorsi* across the frontier.

Brecht's masterpiece shows the scientist Galileo as a sensualist, for whom even the quest for knowledge is a pleasure of the senses. The representatives of the Church are drawn as brilliantly intelligent men who argue their case with consummate skill. The other characters – Galileo's daughter Virginia, who loves her father, becomes an old maid because of his addiction to science, yet cannot understand him; his motherly old housekeeper, Mrs Sarti, her son Andrea, and a large cast of minor figures are finely observed and presented in the round with a wealth of detail.

DER GUTE MENSCH VON SEZUAN (The Good Soul of Setzuan)

Written: 1938–40.
First performance: Zurich, 4 February 1943.
Music by Paul Dessau.
A parable play, set in modern China.

Three gods have come to earth to look for a really good human being. Unless at least one can be found, the world cannot continue to exist. They are weary from their fruitless search. As they enter the town of Setzuan they ask Wang the water-seller to find someone who will give them shelter for the night. The hard-hearted and selfish people of the town refuse to take them into their houses. Only Shen Te, the prostitute, offers them a place to rest their weary limbs. She even sends away a customer to keep her room free for them. In the morning the gods reward her with a gift of money, sufficient to enable her to buy a small tobacco shop.

But as soon as the news spreads that the kindly Shen Te has come into a fortune an army of parasites, would-be relatives, and debtors descend upon her. To protect herself she assumes the personality of a ruthless male cousin, Shui Ta. This brash and brutal young man drives the spongers away.

Shen Te meets an unemployed airman, Yang Sun, and saves him from suicide. She falls in love with him; they plan to get married. But when Yang is alone with the ruthless Shui Ta, he admits, speaking as man to man, that he is after her money. He wants it to bribe himself into a job as a mail pilot and is not going to marry her. Having lost her fiancé, Shen Te is also about to lose her shop, when she learns that she is pregnant.

Shui Ta reappears. Shen Te is said to be away on a journey, and so her ruthless cousin can restore her fortunes: he starts a tobacco factory and employs the ex-airman Yang, who soon becomes a foreman, because he too is ruthless and astute in exploiting the workpeople and making them toil harder.

Wang the water-seller, whom the gods have asked to keep them informed on the fortunes of the one good human being they have as yet encountered, is worried about Shen Te's long absence. He suspects Shui Ta of having murdered her. Shui Ta is arrested and the gods themselves appear to act as judges at the trial. Shui Ta reveals that he is Shen Te in disguise. Only under the mask of ruthlessness and greed could the good soul of Setzuan ever hope to provide for herself and her unborn child. For the good cannot live in our world and *stay* good.

The foolish and ineffectual gods are relieved that the good human being they have found is still alive. When Shen Te draws their attention to her dilemma they avoid the issue. Somehow or other, they say, she will manage. Having convinced themselves that they have after all found one good soul in the world they float away into the heavens. And yet, the epilogue insists, a world where the good cannot live surely ought to be changed.

HERR PUNTILA UND SEIN KNECHT MATTI
(Mr Puntila and his Hired Man, Matti)

Written: 1940–1.

First performance: Zurich, 5 June 1948.

Music by Paul Dessau.

Based on the Finnish folk-tales and the draft of a play by Hella Wuolijoki.

A folk play (*Volksstueck*) in the tradition of Austrian and Bavarian popular drama. Although the action is laid in Finland the speech of common people used is a South German idiom.

Mr Puntila is a rich farmer. Like the millionaire in Chaplin's *City Lights*, he overflows with good humour and kindness when he is drunk, but reverts to a 'reasonable' attitude, mean and businesslike, when he is sober.

Mr Puntila is about to marry his daughter to an attaché in the diplomatic service, a degenerate fop. But when he gets drunk he scolds

Eva for even contemplating such a match merely for money, and draws her attention to the manly figure of his driver and handy-man, Matti. Eva herself does not relish the idea of her engagement to the attaché, and induces Matti to compromise her by being seen emerging from a bathing hut with her. But the attaché is too mean to worry about so trivial a matter.

The morning of the engagement party: four girls of the neighbourhood to whom Puntila proposed during the night, when he was drunk, appear. Now he is sober: he turns them away. But as the engagement party progresses he gets drunk again and keeps on insulting the attaché, till even he notices that he is not wanted. Puntila wants Matti to take the attaché's place and marry Eva. Matti has his doubts: he puts her through an examination to see if she is qualified to be a workman's wife. She fails. Matti decides the time has come when he must leave: friendship or family ties between a landowner and a hired man can only end in disaster.

Puntila is marred by some tactless pinpricks against the anti-Communist Finns, but it contains some masterly scenes. Puntila himself is a great character: the transitions between his sober and drunken selves are brilliantly managed. Very much against Brecht's own intention, Puntila steals the play. Matti who has some witty speeches of Schweikian wisdom in the opening scenes turns out rather a prig, when he refuses the girl who loves him for very arid and pedantic reasons.

DER AUFHALTSAME AUFSTIEG DES ARTURO UI
(The Resistible Rise of Arturo Ui)

Written: 1941.

First performance: Stuttgart, November 1958.

A very long play (seventeen scenes) in mock-heroic blank verse. It attempts to transfer the story of Hitler, from his beginnings to the occupation of Austria, into the world of gangsters of Chicago. This ambitious project, however, with its studied parallels to Shakespeare's *Richard III*, fails: the parallels between Hitler's dealings with the German capitalists and the connexion between Chicago gangsters and business men (vegetable dealers) are laboured and unconvincing. Brecht knew Hitler; he knew very little about Chicago.

DIE GESICHTE DER SIMONE MACHARD (The Visions of Simone Machard)

Written (in collaboration with Lion Feuchtwanger): 1941–3.

First performance: Frankfurt, 8 March 1957.

Another play on the subject of St Joan: Simone Machard, an adolescent girl, works as a servant for the *patron* of an hotel, petrol station, and transport business in Central France. It is June 1940; the Germans are advancing. Simone is worried about her brother, who is serving in a front-line army unit. She has been reading the story of Joan of Arc. In her dreams her brother keeps appearing as an angel, calling upon her to save France.

In the confusion, greed, and selfishness of panic and collapse, Simone alone tries to help the starving refugees, to prevent supplies from falling into the hands of the Germans and to save her country's dignity and honour. In her dream-world Monsieur le Maire has become King Charles VII; the owner of the hotel, the Connétable; his miserly mother, Queen Isabel. The Germans occupy the village; and the *patron*'s mother is collaborating with them. Simone learns that she is about to sell their secret hoard of petrol to the Germans and sets fire to it. In her visions she is tried and sentenced to death. In the real world she is certified insane and taken to a mental home.

The charm of this play lies in the skill with which the dreams and visions of the little girl show history through the eyes of a naïve and simple person – with a touching mixture of anachronisms and naïve clichés. At times the language of the dream dissolves into a dream-like Joycean idiom.

SCHWEIK IM ZWEITEN WELTKRIEG (Schweik in the Second World War)

Written: 1941-4.

First performance (in Polish): Warsaw, 17 January 1957; (in German) Erfurt, March 1958.

Music by Hanns Eisler.

The immortal good soldier is here transferred to German-occupied Prague. He still meets his friends in the same public house, Zum Kelch (The Goblet). But this now has an attractive landlady, Mrs Kopecka, a young widow and ardent Czech patriot. The informer Bretschneider is now a Gestapo agent. Schweik's friend Baloun still has an insatiable appetite and the plot revolves round Schweik's attempts to satisfy it, lest Baloun feel compelled to join the German Army for the sake of a square meal. Asked to steal a certain handsome dog, wanted by an SS leader for his wife, Schweik eventually lands in the German forces himself.

The action is interrupted by interludes, during which the Nazi leaders appear as figures of more than life-size (except Goebbels, who is less than life-size) and proclaim their faith in the undying readiness of the small man to die for them. In the final scene of the play Schweik, the embodiment of the small man, meets Hitler on the snow-covered battlefield of Stalingrad, and shows himself entirely unconcerned about the latter's fate.

Brecht's pastiche of Hašek's language and characterization is most successful. There are also a number of beautiful songs.

LEBEN DES KONFUTSE (Life of Confucius)
Written before 1944.

Only one scene of this curious play has been published posthumously. It deals with the life of Confucius and is written to be acted by children. 'It might appear that it would be impossible to do justice to the high theme if it were entrusted to children. But one might reply that for children only the highest themes are high enough.' Besides, having the life of the great philosopher performed by children will increase the 'distance' between the actors and the public. The short scene itself shows Kung in his early youth instructing some playmates. He teaches them how to subdue their instincts by the self-control of perfect manners.

DER KAUKASISCHE KREIDEKREIS (The Caucasian Chalk Circle)
Written: 1944–5.
First performance (in English): Carleton College, Northfield, Minnesota, 1947; (in German) Theater am Schiffbauerdamm, Berlin, June 1954.
Music by Paul Dessau.
Based on the old Chinese play, *The Circle of Chalk*, which was successfully adapted by Klabund in Germany in the 1920s.

Prologue. Towards the end of the Second World War members of two collective farms in Soviet Georgia are in dispute about a tract of land that used to belong to the goat breeding collective before it had to be abandoned to the advancing Germans. The neighbouring collective farm, specializing in fruit- and wine-growing, has planned an irrigation scheme for which the land in question would be essential. After discussion it is decided to let the fruit farmers have the land; their plan is likely to make it more productive. To illustrate the ethics of this decision a Georgian folk-singer is invited to sing the old legend of the circle of chalk.

In feudal Georgia a long time ago, there once lived a rich Governor with his wife and little son. On an Easter Sunday the barons rose in revolt against the Grand Duke and murdered his Governor. In the panic the Governor's wife fled, leaving her little son behind. A kitchen maid, Grusche Vakhnadze saved the child and took it with her into the mountains. To conceal its identity and to give it shelter and a name Grusche consented to marry a rich peasant, in the last stages of a fatal illness. But after the wedding the dying man revived. He had only pretended to be ill to avoid being recruited for the army. Now the war was over. Simon the soldier, Grusche's fiancé, returned from service and found Grusche married and mother of a child. Before she could explain the situation soldiers seized the little boy. The Governor's wife was claiming it back and had taken the case to law.

But to understand the trial that followed we must know more about the judge who decided the case. His story takes us back to that same Easter Sunday when the barons rose against the Grand Duke. That night Azdak, a drunken village scribe, gave shelter to a beggar whom he later recognized as the Grand Duke in person. Azdak felt that his unwitting rescue of the rascally ruler was a crime, forced the village constable to arrest him and take him to the city to be tried for it. In the city, however, there was no judge left; the soldiers, who were the only power in the land, were so amused by Azdak's jests that they made him the judge to replace the one whom the people had just hanged. For two years Azdak sat in judgment over the people of Georgia: he took bribes and was a lecherous man. But he favoured the poor and down-trodden.

When Grusche and the Governor's wife appeared before Azdak, however, he was about to be hanged. Now that the Grand Duke was back in power there was no place for him. The noose was already round his neck when a messenger arrived from the Grand Duke himself, who had appointed the man who saved his life to be judge over the city. So Azdak heard the case. Having listened to the pleas of the two women, he drew a circle of chalk on the ground, put the child in the centre, and told them to try and drag it out of the circle. The Governor's wife pulled it towards her with violence. Grusche let it go. Azdak awarded the child to Grusche because her gentleness showed that she loved it more. In the dancing and rejoicing that followed this judgment Azdak disappeared and was never heard of again.

The meaning of the story, the singer concludes, is that things should 'belong to those who are good for them: the children to those who are motherly . . . and the valley to those who will irrigate it and make it fruitful'.

With its poetry, its use of narrators, its two-pronged construction, its stylized action – the negative, wicked characters are masked – *The*

Caucasian Chalk Circle is the outstanding example of the technique of the 'epic' drama. It is one of Brecht's greatest plays.

DIE ANTIGONE DES SOPHOKLES (The Antigone of Sophokles)

Written: 1948.

First performance: Chur, Switzerland, February 1948.

An adaptation, based on Hoelderlin's translation. A prologue relates the play to the period after the Second World War. Two sisters in Berlin during the final phase of the war find their brother outside their home, hanged as a deserter by the SS. The version of the play itself, which treats Hoelderlin's brittle language with great freedom, emphasizes Creon's character as that of a power-drunk tyrant.

DIE TAGE DER KOMMUNE (The Days of the Commune)

Written: 1948–9 at Zurich.

First performance: Chemnitz (Karl-Marx-Stadt), 7 November 1956. Music by Hanns Eisler.

The Days of the Commune was written as an answer to the Norwegian playwright Nordahl Grieg's play *The Defeat*. It uses some of the characters and situations of that play to give Brecht's view on the reasons for the defeat of the Paris Communards.

The personal story of a group of inhabitants of a corner of Montmartre is seen against a background of the activities of the Paris City Council, with brief glimpses of the enemies of the Commune, Thiers and Bismarck. The simple faith and staunch common sense of the people is contrasted with the moral scruples and hesitations of the leaders: in their doctrinaire liberalism they fail to use violence, restrain the masses from marching to Versailles and sweeping away Thiers' government; they leave the Bank of France untouched, because they are hypnotized by the idea of legality; they neglect to impose discipline and unified command upon their forces, because of their anti-militarism, etc. As a result the simple people of Montmarte die in the fighting, while from a hill overlooking the city Thiers and a group of aristocrats watch the spectacle of burning, defeated Paris.

The Days of the Commune is an ambitious play. It has many felicitous touches, but is not wholly successful: the good characters are unduly sentimentalized, while Thiers and Bismarck are savage caricatures. The problem of violence and discipline is stated, but remains unsolved.

DER HOFMEISTER (The Private Tutor)

Written: 1950.
First performance: Berlin, 15 April 1950.

An adaptation of a play by Jacob Michael Reinhold Lenz (1751–92), one of the mad geniuses of eighteenth-century German literature. To pillory the spinelessness and lack of civic courage of German intellectuals under Hitler, Brecht revived this savage portrait of a German schoolmaster: Laeuffer, the poor private tutor, is seduced by Gustchen von der Burg, the daughter of his employers, whose fiancé is away at the university. Gustchen becomes pregnant. Laeuffer is chased by her enraged family and seeks refuge in the house of a village schoolmaster. But here too the sex instinct gets the better of him. Rather than disgrace his benefactor's innocent godchild and thus ruin his career as a teacher for the second time, Laeuffer castrates himself. Nevertheless he marries the girl who drove him to this desperate expedient and, though childless, lives happily ever after – an image of the emasculated German pedagogue.

HERRNBURGER BERICHT (Report on Herrnburg)

Written: 1951.
First performance: East Berlin, summer 1951.
Published: *Neues Deutschland*, East Berlin, 22 July 1951.
Music by Paul Dessau.
Choral cantata.

Written for the Communist World Youth Festival, *Herrnburger Bericht* deals with an incident following the previous year's Communist Youth Rally. West German youths who had attended it were stopped on re-entering the territory of the Federal Republic. Police tried to prevent them from marching through West Germany in closed formation, wanted to take down their names, etc. This is presented as a horrid attack upon human rights and the idea of freedom. The text, consisting largely of witless and abusive doggerel, is one of the low points of Brecht's literary career.

DER PROZESS DER JEANNE D'ARC ZU ROUEN 1431
   (The Trial of Joan of Arc at Rouen 1431)

Written: 1952.
First performance: Berliner Ensemble, 23 November 1952.

Based on a radio drama by Anna Seghers which made use of the protocols of the actual trial of Joan of Arc.

DON JUAN

Written: 1952.

First performance: Berliner Ensemble, 16 November 1953.

A fairly close adaptation of Molière's play.

CORIOLAN (Coriolanus)

Written: 1952–3.

Brecht was working on the preparations for the production of this play at the time of his death.

PAUKEN UND TROMPETEN (Trumpets and Drums)

First performance: Theater am Schiffbauerdamm, 1956.
Music by Rudolf Wagner-Regeny.

An adaptation of Farquhar's restoration comedy *The Recruiting Officer* by Brecht, Elisabeth Hauptmann, and Benno Besson. The time of the action is transferred to the period of the American War of Independence, which gives an opportunity for numerous barbed references to imperialism and colonial conquest. The songs are weak imitations of those of *The Threepenny Opera*.

TURANDOT ODER DER KONGRESS DER WEISS-WAESCHER (Turandot or The Congress of Whitewashers)

An unpublished and uncompleted play, written during Brecht's stay in East Berlin. Set in a mythical China, it attacks Western intellectuals who try to whitewash capitalism.

Narrative Prose

NOVELS

DREIGROSCHENROMAN (Threepenny Novel)

Published: 1934.

The *Threepenny Novel*, developed from Brecht's rejected story outline for the film version of the play. It is, however, very far removed from the original. The Marxist element, which was only hinted at in *The Threepenny Opera*, has become dominant. The scene of the action is London during the South African War. Macheath, no longer a dashing and elegant gangster, but a middle-aged business man, runs a chain of cheap multiple shops, the B-stores, that exclusively sell stolen goods. The theft of these is organized on a mass-production basis. Macheath and Polly are no longer romantic lovers. Polly merely marries him because she has become pregnant by another man. The conflict between Polly's father, the beggar-king Peachum, and Macheath is a purely business affair. It revolves around the rivalry between a number of similar stolen-goods chain stores and a project for the sale of unseaworthy hulls to the Admiralty as troop transports for the war. The only sympathetic character is George Fewkoombey, a veteran soldier who has lost a leg in Africa and has found employment with Peachum. After Macheath and Peachum have happily settled their differences in a profitable merger of their respective enterprises, Fewkoombey is hanged for a murder committed by Macheath.

The *Threepenny Novel* is an uneven work: flashes of Dickensian gusto and Swiftian satire alternate with tedious would-be descriptions of the workings of capitalism and high finance as a system of frauds and thefts. The last chapter, Fewkoombey's dream about a trial of a figure resembling Christ on charges of having misled the poor by giving them false hopes, has a blasphemous grandeur of its own.

DIE GESCHAEFTE DES HERRN JULIUS CAESAR
(The Business Deals of Mr Julius Caesar)

Published: 1957.

This unfinished novel is intended to show a great man through the eyes of his contemporaries: Caesar's banker Mummlius Spicer and his private secretary, the slave Rarus. Caesar is revealed as a debt-ridden puppet of money-lenders, his political career and rise to power as a series of desperate expedients to evade his creditors. Roman life is modernized by the use of present-day terminology of finance and politics (in the manner of Feuchtwanger and Robert Graves). But despite some witty passages the novel fails to convince.

SHORT STORIES

In his early years Brecht wrote a considerable number of short stories to make money. He thought little of them and they were not reprinted in his lifetime. Among the more characteristic of these stories are:

'Bargan laesst es sein' ('Bargan Lets it Be'). Published in *Der Neue Merkur*, Munich, 1921.

This story, which seems the germ of the play *Im Dickicht der Staedte*, describes the infatuation of a pirate captain, Bargan, with an utterly worthless, clump-footed member of his crew, which eventually leads to Bargan's ruin.

'Der Kinnhaken' ('The Hook to the Chin'). Published in *Scherls Magazin*, Berlin, 1 January 1926.

A boxing story. A boxer who has lost confidence in himself, through his manager's constant anxious efforts to keep him from drinking, loses the fight. He realizes that his attempts to keep himself from drinking have sapped his morale. One should always do what one feels like doing. This foreshadows the principle of self-indulgence proclaimed in *Mahagonny*.

'Eine Pleite-Idee' ('An Idea for Lean Times'). Published in *Uhu*, Berlin, 12 September 1926.

A down-and-out financier meets a destitute individual who is so emaciated and miserable in appearance that nobody would give him more than a few days to live. The financier feeds this man till he looks healthy, insures his life for a large sum, lets him starve till he regains his desperate looks, and takes him to the insurance company, who are so alarmed at his appearance that they offer to buy the policy back for a considerable sum. This process is repeated with several insurance companies. The financier, who uses the profits from this scheme to start a prosperous business, is hurt because the poor man is not grateful to him, who has fed him so well for such a long time.

'Die Bestie' ('The Beast'). Published in *Berliner Illustrirte Zeitung*, December 1928.

This story, which won Brecht the first prize of 3,000 marks in a short story competition, deals with the problem of reality versus theatrical illusion. A Soviet film producer making a film on a pre-war pogrom needs a man who resembles the notorious Governor of the province, Muratov, who organized that blood-bath. An old man who bears a striking resemblance to Muratov is found, but when he acts the scene his appearance and manner are far too gentle for so bloody a villain. The producer takes the part away from the old man – who is Muratov himself.

KALENDERGESCHICHTEN (Calendar Tales)

Published: 1948.

A volume of short stories, some of Brecht's narrative verse and a selection of the Keuner anecdotes (see below). The short stories, written in a highly compressed, terse style modelled on the *Novellen* of Heinrich von Kleist, are:

'Der Augsburger Kreidekreis'. The plot of the Caucasian chalk circle transferred to Augsburg in the period of the Thirty Years War.

'Die Zwei Soehne' ('Two Sons'). The final phase of the Second World War: a peasant woman in Thuringia is struck by the resemblance of one of the Russian prisoners-of-war, working on her farm, to her own son away at the front. When her son, an SS man, suddenly returns, having abandoned his unit, it is decided that the Russian prisoner, who would denounce him as a member of the SS when Russian troops occupy the village, must be killed. The peasant woman lets the prisoner escape and hands her own son to the Russians to keep him from continuing the senseless fight. She thus saves both her son's and the Russian prisoner's life.

'Das Experiment' ('The Experiment'). Francis Bacon dies as a consequence of his experiment with a chicken stuffed with snow and teaches the little boy, who helps him, the meaning of the scientific method.

'Der Mantel des Ketzers' ('The Heretic's Coat'). Giordano Bruno, fighting for his life against the Inquisition, is desperately anxious to pay a poor tailor the money he still owes him for an overcoat.

'Caesar und sein Legionaer' ('Caesar and His Legionary'). The lives of the dictator Julius Caesar, his secretary Rarus, and a poor old veteran of Caesar's army are strangely intertwined on the eve of the Ides of March. This story is an early stage of the novel *Die Geschaefte des Herrn Julius Caesar*.

'Der Soldat von La Ciotat' ('The Soldier of La Ciotat'). A shell-shocked French soldier has acquired the ability of standing absolutely motionless. Painted with a bronze colour, he exhibits himself at the fair-ground of La Ciotat as the living statue of the unknown soldier.

'Der Verwundete Sokrates' ('Socrates Wounded'). Determined to run away during the battle of Delion, Socrates gets a thorn into his foot and is immobilized. Surrounded by Persians and unable to escape, he utters loud cries, suggesting the presence of a whole Greek army, and causes the defeat of the Persians. He is carried home in triumph, but eventually he summons up the courage to tell Alcibiades what really happened. Admitting one's cowardice is the greatest of all possible acts of courage.

'Die unwuerdige Greisin' ('The Unworthy Old Woman'). Brecht's grandmother abandons the narrow conventions of petty bourgeois respectability after her husband's death.

GESCHICHTEN VOM HERRN KEUNER (Anecdotes of Mr Keuner)

Written: c. 1930–c. 1956.

The Keuner anecdotes are, as Brecht put it, 'attempts to make gestures quotable'. Keuner is Brecht's *alter ego*, and each anecdote expresses one of his basic personal attitudes, ranging from the need to be punctual to more profound problems, such as his approach to religion, violence, friendship, etc. These anecdotes are very short (from about twenty to a few hundred words) and are among Brecht's most remarkable achievements: witty, concise, paradoxical, and profound, they are a modern equivalent to the work of the great French moralists, lying somewhere between the maxims of La Rochefoucauld and the characters of La Bruyère.

GESICHTE (Visions)

A cycle of dreamlike prose sketches and parables of remarkable power.

FLUECHTLINGSGESPRAECHE (Refugee Conversations)

A series of dialogues between two German refugees (written c. 1940). The idea is clearly taken from Goethe's *Unterhaltungen Deutscher Ausgewanderter* (*Conversations of German Exiles*), but the main character, Ziffel; resembles Schweik and Brecht in his deadpan humour.

ME-TI. BUCH DER WENDUNGEN (Me-ti. The Book of Twists and Turns)

Written between 1934 and 1950. A collection of short prose pieces, anecdotes and reflections, very much in the style of the Keuner stories, but with an ancient Chinese setting which, however, very thinly disguises Brecht's own political and personal preoccupations. Brecht himself appears as Kin, Kin-jeh, Ken-jch or Kien-leh (all clearly derived from Keuner), Stalin as Ni-en, Lenin as Mi-en-leh, the Soviet Union as Su, etc. The book not only gives most revealing insights into Brecht's reactions to the Stalinist terror, the backwardness of the Soviet Union, etc. but also contains some of Brecht's most personal writings about his love for, and relationship with a woman, Lai-tu (presumably Ruth Berlau). These are among the most tender love poems and poetic prose pieces Brecht ever wrote.

DER TUI-ROMAN (The Tui Novel)

Fragments of a novel, written in the thirties and forties, which was to become an indictment of the intellectuals, renamed in the inversion by which Brecht transformed Western names into Chinese ones, *Tellekt-Uell-In*, abbreviated by the opening letter of each section into Tui. Set in a mythical Imperial China, the book was to be a Swiftian satire against intellectuals who live by selling their opinions to the highest bidder. Brecht used much of this material for the play *Turandot or the Congress of Whitewashers*.

Essays and Theoretical Writings

Brecht's voluminous theoretical writings about the theatre are assembled in the latest collected editions in five volumes of the paperback, two of the thin-paper hardcover version. They are divided into *Writings on the Theatre* which run to about thirteen hundred pages of text, *Writings on Literature and Art*, and *Writings on Politics and Society*.

The most important titles of longer works among his theoretical essays on the theatre are:

DER MESSINGKAUF (The Purchase of Brass)
Written: 1937–51.
A compendium of views on epic theatre, which remained unfinished, but was conceived as a series of Platonic dialogues interspersed with poems and short illustrative scenes.

KLEINES ORGANON FUER DAS THEATER (Little Organon for the Theatre)
Written: 1948.
A terse and concise summary of Brecht's view on epic theatre in seventy-seven gnomic paragraphs.

Model Books

Brecht believed that exemplary productions of the 'epic' theatre should be recorded and used as models for subsequent productions of the play concerned, giving the new producer a basis on which to work without tying him down in every detail. Every phase of such productions was photographed during an actual performance. The pictures, together with copious notes, were collected in 'model books'. Some of these have been published:

Antigonemodell 1948. Published 1949, reprinted 1955.
Brecht's production of *Antigone* at Chur.

Die Gewehre der Frau Carrar. Published 1952.

Photographs of productions of this play at Paris, Copenhagen, and Greifswald.

Aufbau einer Rolle, Galilei (Building up a part, Galileo). Published 1958.

The production with Charles Laughton in California and the performance of Ernst Busch with the Berliner Ensemble.

Couragemodell 1949 (Mother Courage). Published 1958.

The Berlin production of 1949.

Photographs from model books of three productions, a full account of three others, and a wealth of material on the Brechtian theatre, written by Brecht and his associates are contained in:

Theaterarbeit, 6 Auffuehrungen des Berliner Ensembles, Dresden, 1952.

A magnificent picture book. The six productions described in detail are: *Puntila, Vasa Zheleznova* (Gorky), *Der Hofmeister, Die Mutter, Biberpelz/Der Rote Hahn* (Hauptmann), *Mother Courage.*

Miscellaneous Publications

Kriegsfibel (Primer of War). Published 1955.

A picture book: photographs covering the period from the Spanish Civil War to the end of the Second World War collected by Brecht from Scandinavian and American newspapers and magazines, each accompanied by a quatrain. A grim but impressive piece of pacifist propaganda. It was intended to supplement it by a second volume, *Friedensfibel (Primer of Peace),* which remained unfinished.

TRANSLATIONS

Together with Margarete Steffin, Brecht translated the childhood memoirs of the Danish writer Martin Andersen-Nexoe: *Die Kindheit,* Zurich, 1945. The translation is prefaced by a dedicatory poem by Brecht.

Brecht made a German adaptation, based on a translation by Ernst Hube, of Sergei Tretyakov's play *Ich will ein Kind haben (The Pioneers).*

Films

Brecht wrote a number of film-scripts, most of which never reached the production stage. He had a hand in the following completed films:

Robinsonade auf Asuncion. Written in collaboration with Bronnen, 1922. A group of characters stranded on a deserted island, which, unlike the island of Robinson Crusoe, contains a giant, modern city – completely abandoned by its inhabitants. The story (published in *Berliner Boersen-Courier*, November 1922, as the winning entry of a film competition) was used as the basis of a silent picture. It was, however, so far removed from the authors' original intentions that they disowned it. The completed film had the title *Die Insel der Traenen (The Isle of Tears)* (see *Arnolt Bronnen gibt zu Protokoll*, p. 115).

Die Dreigroschenoper, 1931. Directed by G. W. Pabst.

Brecht's own story outline for the film *Die Beule (The Boil)* is published in *Versuche 3*. Pabst did not adhere to it, and Brecht disliked the resulting film intensely. Made in parallel German and French versions, this is nevertheless the most Brechtian of all Brecht films.

Kuhle Wampe, 1932. Script by Brecht and Ernst Ottwalt. Music by Hanns Eisler. Directed by Slatan Dudow.

Life among the unemployed in pre-Hitler Berlin. A working-class family is shown in the throes of the economic crisis. The son, out of work, commits suicide. The family are evicted from their tenement and move into a shack in an allotment area, Kuhle Wampe. The daughter and her fiance quarrel because he agrees to marry her only from a sense of duty when he learns that she is pregnant. The lovers are eventually reconciled during a big Communist party sporting gala, which symbolizes the forward-looking hope of the new, revolutionary generation. The film was shown in the United States under the title *Whither Germany?*

Hangmen Also Die, 1942. Directed by Fritz Lang. Music by Hanns Eisler.

'I sold a story to a Hollywood firm but I did not write the screenplay myself' (Brecht at the hearing of the Un-American Activities Committee). The assassination of the Nazi Governor Heydrich by Czech patriots.

Herr Puntila und sein Knecht Matti, 1955. Directed by A. Cavalcanti. The script was written with Brecht's advice.

Made in Vienna, this colour film of *Puntila*, with Curt Bois in the name part, is an interesting experiment which fails. The naturalism of the photography and the realistic background destroy the stylized convention in which the play is written, proof that Brecht's ideas only worked on the stage. This may be the explanation why, in spite of his love for the cinema, Brecht was always unhappy about filmed versions of his work.

Mutter Courage (started 1954, uncompleted).

A Cinemascope production in colour. Originally to be directed by Wolfgang Staudte, later by Erich Engel. Disputes about the casting between Brecht and Staudte and interference by the authorities have hitherto prevented the completion of this ambitious project.

A completely new film version, in black and white *Totalvision*, was directed by Peter Palitzsch and Manfred Wekwerth, 1959–60. This film uses the cast of the Berliner Ensemble and sticks closely to the play.

Diaries and Autobiographical Writings

Tagebuecher 1920–1922. Autobiographische Aufzeichnungen 1920–1954.

The early diaries give a fairly full, day to day account of the thoughts and adventures of Brecht in his early twenties. They are followed by brief notes from the years 1920 to 1954.

Arbeitsjournal (Working Diaries).

These diaries, covering the years 1938 to 1955, contain notes, ideas and reflections. They were obviously written with ultimate publication in mind, but nevertheless give illuminating insights into Brecht's political attitudes, his disillusionment with Stalinism after the Ribbentrop–Molotov pact, his disgust at Hollywood, his contempt for the pettiness and provincialism of East Germany.

Section C

BIBLIOGRAPHY

Brecht Bibliographies

The major undertaking of a complete bibliography of writings by and about Brecht – an immense task – has been started in East Berlin:

> SEIDEL, Gerhard (ed.). *Bibliographie Bertolt Brecht*, Berlin (East) and Weimar, Aufbau Verlag.
> The first volume, *Titelverzeichnis, Band I*, was published in 1975. Others will follow.

An important tool for Brecht research is the catalogue of the manuscripts and editions of Brecht's works in the Brecht Archive in East Berlin:

> RAMTHUN, Herta (ed.). *Bertolt Brecht Archiv/Bestandsverzeichnis des literarischen Nachlasses*, East Berlin and Weimar, 4 volumes, 1969–73.

Further useful bibliographical works on Brecht include:

> NUBEL, Walter. 'Bertolt-Brecht-Bibliographie', *Sinn und Form*, Second Special Brecht Issue, 1957.
> This admirable bibliography lists writings by and on Brecht *in German*, published up to the end of 1956.
> NELLHAUS, Gerhard. 'Brecht-Bibliographie', *Sinn und Form*, First Special Brecht Issue, 1949.
> A much shorter bibliography, but it also lists translations of works by Brecht and articles on Brecht in English. Not completely accurate.
> PETERSEN, Klaus-Dietrich. 'Bertolt-Brecht-Bibliographie', Bad Homburg v.d.H., Berlin, Zurich, 1968.

Principal Editions of Brecht's Works

Brecht's numerous writings first appeared scattered throughout an immense number of separate books, periodicals, anthologies, newspapers, etc. The bibliographies listed above contain details of these.

Listed below are the principal *collected editions* of Brecht's works:

> *Brecht: Versuche*, nos. 1–7, 1930–2; nos. 9–15, 1949–57; no. 8 was never published.
> The earlier series is out of print and very rare. But a reprint of

all the numbers, including the hitherto unpublished number 8, is now available in four volumes. The postwar series is published in parallel editions in West Germany (Suhrkamp) and East Germany (Aufbau Verlag). The East German series contains an additional–special–number (Sonderheft) that reprints *Die Gewehre der Frau Carrar*, the short story *Der Augsburger Kreidekreis*, and the poems *Neue Kinderlieder*.

Another collected edition remained incomplete and is practically unobtainable today:

Brecht: Gesammelte Werke, vols. I and II, Malik Verlag, London, 1938.
This edition does not contain the plays that precede *Mann ist Mann* and ends with *Die Gewehre der Frau Carrar*. It was printed in Prague, although the place of publication is given as London. The two further volumes planned were lost after the German occupation of Prague.

An edition which began to be published in Brecht's own lifetime (1953) by Suhrkamp Verlag in Frankfurt and Aufbau Verlag – under licence from Suhrkamp – in East Berlin, comprises:

Stücke (Plays), 14 volumes.
Gedichte (Poems), 10 volumes.
Schriften zum Theater (Writings on Theatre), 7 volumes.
Prosa (Narrative Prose), 5 volumes.
Schriften zur Literatur und Kunst (Writings on Literature and Art), 3 volumes.
Schriften zur Politik und Gesellschaft (Writings on Politics and Society), 1 volume.
This edition grew rather haphazardly, has few notes and also contains many omissions and repetitious overlaps (the same poems appear several times, the same notes on plays can be found in the volume containing the play itself and then again in the Writings on Theatre). To meet growing criticism, Suhrkamp Verlag, Frankfurt, reassembled Brecht's works in a new collected edition which appeared in 1967 – on the eve of Brecht's seventieth birthday. This edition, which still contains some very noticeable gaps, like the suppression of *Herrnburger Bericht*, must nevertheless be regarded as the most complete now – and probably for a long time to come – available. This is:

Bertolt Brecht, Gesammelte Werke, Frankfurt, 1967.
The edition was issued in two forms: 8 thin-paper, hardcover

volumes or 20 pocket-size paperbacks. But the pagination and indexing are identical in both forms.

They are arranged as follows:

Vol. I (corresponds to vols. 1 and 2 of the paperback version)
STÜCKE 1 (Plays 1):

Baal/Trommeln in der Nacht/Im Dickicht der Städte/Leben Eduards des Zweiten von England/Mann ist Mann/Die Dreigroschenoper/Aufstieg und Fall der Stadt Mahagonny/Der Ozeanflug [i.e. Lindberghflug]/Das Badener Lehrstück vom Einverständnis/Der Jasager/Der Neinsager/Die Massnahme/Die heilige Johanna der Schlachthöfe/Die Ausnahme und die Regel/Die Mutter.

Vol. II (corresponds to vols. 3, 4, and part of 5 of the paperback version)
STÜCKE 2 (Plays 2):

Die Rundköpfe und die Spitzköpfe/Die Horatier und die Kuriatier/ Furcht und Elend des Dritten Reiches/Die Gewehre der Frau Carrar/ Leben des Galilei/Mutter Courage/Das Verhör des Lukullus/Der gute Mensch von Sezuan/Puntila/Arturo Ui/Die Gesichte der Simone Machard/Schweyk im Zweiten Weltkrieg/Der Kaukasische Kreidekreis.

Vol. III (corresponds to part of vol. 5 and vols. 6 and 7 of the paperback version)
STÜCKE 3 (Plays 3):

Die Tage der Kommune/Turandot/Adaptations: *Antigone/Der Hofmeister/Coriolan/Der Prozess der Jeanne d'Arc zu Rouen/Don Juan/Pauken und Trompeten*/One-Act-Plays/Adaptations/Practice Scenes for Actors.

Vol. IV (corresponds to vols. 8, 9, and 10 of the paperback version)
POEMS

Vol. V (corresponds to vols. 11 and 12 of the paperback version)
NARRATIVE PROSE 1:
Short Stories/*Geschichten vom Herrn Keuner/Me-ti/Der Tui-Roman.*

Vol. VI (corresponds to vols. 13 and 14 of the paperback version)
NARRATIVE PROSE 2:
Dreigroschenroman/Die Geschäfte des Herrn Julius Caesar/ Flüchtlingsgespräche.

Vol. VII (corresponds to vols. 15, 16, and 17 of the paperback version)
THEORETICAL PROSE 1:
Writings on the Theatre.

Vol. VIII (corresponds to vols. 18, 19, and 20 of the paperback version)

THEORETICAL PROSE 2:

Writings on Art and Literature/Writings on Politics and Society.

There is an additional volume (two volumes in the paperback edition):

Texte für Filme (Screenplays and other writings for the cinema, edited by Wolfgang Gersch and Werner Hecht) 1969.

Also as supplementary volumes to the Suhrkamp edition there has been issued Brecht's 'Working Diary':

Arbeitsjournal
volume 1: 1938–1942.
volume 2: 1942–1955.
Edited by Werner Hecht, 1973.

A further volume, mainly of earlier diaries has also been published by Suhrkamp:

Tagebücher 1920–1922. Autobiographische Aufzeichnungen 1920–1954 (edited by Herta Ramthun), 1975.
A translation of this book was published in English, translated by John Willett. Eyre Methuen, 1979.

CRITICAL EDITIONS AND COLLECTIONS OF MATERIAL FOR SINGLE PLAYS ETC.

The editorial principle on which the collected edition is based is a somewhat doubtful one: it is to present Brecht's final versions which means that early works are presented in the form which Brecht deemed politically advisable during his East German period. Moreover there is a multitude of different versions, drafts and alternatives, which make the preparation of a truly critical edition both important and extremely difficult. As a first step in this direction, Suhrkamp, Brecht's West German publisher, has brought out a number of editions of single plays which give space to at least some variants; as well as books of 'materials' on the plays, which include sketches, utterances by Brecht, and critical material. Those at present available are:

Baal. Drei Fassungen, ed. Dieter Schmidt, Frankfurt, 1970. Contains the texts of the versions of 1918, 1919, and 1926 with variants and critical apparatus.

Baal. Der böse Baal, der Asoziale, ed. Dieter Schmidt, Frankfurt, 1968. The last version (1955) with variants and details of earlier texts.

Im Dickicht der Städte. Erstfassung und Materialien, ed. Gisela E. Bahr, Frankfurt, 1968. First version of the play (1922) with variants and other critical apparatus.

Leben Eduards des Zweiten von England. Vorlage, Texte und Materialien, ed. Reinhold Grimm, Frankfurt, 1968. Marlowe's play in the translation Brecht used, variants, and other critical apparatus.

Der Jasager und Der Neinsager. Vorlagen, Fassungen und Materialien, ed. Peter Szondi, Frankfurt, 1966.

Der Brotladen. Stückfragment. Bühnenfassung und Texte aus dem Fragment, Frankfurt, 1969. Text of the version of this uncompleted play as performed by the Berliner Ensemble, 1967, with additional scenes.

Die Heilige Johanna der Schlachthöfe. Bühnenfassung, Fragmente, Varianten, ed. Gisela E. Bahr, Frankfurt, 1971.

Die Massnahme. Kritische Ausgabe mit einer Spielanleitung, ed. Reiner Steinweg, Frankfurt, 1972.

Materialien zu Brechts 'Leben des Galilei', ed. W. Hecht, Frankfurt, 1963.

Materialien zu Brechts 'Mutter Courage und ihre Kinder', ed. W. Hecht, Frankfurt, 1964.

Materialien zu Bertolt Brechts 'Schweyk im Zweiten Weltkrieg', ed. Herbert Knust, Frankfurt, 1974.

Materialien zu Brechts 'Der Gute Mensch von Setzuan', ed. W. Hecht, Frankfurt, 1968.

Materialien zu Bertolt Brechts 'Die Mutter', ed. W. Hecht, Frankfurt, 1969.

Brechts Modell der Lehrstücke. Zeugnisse, Diskussion, Erfahrungen, ed. Reiner Steinweg, Frankfurt, 1976.

Kuhle Wampe. Protokoll des Films und Materialien, ed. W. Gersch and W. Hecht, Frankfurt, 1969.

Translations into English

There are numerous translations of Brecht's works scattered in periodicals and editions which have now become difficult to obtain. Only the most comprehensive – and most easily accessible – editions are listed below.

A collected edition, planned to include all plays and Brecht's principal prose works and poetry, is currently appearing in parallel but by no means identical form in London and New York. Due to the differences between English and American idiom, some plays appear in different versions on either side of the Atlantic.

The U.S. edition is:

Bertolt Brecht, *Collected Plays*, ed. Ralph Manheim and John Willett, New York, Vintage Books (Random House).

The British edition is:

Bertolt Brecht, *Plays, Poetry and Prose*, annotated and edited in hardback and paperback by John Willett and Ralph Manheim, London, Eyre Methuen:

Collected Plays

Vol. 1	Baal; Drums in the Night; In the Jungle of Cities; The Life of Edward II of England; A Respectable Wedding; The Beggar; Driving Out a Devil; Lux in Tenebris; The Catch (*hardback only*)
Vol. 1i	Baal (*paperback only*)
Vol. 1ii	A Respectable Wedding and other one-act plays (*paperback only*)
Vol. 1iii	Drums in the Night (*paperback only*)
Vol. 1iv	In the Jungle of Cities (*paperback only*)
Vol. 2i	Man equals Man; The Elephant Calf
Vol. 2ii	The Threepenny Opera
Vol. 2iii	The Rise and Fall of the City of Mahagonny; The Seven Deadly Sins
*Vol. 3i	Saint Joan of the Stockyards
*Vol. 3ii	The Baden-Baden Cantata; The Flight over the Ocean; He Who Said Yes; He Who Said No; The Decision
*Vol. 4i	The Mother; The Exception and the Rule; The Horatii and the Curiatii
*Vol. 4ii	Round Heads and Pointed Heads
*Vol. 4iii	Señora Carrar's Rifles; Fear and Misery of the Third Reich
Vol. 5i	Life of Galileo
Vol. 5ii	Mother Courage and her Children
*Vol. 5iii	The Trial of Lucullus; Dansen; What's the Price of Iron?
*Vol. 6i	The Good Person of Szechwan
*Vol. 6ii	The Resistible Rise of Arturo Ui
*Vol. 6iii	Mr Puntila and his Man Matti
Vol. 7	The Visions of Simone Machard; Schweyk in the Second World War; The Caucasian Chalk Circle; The Duchess of Malfi
*Vol. 8i	The Days of the Commune
*Vol. 8ii	Turandot; Report from Herrnburg

Vol. 8iii   Downfall of the Egoist Johann Fatzer; The Life of
Confucius; The Breadshop; The Salzburg Dance of
Death

Poetry
Poems 1913–1956
Prose
Brecht on Theatre
Diaries 1920–1922
*Selected Prose
*Selected Essays

* in preparation

Another series of translations is published by Grove Press, New York:

Seven Plays by Bertolt Brecht, edited and with an introduction by
Eric Bentley, New York, Grove Press, 1961. Contains: *In the
Swamp/A Man's a Man/St. Joan of the Stockyards/Mother Courage/
Galileo/The Good Woman of Setzuan/The Caucasian Chalk Circle.*

Grove Press also publishes a paperback edition of Brecht's plays under
the general editorship of Eric Bentley. The following volumes are
available:

Baal, A Man's a Man, and *The Elephant Calf*
The Jewish Wife and Other Short Plays (contains three sketches from
Furcht und Elend des Dritten Reichs: 'The Jewish Wife', 'In Search
of Justice', 'The Informer'; also: 'The Elephant Calf', 'The
Measures Taken', 'The Exception and the Rule', and 'The Salzburg
Dance of Death')
Mother Courage
Parables for the Theatre (*The Caucasian Chalk Circle* and *The Good
Woman of Setzuan*)
Jungle of the Cities and Other Plays (also contains *Drums in the Night*
and *Roundheads and Peakheads*)
Galileo
The Visions of Simone Machard
The Threepenny Opera
Edward II
The Mother

The hitherto most comprehensive translation of Brecht's poetry is the
one published in the framework of the Eyre Methuen collected
edition:

Poems 1913–1956, ed. John Willett and Ralph Manheim, with the
co-operation of Erich Fried, London, Eyre Methuen, 1976; New

York, Methuen Inc, 1979. The hardback edition contains a comprehensive critical apparatus, superior to that in any German edition.

Other collections of poems by Brecht in English are:

Selected Poems, translation by H. R. Hays, New York, Grove Press, 1959.

Manual of Piety (*Die Hauspostille*), bilingual edition, translations by Eric Bentley.

Of Brecht's prose works the following are accessible in English:

Tales from the Calendar, translated by Yvonne Kapp and Michael Hamburger, London, 1961.

Threepenny Novel, translated by Desmond I. Vesey and Christopher Isherwood, New York, 1956, London, 1958.

Brecht on Theatre, translated by John Willett, London, 1964, New York, 1964.

The Messingkauf Dialogues, translated by John Willett, London, 1965.

Diaries 1920–1922, translated by John Willett, London, 1979, New York, 1979.

Books on Brecht

The literature about Brecht has grown so large that only some of the principal books and special issues of periodicals can be listed here.

BIOGRAPHICAL

AUFRICHT, Ernst Josef, *Erzähle, damit du dein Recht erweist*, Berlin, 1966.
The autobiography of the manager of the Schiffbauer Damm Theatre where the *Threepenny Opera* was first produced in 1928.

BUNGE, H., *Fragen Sie mehr über Brecht. Hanns Eisler im Gespräch*, Munich, 1970.
Conversations about Brecht with the composer Hanns Eisler, one of Brecht's closest collaborators and friends.

ENGBERG, Harald, *Brecht paa Fyn*, 2 vols., Odense, 1966.
A detailed account of Brecht's exile in Denmark.

EWEN, Frederic, *Bertolt Brecht. His Life, His Art and His Times*, New York, 1967; London, 1970.

FASSMANN, Kurt, *Brecht: Eine Bildbiographie*, Munich, 1958.

FRISCH, W. and OBERMEIER, K. W., *Brecht in Augsburg*, Frankfurt, 1976.
Documents on Brecht's childhood and youth in his native city.

HECHT, W. (ed.), *Bertolt Brecht. Sein Leben in Bildern und Texten*, Frankfurt, 1978.

A sumptuous coffee-table book, issued by Suhrkamp to celebrate Brecht's 80th birthday, with numerous photographs and quotations from Brecht's letters and diaries. Max Frisch has written the preface.

HECHT, W. (ed.), *Brecht im Gespräch. Diskussionen. Dialoge. Interviews*, Frankfurt, 1975.

Conversations, discussions, interviews.

HECHT, W., BUNGE, H., RÜLICKE-WEILER, K., *Bertolt Brecht. Sein Leben und Werk*, East Berlin, 1969.

KESTING, Marianne, *Bertolt Brecht in Selbstzeugnissen und Dokumenten*, Hamburg, 1959.

A short paperback monograph based on autobiographical passages from Brecht's works. Illustrated.

MÜNSTERER, H. O., *Bert Brecht. Erinnerungen aus den Jahren 1917–1922*, Zurich, 1963.

Recollections by one of Brecht's school friends.

STERNBERG, Fritz, *Der Dichter und die Ratio. Erinnerungen an Bertolt Brecht*, Göttingen, 1963.

Reminiscences of the sociologist from whom Brecht learned some of his Marxism.

VÖLKER, Klaus, *Brecht Chronik*, Munich, Hanser, 1971.

An excellent chronology of Brecht's life. Also available in an English translation.

VÖLKER, Klaus, *Bertolt Brecht. Eine Biographie*, Munich, 1976.

English translation by John Nowell, New York, 1978; London, 1979.

CRITICAL

BENJAMIN, Walter, *Versuche über Brecht*, Frankfurt, 1966.

Essays about Brecht and Conversations with Brecht by the great German critic who was a close friend of Brecht's.

English translation: *Understanding Brecht*, London, 1973.

CHIARINI, P., *Bertolt Brecht*, Bari, 1959.

——, *Brecht e la Dialettica del Paradosso*, Milan, 1969.

DEMETZ, P. (ed.), *Brecht. A Collection of Critical Essays*, Englewood Cliffs, N.J., 1962.

ESSLIN, M., *Bertolt Brecht*, New York and London, 1969. (Columbia Essays on Modern Writers, No. 42.)

FUEGI, John, *The Essential Brecht*, Los Angeles, 1972.

GERSCH, Wolfgang, *Film bei Brecht*, East Berlin, 1975.

GRAY, Ronald, *Brecht the Dramatist*, Cambridge, 1976.

GRIMM, Reinhold, *Bertolt Brecht, die Struktur seines Werks*, Nuremberg, 1959.

——, *Bertolt Brecht und die Weltliteratur*, Nuremberg, 1961.

——, *Brecht und Nietzsche*, Frankfurt, 1979.

HINCK, Walter, *Die Dramaturgie des späten Brecht* (Vol. 229 of 'Palaestra,' Untersuchungen aus des deutschen und englischen Philologie und Literaturgeschichte), Göttingen, 1959.
A thorough and scholarly analysis of Brecht's dramatic technique.

HULTBERG, Helge, *Die aesthetischen Anschauungen Bertolt Brechts*, Copenhagen, 1962.

IHERING, Herbert, *Bertolt Brecht und das Theater*, Berlin, 1959.
A short essay followed by 64 illustrations.

JENDREIEK, H., *Bertolt Brecht. Drama der Veränderung*, Düsseldorf, 1969.

KLOTZ, Volker, *Bertolt Brecht, Versuch über das Werk*, Darmstadt, 1957.
A lucid and penetrating study of Brecht's style and poetic method.

KNOPF, Jan, *Bertolt Brecht. Ein kritischer Forschungsbericht*, Frankfurt, 1974.
A survey of Brecht research in Germany.

LYON, James K., *Bertolt Brecht and Rudyard Kipling*, The Hague, 1975.

LYONS, Charles R., *Bertolt Brecht, the Despair and the Polemic*, Carbondale, Ill., 1968.

MANN, Otto, *Mass oder Mythos: Ein kritischer Beitrag über die Schaustücke Bertolt Brechts*, Heidelberg, 1958.
An attack on Brecht from the point of view of the traditional conception of the German classical drama.

MAYER, Hans, *Anmerkungen zu Brecht*, Frankfurt, 1965.

——, *Bertolt Brecht und die Tradition*, Pfullingen, 1961.

——, *Brecht in der Geschichte*, Frankfurt, 1971.

MITTENZWEI, Werner, *Bertolt Brecht. Von der Massnahme zu Leben des Galilei*, East Berlin, 1962.

MUELLER, Klaus-Detlef, *Die Funktion der Geschichte im Werk Bertolt Brechts*, Tubingen, 1967.

MUNK, Erika (ed.), *Brecht. 18 articles from the TDR*, New York, 1972.

NIESSEN, Carl, *Brecht auf der Bühne*, Cologne, 1959.
A detailed and profusely illustrated catalogue of an exhibition of pictures and documents relating to the stage history of Brecht's plays, arranged by the Institute of Theatre Studies of Cologne University and held at Munich in the autumn of 1959.

PIETZKER, Carl, *Die Lyrik des jungen Brecht*, Frankfurt, 1974.

REICH, B., *Brecht* (in Russian), Moscow, 1966.

RISCHBIETER, Henning, *Brecht*, 2 vols., Velber bei Hannover, 1966.

ROSENBAUER, H., *Brecht und der Behaviorismus*, Bad Homburg, 1970.

RÜLICKE-WEILER, Käthe, *Die Dramaturgie Brechts*, East Berlin, 1966.

SCHMIDT, Dieter, '*Baal*' *und der junge Brecht*, Stuttgart, 1966.

SCHUHMANN, Klaus, *Der Lyriker Bertolt Brecht 1913–1933*, East Berlin, 1964.

SCHUMACHER, Ernst, *Die dramatischen Versuche Bertolt Brechts 1918–1933*, East Berlin, 1955.
     A voluminous study of the early Brecht from a strictly Marxist point of view. Contains a wealth of valuable factual material but also demonstrates the effect of the rigid Marxist orthodoxy on the critical faculties of an acute intelligence: the plays are most predictably judged according to their political content.

——, *Bertolt Brechts 'Leben des Galilei' und andere Stücke*, East Berlin, 1965.

——, *Der Fall Galilei. Das Drama der Wissenschaft*, East Berlin, 1964.

SERREAU, Genevieve, *Brecht*, Paris, 1955 (Les Grands Dramaturges no. 4).

SPALTER, Max, *Brecht's Tradition*, Baltimore, 1967.

STEINWEG, Reiner, *Das Lehrstück*, Stuttgart, 1972.

SUBIOTTO, A., *Bertolt Brecht's Adaptations for the Berliner Ensemble*, London, 1975.

WALBERN, J. H., *Brecht and Ionesco*, Urbana, Ill.

WEKWERTH, Manfred, *Schriften. Arbeit mit Brecht*, East Berlin, 1973.

——, *Notate. Über die Arbeit des Berliner Ensembles 1956–1966*, Frankfurt, 1967.

WILLETT, John, *The Theatre of Bertolt Brecht*, London, 1959. Revised paperback edition: London, 1977.

SPECIAL NUMBERS OF PERIODICALS

Adam & Encore, London, Autumn 1956. A joint Brecht issue of the literary magazine *Adam* and the theatre quarterly *Encore*.

Cahiers du Cinéma, Paris, No. 114, December 1960.

The Drama Review, New York, Fall 1967.

The Drama Review, New York, Winter 1968.

Europe, 35e année, nos. 133–4, Paris, January/February 1957.

Sinn und Form, East Berlin, Sonderheft Bertolt Brecht, 1949.

Sinn und Form, East Berlin, Zweites Sonderheft Bertolt Brecht, 1957.
     This 'Second Special Brecht Issue' of *Sinn und Form* contains a

wealth of excellent contributions and much interesting material by Brecht.

Text + Kritik (ed. H. L. Arnold), Sonderheft Brecht 1, Munich, 1972.
Text + Kritik (ed. H. L. Arnold), Sonderheft Brecht 2, Munich 1973.
Théâtre Populaire, Paris, No. 11, January/February 1955.
The Tulane Drama Review, New Orleans, September 1961.

INDEX

I. INDEX OF WORKS BY BRECHT

This index lists all references to Brecht's writings mentioned in the text. Where a full description of a work is given in the 'Descriptive List of Brecht's Works' it appears in bold figures. The type of work listed is indicated by the following abbreviations: s (Stage works); N (Narrative prose); E (Essays and Theoretical writings); F (Films); P (Poems) and CP (Collections or Cycles of Poems); M (Model books).

No separate references to characters in plays and fiction are given. They can be found by referring to the titles of the works in question.

II. GENERAL INDEX